Peter and

Wisdom's Children

With love and blessings

from

Nick

Wisdom's Children

Celebrating Men and Women of Faith and Genius

Nicholas Jowett

Nicholas PAdowell

inspire

Copyright © Nicholas Jowett 2007

British Library Cataloguing in Publication data

A catalogue record for this book is available from the British Library

ISBN 978-1-905958-00-9

First published by Inspire
4 John Wesley Road
Werrington
Peterborough PE4 6ZP

Printed and bound in Great Britain by
Athenaeum Press Ltd, Gateshead, Tyne & Wear

Foreword

When I was living in Sheffield some years ago, I discovered that a near-neighbour had died. I had never met him, but his obituary was carried in the *Independent*. The Revd Kenneth Hayes was, in many ways, a rather unremarkable man. He had been a pastor in a small mining village in Wales, which no-one would ever have heard of but for the name of Aberfan. It was Hayes who, on 21 October 1966, had been shaken that morning by a terrible sound followed by an even more terrible silence. It was he who had opened up his chapel, organized the relief work. It was he who kept the community afloat in the months ahead, organizing appeals for toys, arguing with the Coal Board for compensation, and taking Aberfan to Downing Street.

But it was also he, a 36-year-old clergyman, who on that morning, had lost his own son somewhere under the silt and slurry. In spite of his loss, he had worked for his community, holding everyone up when he should have been breaking down. In all of that unbearable anguish, he had still bestowed a calm sincerity and spirituality to a community searching for meaning in the midst of unimaginable grief.

He is a kind of hero. He fought the government and Coal Board for Aberfan when many would have given up. He pushed Harold Wilson hard for compensation, but only won a partial victory. The Coal Board refused to move its tips unless it was compensated for this, so the Aberfan Disaster Fund was compelled to dig into its own disaster fund and make-over, in 1966, £150,000 back to the Coal Board, so it could make Aberfan 'safe'. Up until the last minute, it had demanded £235,000. The negligence that killed 100 children cost the Coal Board virtually nothing. They paid £500 to each bereaved family, and £160,000 to the village, but then got most of it back from the coerced donation. You might like to know that the present government was swift to acknowledge how wrong their predecessors had been. In July 1997, the new Secretary of State for Wales paid the money back to the fund, in full.

It would be churlish to call Kenneth Hayes a 'saint' in the way that the Anglican or Catholic churches normally might mean it. Hayes was a Baptist. Yet there was something extraordinarily saintly about his conduct throughout life, a stature of grace that meant that he became an icon for his community, a beacon of hope in a dark place.

On the Sunday after his son's death, Hayes preached in his chapel on Romans 8, the passage on 'who can separate us from the love of God'. He said 'as far as I'm concerned we've still got two boys. We're only separated for a time. One day we're going to meet. The parting and the loneliness and being without him is terrible, but it is not forever.'

In Nicholas Jowett's prescient and engaging book we meet a 'cloud of witnesses' who are, like Kenneth Hayes, not necessarily 'saints' in the conventional understanding of the term. Nicholas introduces us to figures who have inspired, enchanted and illuminated humanity down the ages, and have offered their lives and gifts in ways that continue to speak to us. We meet heroes, heretics, poets, novelists, artists, scientists – and many others who have simply served. Not all the 'saints' are Christian – but these are lives that have nonetheless touched and inspired those of faith, and many who have no religious affinity at all. But these are people whose righteousness and giftedness can help inspire us to live a different kind life.

According to one Jewish tradition, we are all in the hands of God. But it is the righteous souls – the saints – who 'glow like sparks in the stubble'. It is an enchanting image. Saints, rather like the embers of a fire, continue to give off light and heat, and may still illuminate life. But they are also thrown out of the fire into the world. They are on loan there, setting light to life, but illuminating us with their artistry, imagination, wisdom, sacrifice and holiness. Although they are dead, it is because of their deeds that they are not forgotten. But more than that, their lives – often flecked with shards of sacredness – still speak to us today, and ask us what we think our lives are really about.

Martyn Percy
Ripon College Cuddesdon
Advent 2006

Preface

This book has its origin in my attempts to diversify from the official saints celebrated at a midweek service of Holy Communion in my church, St Andrew's Psalter Lane, an Anglican–Methodist partnership in Sheffield. Over several years we had remembered all the saints in the Anglican calendar, but I began to feel that it would be interesting to look at the lives of those who, without being 'saints', had been significant or challenging in the history of the Church. This certainly proved stimulating, and in 2004, during a period of sabbatical study, I decided to follow up some of these characters in a more systematic way.

I began to see that there were clear categories of 'brilliant Christians' which had been ignored or neglected in the calendars of the saints. I felt that it was somewhat small-minded of the Church not to honour heroes of the Old Testament or some of the 'great souls' of other faiths, especially when they had had a positive influence on or relationship with Christianity. This set the shape of the present book.

I am grateful to Professor Martyn Percy for his ongoing encouragement for this project and to St Deiniol's Library, Hawarden, for several periods of research in their ideal facilities. I am thankful for the support and stimulus of the congregation at St Andrew's Psalter Lane, especially the small midweek Communion congregation. Thanks are also due to my editor, Dr Natalie Watson, for many helpful suggestions for improving the format and content of what I wanted to write.

I dedicate this book to the memory of my father and mother, Alfred and Margaret Jowett, who read, enjoyed and commented on some of the sections before their deaths in 2004 and 2006, and to my wife Hilary and my daughter Abigail, with much love and gratitude.

Nicholas Jowett
6 December 2006

The name of Josiah is like blended incense prepared by the skill of the perfumer; his memory is as sweet as honey to every mouth, and like music at a banquet of wine.

Sirach 49.1

Contents

*All the chapter headings are taken from
Sirach (Ecclesiasticus) chapters 38 and 44*

Introduction

Sometimes I dream of revolution, a coup d'état by the second rank – troupes of actors slaughtered by their understudies, magicians sawn in half by indefatigable smiling glamour girls, cricket teams wiped out by marauding bands of twelfth men – comedians die on provincial stages, robbed of their feeds by mutely triumphant stooges – an army of assistants and deputies, the seconds-in-command, the runners-up, the right-hand men, storming the palace gates wherein the second son has already mounted the throne having committed regicide with a croquet mallet – stand-ins of the world, stand up![1]

So the second-string theatre critic, Moon, fantasizes in Tom Stoppard's play *The Real Inspector Hound*. I have to admit that my motivation for this collection of 'alternative' heroes of faith was initially somewhat similar. I share with the church historian, W.H.C. Frend, 'an instinctive sympathy for history's runners up'. They, of course, can no longer stand up and fight their corner for our attention, and history is written by the victors, or by their heirs, and this is nowhere more evident than in the history of the Church. And yet as centuries go by and new evidence comes to light, people with radically different sensibilities tell the old stories in different ways. In the last two centuries, for example, we have seen a determined investigation into the historicity of holy scripture and a corresponding interest in the theological and political interests of the writers. One result of that has been the emergence, in broad outline, of the historical figure of Jesus, the prophet from Nazareth, from behind the gospels' 'wall of narrative theology', challenging us once again to express an understanding of the incarnation.

Another has been the release for positive attention of the role of women and feminine imagery in the Bible.

What about the saints? There is no doubt that, in the western Church, they have been regarded in the past in very different ways from how they are thought of today. The earliest Christian saints were martyrs to their faith; their deaths were celebrated, their remains venerated, and their intercession in heaven sought in prayer. The Protestant Reformation rejected the cult of the saints because of many abuses that had become associated with it – the bogus relics, the veneration of images, the 'use' of saints as miracle-workers. When, after the fourth century, martyrdom became much less common, people of heroic and exemplary faith were honoured, and many monks and nuns, priests, bishops, missionaries and teachers of the faith, were proclaimed as saints. In more recent centuries, Christians who have served the needs of the suffering and the poor in the secular world have been regarded as saints.

In the early centuries sainthood was a matter of local acclaim but by the later Middle Ages canonizations were increasingly reserved for the pope to declare and authorize, after a process of investigating the quality of the saint's life and the miracles wrought by his or her influence. The Roman Catholic Church has conducted a number of rationalizations and revisions of its saints, and is much more sceptical towards the extravagant and fantastic stories in the earlier accounts of saints' lives and martyrdoms (hagiographies). At the Reformation the Church of England declared that the saints were to be commemorated not for their intercession or for miracles, but rather for the holiness of their lives and for the example that they offered to the living. It retained some saints' days in its calendar, but of course now had neither the mechanism nor the desire for further canonizations. Only in the twentieth century did it add new names of saints to its calendar. The principles behind these additions to the calendar, mainly derived from a 1958 commission report to the Lambeth Conference and recognizing that 'canonization' as such was no longer possible, were that the individuals chosen should be people whose lives were well attested, whose sanctity was not in doubt and whose example had been an inspiration to others. Except in the case of martyrdom, the individuals selected should have been dead for 50 years, thus avoiding the 'cult of the passing moment'. Other Protestant churches adhered to the New Testament concept that the saints are the whole people of God, although even in them there was celebration of great founding figures, such as John and Charles Wesley in the Methodist Church.

There have, then, been many different attitudes and approaches to the saints throughout Christian history, and many different descriptions of their status and role.

Robert Atwell, in his book *Celebrating the Saints: Daily Spiritual Readings for the Calendar of the Church of England*, writes:

> In the stories of individual saints it is as if the intense white light of the gospel has passed through a prism and been refracted into its constituent colours, making visible the spectrum of God's call to holiness. As we ponder their lives we glimpse little by little the face of the Christ who is coming to gather up all things in himself. The saints celebrate the vocation of the whole people of God to share in his very being.[2]

Karl Rahner, too, offered a helpful definition of the saints:

> They are the initiators and the creative models of the holiness which happens to be right for, and is the task of, their particular age. They create a new style; they prove that a certain form of life and activity is a really genuine possibility; they show experimentally that one can be a Christian even in *this* way; they make

such a type of person believable as a Christian type.[3]

And yet, looking at this question from an Anglican or Roman Catholic point of view, I feel that the roll-call of 'official' saints does not cover the whole spectrum, and does not include significant forms of life and activities in which individuals have expressed a passionate commitment of faith and a different model of holiness.

I recently did a little counting in the calendar authorized by the Church of England in 1997. Not counting the biblical saints, there are just over 200 names. Of these, over 80 are priests or bishops, and a further 48 are monks or nuns. Only just over 40 are women. There are significant numbers of martyrs and missionaries and theological writers, as one might expect, and some who were pioneers in charitable and social work. There are eight 'saintly monarchs', and when I tried to make a distinction between those from an aristocratic or comfortable upper-class background and those whose provenance was poor or disadvantaged, I came up with 146 of the former against 27 of the latter! That may not be an entirely accurate piece of sociological judgement, but it shows where our Christian saints come from. If we add to these findings certain other problems – the legendary stories that accreted round many of the earlier saints; the world-denying, body-punishing values that dictated definitions of holiness in earlier centuries; the completely changed judgement of history on certain characters (for example, Thomas Beckett) – then it becomes clear that the saints often need to be approached with a 'health warning'. They may no longer properly represent a rounded picture of holiness and heroic faith. Robert Atwell claims that the most recent Anglican calendar of saints is more inclusive, more catholic and more ecumenical. This is true, since it now includes more contemporary figures and people from other denominations and other parts of the world. But there is still, I believe, a long way to go.

This means that the range of people in the calendar of saints may actually be quite narrow. In what I admit is something of a caricature, you could draw the general conclusion that, to have the best chance of becoming a saint, you have to be male, upper-class, institutionally ultra-loyal, preferably a monk or a bishop, or failing that, a missionary or theological writer, and if at all possible, a virgin. Of course, I've left out the essentials – of being heroically and practically good, faith-full and loving unto death – and yet, in spite of that, the odd, lopsided profile of the 'ideal Christian' remains.

In 1997 Robert Ellsberg produced a pioneering volume entitled *All Saints,* in which he provided a short biography of a saint for every day of the year, including many un-canonized and interesting personalities. In his introduction he wrote:

> Previous models of sanctity tended to emphasize a world-denying asceticism; today we need examples of discipline and self-denial in service to the world and in solidarity with a suffering humanity. There are countless saints who exhibited the virtue of charity; we need saints who combine charity with a prophetic thirst for justice. Much of Christian history has been written with male hands; we need to recall the example and the gifts of holy and prophetic women. The traditional list of saints has been dominated by the clergy and those in religious life; we need to give special attention to the witness of lay people ... Church history tends to be written in Western terms; in this era of ... the 'world church' we need to remember the struggle of saints who translated the gospel into the idiom of local, non-Western cultures, who engaged the wisdom of other religious paths, and who tried to understand their faith in terms of new

intellectual and cultural horizons. We need examples of holiness beyond the cloister: saints immersed in the worlds of art, literature, scholarship, in political struggle, and in everyday life. We need prophets who challenge the church as well as the world to better reflect the justice and mercy of God. We need the witness of the martyrs, ancient and new, who have laid down their lives for their faith and for their neighbours. We must attend the visions of the mystics, who see through the shade of everydayness and so remind us of the God who is ever-greater than our theologies or our imaginations.[4]

There is no doubt that the Church *is* beginning to address some of these issues. Those who struggled prophetically against injustice, lay people, women pioneers, today's martyrs – these *are* remembered and celebrated. Robert Ellsberg himself provided a fascinating selection of heroes of faith, mainstream and eccentric. What has seemed to me to be absent, however, has been a precise analysis of the blind spots in the Church's collective memory and celebration. Who is being systematically left out? This book attempts to answer that question, and it does so in eight chapters, each chapter representing a 'category of the unregarded'.

These eight chapters can be further divided into two groups.

The first group is those who could be described as 'not for us'[5]: the heroes of the Hebrew scriptures; those who were condemned and marginalized as 'heretics', accused of destroying rather than building up the faith; and the outstanding figures of other faith traditions. My sympathy is with the underdog, and it proves remarkably easy to select a good number of individuals from all these categories who may not be 'for us', but who are certainly not against us; they are admirable people, deeply sympathetic to thoughtful Christians, and, in the case of a number of the heretics, seriously wronged by the Church. To begin to reinstate and remember them will be an act of magnanimity and contrition by today's Church, and an opportunity to challenge our theology and see how it stands up to questions from unexpected angles.

The 'alternative heroes' of the other group are 'underdogs' and 'unregarded' only in relation to the Church; in themselves they are masterful and glorious. They are the creative artists, the novelists and poets, the artists and architects, the composers and musicians; the pioneers of science; and a host of others, pioneers in the communication of the faith, who just got lost, for a whole variety of reasons. Their faith was not perhaps expressed *primarily* in holiness of life or in activities approved by the Church, but in a skill or talent, a gift from God, pursued and developed with total passion and conviction to the glory of God. When the footballer George Best died, there was a huge public demonstration of the awe and respect in which he was held, with great crowds celebrating his remembered footballing prowess, at Old Trafford and at his funeral. No one could claim that George Best had led a morally admirable life – he had extravagantly wasted his vast wealth, his relationships and his very life – and yet what people remembered was his almost godlike skill on the football field, those few years when he ran rings round oppositions and dazzled the spectators. Similarly, not all the creative artists and scientists I celebrate led pure Christian lives, but when they came to exercise their special gift, they did it with something like the perfection of saints. I find it strange that the Church has honoured those with great gifts of spirituality or charity or theological skill but has largely ignored those with gifts of music, art or science. Perhaps, as I try to show, there has been a tendency to see them as dangerously free and potentially 'against us'. But how fair is it to celebrate Ignatius Loyola each year, but not Johann

Sebastian Bach? It would be hard to say which of them had done more to inspire faith over the centuries.

This book, then, is a challenge to the Church and to Christians, to put aside institutional fears and small-mindedness and to celebrate goodness and beauty and truth wherever we find it. Incidentally, this very much affirms the role of all the saints: we may learn more about true discipleship from lived lives than from many an abstract catechism. The saints, of course, always struggled and wavered in their progress; the people pictured here did just the same, and we can take comfort and inspiration from that. Do I want to see a whole new raft of official saints, along the lines I'm suggesting? As an Anglican, I think the Church of England would capture people's imagination if it did something a little brave like this. I also believe there may be increased scope now for something more like the Early Church situation, in which saints were celebrated locally and by local choice. Anglican diocesan bishops actually have the power to authorize local celebration of saints. In my own church we recently celebrated the life of a wonderful member of the church who had died a year earlier. More important, however, is that Christians of all denominations discover and rediscover saints official and unofficial, and receive the richness of their embodied, completed faithfulness. And so my hope and my second main goal is that, providing some depth of biographical detail of just three figures within each of my eight categories, I may delight, stimulate and edify, and so inform and strengthen faith in God through Jesus Christ. To that end I have provided a prayer at the end of each life and each chapter, to be used perhaps as a response by the reader.

What I offer here will have succeeded if it prompts the reader to think of other heroes of faith, famous or unknown, who could and should be celebrated within the Christian community. In relation to perceived omissions, I should say that, because this book is as much a manifesto as a celebration, I have not aimed to 'plug every hole' in the catalogue of saints. Far from it; and I am conscious that much more could be done than I have here done to promote the cause – to take some of the types mentioned by Robert Ellsberg – of those who have struggled alongside the powerless for political justice, of those whom the Spirit has powerfully moved in the 'world church' far beyond the European frame, of those whose insights have been those of the mystic, and of those who happened to be women not men. For the purposes of this book, and because none of those categories is actually completely ignored by the Church, I decided not to tackle them. But it is of real importance that we tackle all these 'omissions' as they become clear to us, for as Mark Santer has written:

> There is a connection between our self-identification as members of particular communities and the stories we tell about the past. It is by the things we remember, and the way we remember them, and by the things we fail to remember, that we identify ourselves as belonging to this or that group. What we remember, or do not remember, moulds our reactions and our behaviour towards others at a level deeper than that of conscious reflection.[6]

I hope, at all events, that this book will go a small way to enabling us as contemporary Christians to have a richer, deeper memory of the past and a more generous attitude to the world in which we are set.

As an epilogue I have included some thoughts about that 'classic villain', Judas Iscariot, as a sort of ultimate test-case of possible rehabilitation. My conclusion may be surprising in a book like this, but in the end we have to respect the limits of what historical evidence can tell us, make a provisional judgement and commend a life to the mercy of God.

Kathleen Jones wrote, about the Celtic saints:

> They are unusual people: dedicated, and full
> of the Holy Spirit. They are sometimes anti-
> social, quirky and plain obstinate. They love
> remote islands, where they can contemplate
> the Creator through the creation ... They bless
> freely, and they curse freely. They live plainly
> and pray much. Though the outlines of their
> story are blurred by time or distorted by
> inaccurate reportage, it is often in the details
> of their lives that we can make direct contact
> with them.[7]

I hope that the reportage which follows here is not too
inaccurate and that through the details offered you will
encounter some more unusual people – quirky, gifted,
single-minded, and lights for our faith.

> It is a maxim that those to whom everyone
> allows the second place, have an undoubted
> title to the first.[8]

Chapter 1

Those who 'spoke in prophetic oracles'
The heroes of the Hebrew scriptures

There are three 'Old Testament saints' listed in the *Oxford Dictionary of Saints*. Would you guess they might be Abraham, Moses and Elijah? Or Ruth, Isaiah and Esther? Not at all. It turns out that none of them is human, and two of them also have small walk-on parts in the New Testament. They are, of course, the three archangels, Michael, Raphael and Gabriel. Michael is the special protector of Israel in the book of Daniel, and he leads the great fight against the devil (the dragon) and his angels in Revelation 12. (Well, perhaps a bit more than a walk-on part.) Gabriel's starring Christmas role in Luke's nativity story is well known: he announces births to both Zechariah and Mary; but he had also earlier helped Daniel understand his visions. Raphael gets his moment of glory as the heavenly helper in the apocryphal book of Tobit; he heals Tobit's blindness.

There are, of course, some positive aspects in this strange situation: to cast these older Jewish heavenly figures into roles in the Christian story – which is what Luke and John of Patmos do – is to proclaim strongly the continuity from Old to New (in other words, in spite of Marcion and the Gnostics, it's the same God and the same basic purposes we're dealing with in both); and to put St Michael alongside, say, St Matthew in the same category is to make an interesting claim for God's grace in Christ upon the latter: both are saints, that is, holy. But whatever you think about the literal (as opposed to the symbolic) reality of angels, it seems odd to put them in the same category with struggling human beings. It seems to be a confusion of categories, and it certainly adds an extra burden to the average failing Christian wondering whether they can aspire to such heights of holiness. Further, if the real continuity of the testaments was to be expressed, why not take Abraham or Moses, Elijah or Isaiah, figures of huge importance as the early Christians developed their self-understanding as the true heirs and fulfilment of what had gone before in the Hebrew tradition?

The earliest Christians continued the Jewish custom of building monuments over the burial places of patriarchs, prophets or martyrs, and even of joining in the veneration of Jewish heroes of the faith, particularly the prophets and the Maccabaean martyrs, as well as their own martyrs. Why, then, only angels from the Hebrew scriptures were honoured as saints in the later tradition of the Church must remain a matter of speculation, but a likely reason must be that the truths of the people of the old covenant were seen as superseded by the new revelation in Christ. Salvation was now by God's grace through faith in Christ, and the old prophecies had been fulfilled and the old law superseded. A strong expression of this is given by the words Jesus utters about John the Baptist: 'Truly I tell you, among those born of women no one has arisen greater than John the Baptist; yet the least in the kingdom of heaven is greater than he ... For all the prophets and the law prophesied until John came; and if you are willing to accept it, he is Elijah who is to come.'[1] This seems to put even the great forerunner John on the 'wrong' side of a sharp dividing line between the old and the new: all the greatness of the old is as nothing now Christ has come with the new dispensation. It suddenly makes you wonder how John the Baptist ever made it to being recognized as a saint; perhaps we could after all count him as the one human Old Testament saint? Nevertheless, it's John's role and closeness in relation to *Jesus* which really count in terms of his canonization; he is regarded as a sort of 'honorary Christian' because of that.

There is, however, a stronger affirmation of the 'real Old Testament saints' in the eleventh chapter of the letter to the Hebrews. This actually lists in a most solemn manner all the great people of the Old Testament who lived by faith and accomplished great deeds and great suffering, from Abel through Abraham and Moses right down to Samuel and David and then on into a great catalogue of the torments, trials and faithfulness of others; but the author ends the chapter with these words: 'Yet all these, though they were commended for their faith, did not receive what was promised, since God had provided something better so that they would not, without us, be made perfect.'[2] In other words, that roll-call of ancient saints, those whom the writer now immediately calls a 'great cloud of witnesses', will finally have the reward of their faith along with us Christians who know about it directly; they will be redeemed 'from the transgressions under the first covenant'.[3] And it is definitely worth remembering them, the writer insists, because of their great faith and hope, which can be an inspiration for Christians, and because they still surround us with their invisible support.

But the ambivalence remains: these *are* the people of the old covenant, these are the people of that ethnic identity from which the Church was rapidly separating itself, and although Abraham's faith was much quoted by Paul, although Moses' giving of the law and Elijah's promised return were enormously important to the first Christians, and although they quoted from Isaiah and the other prophets to justify their new theological narrative, yet, in spite of that, the practice of using a monument as a focus of thankfulness and remembrance and prayer to figures from pre-Christian times clearly did not survive. Meanwhile, of course, the Early Church was suffering its first martyrdoms, and the new martyrs, their relics and their shrines, inevitably took precedence in the roll of those to be remembered, honoured and prayed to. Official, papally recognized canonizations only took over from locally approved cults in the thirteenth century, and the Second Vatican Council set in motion a major rationalization of the cult of the saints, and at that point

(1969) only the three archangels were recognized in the calendar, all to be celebrated with Michael on 29 September. The Church of England just has St Michael and All Angels on that day.

But is there any good reason for our *not* recalling some of the human heroes of faith in the Hebrew world before the Common Era? I think not; and in fact there are some good reasons *for* doing so: it will help us focus on the particular courage of an individual, rather than just seeing them as part of the sweep of salvation history; it will bring some obscure (and often female) figures out into the light; and it will help us to see something very important – that there was Christlikeness before Christ, something already incarnated and lived out in different ways, just as Jesus' ethic itself can be found paralleled in Jewish scripture. So the pernicious myth that everything before him is somehow superseded in Christ will be rightly undermined.

Justin, the second-century Christian apologist, can support our purpose here. He pondered on the idea, from John's Gospel, of Christ as the Logos (God's Word or fundamental purpose), and making use of Stoic and Platonic philosophy, he saw that each person shared in this divine Logos, having as it were a tiny seed (sperma) of it as a result of the action of the seed-giving or generative Word (spermatikos logos). Since Christ was God's first-born, the Logos, everyone throughout history, whether or not they had known Christ, could have a share or seed of his infinite truth and wisdom, even if it were often obscured or imperfectly realized:

> We have declared above that he [Christ] is the Logos of whom every race of men were partakers; and that those who lived reasonably (that is, with logos) are Christians though they have been thought atheists: as, among the Greeks, Socrates and Heraclitus, and men like them; and among the

barbarians, Abraham, Ananias, Azarias,
Misael and Elias [Elijah] and many others.[4]

This encourages us to celebrate the outstanding figures
of the 'old covenant' (and of course figures of other faiths
– see chapter seven) as those in whom was planted the
divine seed, God's Word, who was there in the beginning
and who became flesh in Jesus the Christ.

Of the three Old Testament 'saints' here presented, I
have chosen one of the great prophets, about whom we
seem to know more than most others, but then I have
flanked him with two lesser-known women, who played a
small but heroic part in the long history of God's ancient
people. We are told so much more about men than women
in the Bible, and that reflects the balance of public and
private roles; but it is good to dwell on some women of
character and integrity from those pre-Christian times,
and I might just as well have chosen Rahab the prostitute,
Ruth the loyal foreigner or Huldah the prophet. God's
generative Word was at work in them, too.

Abigail
Eleventh century BC

Abigail is one of the unknown stars of the Old
Testament. She survives in later Jewish oral commentary,
her story appears in the works of Chaucer, Milton and
Dryden, and her name had once again become favoured by
the end of the twentieth century, but she herself has
disappeared from the consciousness of many, if not most,
churchgoing Christians. Recent lectionaries, even where
they were, in principle, reading through a whole book of
the Bible continuously from day to day, simply omitted the
chapter (1 Samuel 25) in which she so stunningly appears.
She therefore found herself dumped into oblivion along
with the likes of Shechem, who, it turns out, raped Jacob's
daughter Dinah and was then murdered by Dinah's
brothers shortly after undergoing a painful circumcision
(Genesis 34), or along with the Levite of Judges 19 who

decided it would be all right to send out his concubine to be gang raped by the Benjaminites of Gibeah. Abigail does not deserve this.

She should rather be enrolled in the ranks of intelligent, decisive women, who, in a crisis, know exactly what to do. Where the men were about to sort out a problem in the only way they knew – by fighting – she found a better solution. She saved lives – but also kept her eye on the main chance. And it should be mentioned, just in passing, that she was very, very sexy. The Bible simply calls her 'of good understanding and beautiful', but the Haggadah (Jewish non-legal literature) counts her among the four women of surpassing loveliness in the world (the other three were Sarah, Rahab and Esther) and says that it was reported that even the memory of her inspired lust. Not altogether surprising, then, if she didn't take too long to convert the lusty young David to her point of view.

As the story begins, David has had his life threatened and has escaped from the court of king Saul, who is in pursuit of him. David has no power base, but moves around from place to place in the south of the country with a gang of men who have a variety of grievances against Saul. Their similarity to Robin Hood and his merry men is not altogether far-fetched. Abigail is the wife of one Nabal, a very rich man, who owns vast numbers of sheep and goats. We can only presume that Abigail had little say in the choice of a husband, because he is described as 'churlish and ill-behaved'; in fact his very name means 'fool'. When St Jerome came to comment on this passage, he compared him with the 'rich fool' of Jesus' parable, who thought he could live long on his stored-up wealth but was sadly mistaken – an apt comparison, as we shall see. Abigail, by contrast, seems almost to personify the lady Wisdom of Proverbs, for she will offer the young man David long life and prosperity if he follows her.

Nabal's shepherds have been shearing the sheep, and it seems that David's men have been 'helping' them. This 'help' may have been little better than a protection racket, but at all events David then sends 10 of his men to ask Nabal for a little consideration for the 'help' given, a little share in the sheep-shearing festival perhaps. True to form, Nabal sends them away with a flea in their ear: 'Who is this son of Jesse anyway? Haven't I got enough of my own workers to feed and water?' At this the red mist comes down on David, and he and 400 fighters set off with swords at their belts to get even with Nabal.

David heard in the wilderness that Nabal was shearing his sheep. So David sent ten young men; and David said to the young men, 'Go up to Carmel, and go to Nabal, and greet him in my name. Thus you shall salute him: "Peace be to you, and peace be to your house, and peace be to all you have. I hear that you have shearers; now your shepherds have been with us, and we did them no harm, and they missed nothing, all the time they were in Carmel. Ask your young men, and they will tell you. Therefore let my young men find favour in your sight; for we have come on a feast day. Please give whatever you have at hand to your servants and to your son David."'

When David's young men came, they said all this to Nabal in the name of David; and then they waited. But Nabal answered David's servants, 'Who is David? Who is the son of Jesse? There are many servants today who are breaking away from their masters. Shall I take my bread and my water and the meat that I have butchered for my shearers, and give it to men who come from I do not know where?' So David's young men turned away, and came back and told him all this. David said to his men, 'Every man strap on his sword!' And every one of them strapped on his sword; David also strapped on his sword; and about four hundred men went up after David, while two hundred remained with the baggage.

1 Samuel 25.4–13

Now Abigail finds out the situation from one of Nabal's men, who, it must be admitted, paints a very positive picture of the 'protection' that David has offered them in the fields. She acts swiftly and decisively to avert the violent clash that is now almost inevitable. David is marching down a valley breathing blood and vengeance on Nabal and his men. 'He has repaid me bad for good. May God bring unnameable ills on David and worse ones, too, if by morning I leave a single manjack alive of all who belong to him!' But then he encounters Abigail. Or rather, he encounters first of all a series of asses laden with food: bread, wine, mutton, grain, raisins and figs. In the same way that Jacob propitiated Esau with an advance gift of sheep, goats, camels and cattle after their long separation, so Abigail softens up David with the sight of all the delights he must have assumed he would not now receive from Nabal. She follows this up quickly by jumping off her donkey and bowing deeply before David; it must have been a pretty sight to the rough men marching out of the wilderness. Now follows Abigail's speech, which is at once gentle, flattering, honest and diplomatic – just what the situation needs. She begins by referring to herself as David's 'handmaid' and asking that the guilt of the situation fall on her. Since this is clearly not going to happen, she then feels free to put all the blame for the discourtesy on to her husband and even to call him 'fool'. She goes on more or less to prophesy David's future success and kingship, and subtly reminds him that, when he has got to the top, he will be rather glad he did not stain his hands with the blood of Nabal's innocent men. At the very end of the speech – and one can almost see her flashing her eyes boldly up at the wide-eyed David – she says, 'And when God has given you success, don't forget me.'

'Now then, my Lord, as the LORD lives, and as you yourself live, since the LORD has restrained you from blood-guilt and from taking vengeance with your own hand, now let your enemies and those who seek to do evil to my Lord be like Nabal. And now let this present that your servant has brought to my Lord be given to the young men who follow my Lord. Please forgive the trespass of your servant; for the LORD will certainly make my Lord a sure house, because my Lord is fighting the battles of the LORD; and evil shall not be found in you as long as you live. If anyone should rise up to pursue you and to seek your life, the life of my Lord shall be bound in the bundle of the living under the care of the LORD your God; but the lives of your enemies he shall sling out as from the hollow of a sling. When the LORD has done to my Lord according to all the good that he has spoken concerning you, and has appointed you prince over Israel, my Lord shall have no cause of grief, or pangs of conscience, for having shed blood without cause or for having saved himself. And when the LORD has dealt well with my Lord, then remember your servant.'

1 Samuel 25.26–31

There is little chance that David will forget her, and none at all that he will reject what can only be called a handsome apology. It is as though your breakfast bacon were slightly burnt at the Hilton Hotel and the company offered you, in compensation, a free weekend in the best bedroom with a charming young escort thrown in. David accepts with grace, and Abigail returns home. She has done a good day's work, saving her husband's men from death and implanting her image firmly in David's mind. That she is a humble, loyal wife cannot be said; she hasn't even told Nabal what she's done. He, meanwhile, goes on a bit of a sheep-shearing festival binge, and only when he sobers up a little in the morning does Abigail tell him what she has done. Nabal at once suffers some kind of heart attack or seizure ('his heart died within him; he became like a stone') and in 10 days he's dead. Abigail has shown her intelligence in choosing the right moment to tell her tale to Nabal.

When he hears of Nabal's death, David is, understandably, rather pleased, both because he is after all avenged on him without having to dirty his hands, but possibly even more at the sudden availability of Abigail. He sends messengers to woo her, and she takes no persuading. With her five maids, she goes 'off to the woods' to be Maid Marian to David's Robin Hood.

We don't hear much more of Abigail in the Bible. We hear that David had to rescue her along with his other wife, Ahinoam, when they were snatched from Ziklag (1 Samuel 30.5), that she was with him when he became king in Hebron and that she bore him at least one son (called Chileab in 2 Samuel 3.3 or Daniel in 1 Chronicles 3.1). David, of course, had many more wives, including many later who were married for dynastic purposes, but it may be guessed that he retained a special affection for the gorgeous, brilliant woman who fell at his feet and saved him from murder.

> She met him in a wild pass of the mountains,
> David, whom she called her Lord, and said:
> 'I bring you bread and wine, I bring you raisins.
> Sheep I bring, and corn, and cakes of figs.
> Accept all these, my Lord; I am your servant;
> I save you from blood-guilt. For you are bound
> Where Nabal is, my husband, who insulted
> Certain of your soldiers. Do not kill him.
> Nabal's very name, my Lord, is Fool.
> Then do not kill him. When my Lord is king,
> What pity if a fool's blood blights his conscience.
> I am your servant, saving you.' He looked,
> Beautiful himself, upon her beauty,

And said: 'So shall it be. Blessed are you
That kept me from revenge. I would have killed him,
Surely. Go in peace.' And David left her.
Then was it with his beauty in her heart
That she went straight to Nabal, who was drunk,
And told him of the danger there had been,
So that his spirit sank in him, like stone,
And in ten days he died?
For she was ready at Carmel
When those messengers came in
With word that David wanted her for wife.
She mounted up at once and rode to him,
And married him forever, and forgot,
Or did you, Abigail, that first one's fall?

Mark van Doren[5]

Does it seem fair that Abigail was edited out of our lectionary when we had to plough through so many of the grizzlier episodes of the books of Joshua and Judges? This begins to look like the modern censor's greater objection to sex than violence, an extremely dubious preference. It could be argued that David's meeting with Abigail was not a historic event like the annihilation of the cities of Canaan or the endless cycle of violence in the time of the Judges. Nothing much changed, as in: no one was brutally murdered, a woman used her ingenuity and her beauty to avert disaster, and two beautiful young people were brought together in sexual union. But actually quite a lot happened, as in: a story in which the 'weaker sex' by subtlety gains mastery over the situation, a parable in which a woman stops men doing something stupid which they will regret and proves that saying sorry is usually a good thing, and a terrific tale told in masterly fashion by one of the great chroniclers of David's life.

Let us praise Abigail for her beauty, her wisdom and her great foresight.

Jesus,
living openly and without protection,
you were willing to respond to a Caananite
woman because of a sudden flash of
intelligence and hope in her.
As we thank God also for the decisive wisdom
of Abigail,
we pray that we may use our gifts of body
and mind with good sense
and always be ready to be diverted from
over-hasty reactions.
We ask this in your name.

৪০ ৫৪

Jeremiah
Seventh century BC

> O LORD, you have enticed me, and I was enticed; you
> have overpowered me, and you have prevailed. I have
> become a laughing-stock all day long; everyone mocks
> me. For whenever I speak, I must cry out, I must shout,
> 'Violence and destruction!' For the word of the LORD
> has become for me a reproach and derision all day long.
> If I say, 'I will not mention him, or speak any more in
> his name', then within me there is something like a
> burning fire shut up in my bones; I am weary with
> holding it in, and I cannot.
>
> Jeremiah 20.7–9

The prophet Jeremiah gave his name to the *jeremiad*, a
literary form popular in Puritan America, in which a writer
laments the causes of current calamities and demands
reform if the future is to be brighter. That is still how we
think of Jeremiah, 'the weeping prophet', who had a divine

compulsion to speak but could only bring news of gloom and disaster for God's wayward people.

It is probably true that people think they know more about Jeremiah's personal history than any other of the Old Testament prophets. We seem to have a good deal of personal 'confessional' material in the book of his prophecy, like the passage quoted above. But perhaps we should be cautious, in the same way that thoughtful people no longer ascribe everything contained in the gospels to the historical Jesus. For it is clear, when scholars look at the text of Jeremiah, that his sayings and traditions have been thoroughly worked over by later writers to fit them into a theological scheme derived from Deuteronomy, in which the people of Judah suffer terminal calamity because they failed to keep their part of the covenant with God. Has the historical Jeremiah disappeared behind the work of many later editors?

Robert Carroll certainly believed so. In his commentary on Jeremiah he writes:

> The refraction of the figure of Jeremiah due to the editing and developing of many discrete traditions over a long period of time must be recognized as creating Jeremiah in a different image from whatever may have been the case before the tradition developed.[6]

Carroll criticizes those many writers who have turned Jeremiah into some kind of modern, tortured existential hero. He quotes a typical over-the-top claim by Jean Steinmann who wrote that Jeremiah 'was truly the genius of torment and disharmony, the Euripides, the Pascal or the Dostoyevsky of the Old Testament'. By contrast, the commentary of William L. Holladay, published in 1986, the same year as Carroll's, believes that many of the texts in the book of Jeremiah can be fitted into the historical chronology of a real individual and that there is a real person very visible there. The truth is almost certainly somewhere between the extremes of Carroll and Holladay, with the added bonus that, as with the figure of Jesus, the 'literary remains', although not always historically reliable, portray a human being struggling to be faithful to a vision, and that still has the power to stimulate and inspire us, irrespective of history.

So who was Jeremiah? He came from Anathoth, a village just north of Jerusalem, he died in exile in Egypt, and he lived through those fateful years in Jerusalem at the very end of the seventh century and the beginning of the sixth century BC, during which the people of Judah finally lost their political autonomy. It fell to him to speak the mind of God when it could only be bad news to his hearers.

When the power of the Assyrian empire began to fade and the power of Babylon to grow in the last years of the seventh century, Judah, the surviving Jewish kingdom, found itself trapped between the hammer of Babylon and the anvil of Egypt. King Jehoiakim (609–598) tried to play a game of international roulette between Babylon and Egypt, but Nebuchadnezzar finally lost patience and invaded Jerusalem in 598. The king was killed, and many of the leading citizens were deported to Babylon, together with a new king-in-name, Jehoiachin, the son of the dead king. Those who were left behind in Jerusalem had another son of Jehoiakim, Zedekiah, as their king, and for some 11 years there was intense rivalry between the communities in Jerusalem and Babylon. Zedekiah struggled to free Judah from Babylonian overlordship, and in 587, encouraged by the promise of Egyptian help (which did not materialize), he began a rebellion. This brought down Babylonian military might on Judah: Jerusalem and the Temple were destroyed, and most of the rest of the ruling class was taken off into exile in Babylon. A governor, Gedaliah, was left behind in Jerusalem, but when he was assassinated together with some Babylonian soldiers many of the remaining Jewish citizens fled to Egypt, fearing reprisals. They took a very unwilling Jeremiah with them.

The word that came to Jeremiah from the LORD: Stand in the gate of the LORD's house, and proclaim there this word, and say, Hear the word of the LORD, all you people of Judah, you that enter these gates to worship the LORD. Thus says the LORD of hosts, the God of Israel: Amend your ways and your doings, and let me dwell with you in this place. Do not trust in these deceptive words: 'This is the temple of the LORD, the temple of the LORD, the temple of the LORD.'

For if you truly amend your ways and your doings, if you truly act justly one with another, if you do not oppress the alien, the orphan, and the widow, or shed innocent blood in this place, and if you do not go after other gods to your own hurt, then I will dwell with you in this place, in the land that I gave of old to your ancestors for ever and ever. Here you are, trusting in deceptive words to no avail. Will you steal, murder, commit adultery, swear falsely, make offerings to Baal, and go after other gods that you have not known, and then come and stand before me in this house, which is called by my name, and say, 'We are safe!' – only to go on doing all these abominations? Has this house, which is called by my name, become a den of robbers in your sight?... And now, because you have done all these things, says the LORD, and when I spoke to you persistently, you did not listen, and when I called you, you did not answer, therefore I will do to the house that is called by my name, in which you trust, and to the place that I gave to you and to your ancestors, just what I did to Shiloh. And I will cast you out of my sight, just as I cast out all your kinsfolk, all the offspring of Ephraim.

Jeremiah 7.1–15

The priests and the prophets and all the people heard Jeremiah speaking these words in the house of the LORD. And when Jeremiah had finished speaking all that the LORD had commanded him to speak to all the people, then the priests and the prophets and all the people laid hold of him, saying, 'You shall die! Why have you prophesied in the name of the LORD, saying, "This house shall be like Shiloh, and this city shall be desolate, without inhabitants"?' And all the people gathered around Jeremiah in the house of the LORD.

Jeremiah 26.7–9

Jeremiah represents the deepest kind of human heroism – the willingness to stand against a whole hypocritical establishment which does not want to accept painful truth, and to keep speaking, whatever the consequences. The people of Judah were relying on an ideology of the Jewish state which told them that God's covenant with king and people, focused in the Temple, would always protect them, but they had failed to reckon with the righteousness of God and with the certainty that, if they persistently violated the commitments of the covenant in idolatry and social injustice, God would ultimately not intervene to save them from disaster, and indeed would actively bring about their punishment at the hand of foreign invaders (see the curses proclaimed in Deuteronomy 28). Jeremiah's words of anguish, from the times of Jehoiakim and Zedekiah, on the people's sin and the irrevocable doom which is to follow, are recorded in the first 25 chapters of the book of Jeremiah, together with his own miserable ruminations on the utterly thankless task God has given him. Chapters 26–45 contain historical narratives from this period, ending with Jeremiah's exile to Egypt, in which the sufferings of the prophet include: arrest (after the Temple sermon); having his words, painstakingly recorded by the scribe Baruch, systematically torn into strips and burned in a brazier by

King Jehoiakim; a further arrest and imprisonment in the time of Zedekiah, when the Babylonians were besieging Jerusalem, and when, for a time, Jeremiah was left to rot in a mud-filled cistern; and finally being taken off to Egypt against his will. Consistently he advised that there was no avoiding God's decree of doom on an evil people, a doom to be carried out by the hand of Nebuchadnezzar.

> I thought how I would set you among my children, and give you a pleasant land, the most beautiful heritage of all the nations. And I thought you would call me, My Father, and would not turn from following me. Instead, as a faithless wife leaves her husband, so you have been faithless to me, O house of Israel, says the LORD.
>
> Jeremiah 3.19–20

But there is more to Jeremiah than the figure of a Cassandra, doomed to announce nothing but bad news and never to be believed. For, together with the anguish he feels for himself and his people, he also expresses the sadness and misery of God over the people who have turned away from their Father and are bringing disaster upon themselves. But that frustrated love of God contains the seed of hope beyond the time of inevitable disaster, a hope that Jeremiah expresses in several different ways. In the time of Zedekiah he wrote to the exiles in Babylon, advising them that it was God's will that their exile should not end soon, and therefore they should settle and make a permanent home and 'seek the welfare of the city where I have sent you into exile and pray to the LORD on its behalf, for in its welfare you will find your welfare' (29.7). The outlook for the people of God might have changed drastically, but God still had a will and purpose for their good. Later, while the Babylonians were besieging Jerusalem and when Jeremiah himself was still in prison, he actually purchased a field at Anathoth from his cousin

Hanamel, and proclaimed the symbolic significance of such an action: 'For thus says the LORD of hosts, the God of Israel: Houses and fields and vineyards shall again be bought in this land' (32.15). After the final catastrophe had happened to Judah, Jeremiah could paint pictures of future return and restoration; God had certainly not finished with them. They had suffered the inevitable consequence of their sin, but now there was to be a new kind of start.

The days are surely coming, says the LORD, when I will make a new covenant with the house of Israel and the house of Judah. It will not be like the covenant that I made with their ancestors when I took them by the hand to bring them out of the land of Egypt – a covenant that they broke, though I was their husband, says the LORD. But this is the covenant I will make with the house of Israel after those days, says the LORD: I will put my laws within them, and I will write it on their hearts; and I will be their God, and they shall be my people. No longer shall they teach one another, or say to each other, 'Know the LORD', for they shall all know me, from the least of them to the greatest, says the LORD; for I will forgive their iniquities, and remember their sin no more.

Jeremiah 31.31–34

That passage almost certainly comes, in its present form, from a later time than Jeremiah's, but it is true to Jeremiah's theme of the absolute reliability and inevitability of God's justice *and* God's love. It was taken over by the New Testament writer to the Hebrews (8.8–12; 10.16–17) as a way of describing what God had done in Christ.

We leave Jeremiah as we found him, lamenting the times in which he was born and the task that God had thrust upon him. He is far from the only saint who has complained bitterly to God about the good he was inwardly compelled to say and to do, in 'interesting times'.

> Cursed be the day on which I was born! The day when my mother bore me, let it not be blessed! Cursed be the man who brought the news to my father, saying, 'A child is born to you, a son', making him very glad. Let that man be like the cities that the LORD overthrew without pity; let him hear a cry in the morning and an alarm at noon, because he did not kill me in the womb; so my mother would have been my grave, and her womb forever great. Why did I come forth from the womb to see toil and sorrow, and spend my days in shame?
>
> Jeremiah 20.14–18

Father of sternest love,
you never let humanity escape the
consequence of its sin,
but you speak to us through prophets who,
like Jeremiah, look at the world through your
sad eyes
and speak uncomfortable messages
to those who do not want the truth.
May powerful people everywhere
be willing to listen to the lone voices and the
minority reports
and so fulfil your will of salvation
even in the teeth of impending catastrophe.

ᛞ ᚳ

The Mother of Seven Sons
Second century BC

It happened also that seven brothers and their mother were arrested and were being compelled by the king, under torture with whips and thongs, to partake of unlawful swine's flesh. One of them, acting as their spokesman, said, 'What do you intend to ask and learn from us? For we are ready to die rather than transgress the laws of our ancestors.'

The king fell into a rage, and gave orders to have pans and cauldrons heated. These were heated immediately, and he commanded that the tongue of their spokesman be cut out and that they scalp him and cut off his hands and feet, while the rest of the brothers and the mother looked on. When he was utterly helpless, the king ordered them to take him to the fire, still breathing, and to fry him in a pan. The smoke from the pan spread widely, but the brothers and their mother encouraged one another to die nobly, saying, 'The Lord God is watching over us and in truth has compassion on us, as Moses declared in his song that bore witness against the people to their faces when he said, "And he will have compassion on his servants." '

2 Maccabees 7.1–6

Like many women in the Bible, we do not know her name. Like many women through the ages, she is defined in terms of her relationship with men: she is the mother of seven sons. And like all the biblical authors, her literary chronicler is a man, who believes that in her moment of deadly trial she needs to 'reinforce her womanly argument with manly courage'.

The year is 167 BC. Palestine is part of the Seleucid Empire. There has been no independent Jewish state for more than 400 years, although the Jews have been allowed the practice of their religion for most of that time. Since the death of Alexander the Great (323 BC), they have been under Egyptian rule (the Ptolemies), but then, for the last 30 years, under the Seleucids, whose rule at its widest stretches from Asia Minor (modern Turkey) to the borders of India. Their king (175–163 BC) has become a unique hate-figure for many Jews and the cause of a battle for freedom. He is Antiochus IV Epiphanes; they believe he wants to wipe out Jewish religion and culture. He is the man behind the Abomination of Desolation. It is beginning to look like the David and Goliath struggle all over again.

But matters are not quite that simple. For one thing, there are Jews and Jews. There are, of course, many in Palestine, but there are many more scattered round the Mediterranean – in Egypt, in Asia Minor, in Greece, in Italy. Increasingly the Diaspora Jews no longer understand Hebrew or Aramaic, and a version of the Old Testament in Greek (the Septuagint) has to be created. They are surrounded by Greek (Hellenistic) culture, spread by the conquests of Alexander the Great and continued by his successors, the Ptolemies and Seleucids. No Jew is more than a stone's throw from people who entertain Greek philosophical ideas (like the immortality of the soul), who indulge in Greek activities (like gymnastics or the theatre) or who worship Greek gods (subtly blended with their own local deities). And for Jewish religion and culture, it's 'killing me softly', just as western products and advertising threaten the indigenous cultures of the globe today. Aristocratic Jews with some political pretensions are increasingly willing to compromise their ancestral faith in exchange for power.

In fact it is Jews who precipitate the violent oppressions of Antiochus IV. The king is desperate for money to hold together his crumbling empire (he's got Parthians to the east, Egypt to the south and Rome to the west, all with their tails up), and, although initially he isn't trying to wipe out local religion and customs, he wants to see a common Hellenistic culture to unify his realm. So he's very happy when the High Priest's brother at Jerusalem, a man called Joshua who, ominously, likes to be called Jason, offers a very large sum of money and full implementation of the hellenizing policy *if* he can have the High Priest's job himself. Antiochus gives him the job, and Jason soon sets up a Greek gymnasium in Jerusalem. (Some of the naked Jewish gymnasts are so embarrassed about their circumcision that they have it surgically disguised!) After three years Jason is ousted by one Menelaus, who promises Antiochus even more money, but when in 169 BC Jason brings an army against Menelaus and almost drives him out, Antiochus himself suddenly turns up on the way back from campaigns in Egypt, re-establishes Menelaus as High Priest and plunders the Temple, removing its sacred furniture and vessels and even stripping the gold leaf from its façade.

From here on it's downhill all the way, as opposition from orthodox Jews begins to grow and Antiochus realizes that to fulfil his policy he will have to stamp out the religion at Jerusalem. He sends a large force which butchers and enslaves many Jews, loots and destroys part of the city and sets up a citadel just to the south of the Temple. With the connivance of Menelaus, Judaism is about to be reorganized as a Syro-Hellenic cult in which Yahweh will be worshipped in complete identification with Zeus *and* King Antiochus himself. And now, for faithful Jews, comes the real shock – horror stuff: the regular Temple sacrifices, observance of the Sabbath and the traditional feasts are forbidden. Copies of the law are to be destroyed. Children are no longer to be circumcised. Pagan altars are erected throughout the land and unclean animals offered on them. Jews are forced to eat pork on pain of death. Worst of all, an altar and image of Zeus, possibly bearing the features of Antiochus himself, is set up in the Temple and pig flesh is offered on it. This is the

Abomination of Desolation of the book of Daniel, written only a year or two later. The book disguises Antiochus all too thinly as Nebuchadnezzar, king of Babylon, or, in the apocalyptic visions, as a blasphemous little horn sprouting from a fearsome beast.

What will be the response of faithful Jews? What form will their defiance take? Militarism or martyrdom? In fact, it is both. The first and second books of Maccabees in the Apocrypha give alternative accounts of the events (and we need to be aware that these are written totally from the point of view of faithful religious Jews; there is no attempt at 'balance' or any kind of sympathy for Antiochus' problems and motivation). The military response begins with the old priest Mattathias, whose son Judas Maccabaeus leads a successful campaign against the Seleucid forces, in December 164 BC, rededicates the Temple with great joy (an event celebrated in the festival of Hanukkah) and inaugurates a final period of religious freedom and political autonomy for Judah.

What of the martyrs?

After the first brother had died in this way, they brought forward the second for their sport. They tore off the skin of his head with the hair, and asked him, 'Will you eat rather than have your body punished limb by limb?' He replied in the language of his ancestors and said to them, 'No'. Therefore he in turn underwent tortures as the first brother had done. And when he was at his last breath, he said, 'You accursed wretch, you dismiss us from this present life, but the King of the universe will raise us up to an everlasting renewal of life, because we have died for his laws.'

After him, the third was the victim of their sport. When it was demanded, he quickly put out his tongue and courageously stretched forth his hands, and said nobly, 'I got these from Heaven, and because of his laws I disdain them, and from him I hope to get them back again.' As a result the king himself and those with him were astonished at the young man's spirit, for he regarded his sufferings as nothing.

2 Maccabees 7.7–12

This is where the mother of seven sons makes her appearance, in 2 Maccabees 7. She and her sons are being forced by King Antiochus to eat pork on pain of torture and death. The woman has to witness the hideous mutilation and death of each of her sons in turn, but she strengthens them to resist the temptation to apostasize and even tricks the king into thinking she is pleading with the youngest to save his life when in fact she is exhorting him to martyrdom. Finally she too is put to death. There is no doubt that this is an 'ideal scene' created long after the persecutions had passed into history, but, like so much of the Bible and of ancient history writing in general, there is a core of history behind the edifying narrative that has been created, and the truth of a martyrdom emerges.

What are the truths of this martyrdom?

First, the truth that violence against those who are defending the very things that give their life meaning and identity will always be futile. In a thousand reruns of Antiochus and the woman with seven sons the outcome will always be the same. We don't have to look far round our world today to see the futile replays of this hideous sport. Secondly there is the truth that martyrdom is usually 'fighting by other means'. The martyr, if you like, heaps a whole pile of wrong on to the perpetrator. We see this in the defiant words of the sons, especially the last son, who threatens the king with God's severest judgement and punishment as he dies. He may have lost the battle of life, but he takes with him the moral high ground and consigns his persecutor to hell. (We can, however, contrast this with the final prayers for forgiveness of their murderers by Jesus and Stephen, an attitude nevertheless not shared by John of Patmos (Revelation 6.10 and 11.1–19).)

> The mother was especially admirable and worthy of honourable memory. Although she saw her seven sons perish within a single day, she bore it with good courage because of her hope in the Lord. She encouraged each of them in the language of their ancestors. Filled with a noble spirit, she reinforced her woman's reasoning with a man's courage, and said to them, 'I do not know how you came into being in my womb. It was not I who gave you life and breath, nor I who set in order the elements within each of you. Therefore the Creator of the world, who shaped the beginning of humankind and devised the origin of all things, will in his mercy give life and breath back to you again, since you now forget yourselves for the sake of his laws.'
>
> 2 Maccabees 7.20–23

A third truth is that of the growing logic of resurrection. 2 Maccabees 7 is one of the earliest witnesses to a new Jewish belief. The agonizing question of how the God of the covenant can allow those who are faithful to it nevertheless to suffer is posed here, and answered with trust and hope; there will be resurrection, to put things right. And it will not be a Greek immortality of the soul, but a restoration/transformation of the psycho-physical unity which, for Jewish thought, was a human being.

> The new life they will receive, which is seen in very 'bodily' terms, is the gift of the creator god who made them and all the world in the first place. And the resurrection they await is not the same as the 'everflowing life' they have already drunk. It is still

> awaited. The writer of 2 Maccabees did not suppose that the brothers and the mother had already been given their hands, tongues and whole bodies back again. Their resurrection would surely happen, but it certainly had not happened yet ... Resurrection is never a redescription of death, but always its overthrow and reversal.
>
> N.T. Wright[7]

With the promise of resurrection, there is also the beginning of an idea of atonement and redemption: the martyrs bear suffering on behalf of the whole people, and the people move into freedom as a result, with the tyrant Antiochus overthrown and killed. The writer of 4 Maccabees, writing more than a hundred years later and reflecting on the meaning of the martyrdom of the seven sons and their mother, had this comment:

> These then, who have been consecrated for the sake of God, are honoured, not only with this honour, but also by the fact that because of them our enemies did not rule over our nation, the tyrant was punished, and the homeland purified – they having become, as it were, a ransom for the sin of our nation. And through the blood of those devout ones and their death as an atoning sacrifice, divine Providence preserved Israel that previously had been mistreated.
>
> 4 Maccabees 17.20–22

But perhaps deeper than all those truths is the image of the 'mater dolorosa', anticipating Mary at the foot of the cross, but also representing the millions of mothers throughout the world who have witnessed the death of their children and cried out, 'Was it for this the clay grew tall?'[8] But the unnamed mother of seven sons ends in trust, not desolation.

My son, have pity on me. I carried you for nine months in my womb, and nursed you for three years, and have reared you and brought you up to this point in your life, and have taken care of you. I beg you, my child, to look at the heaven and the earth and see everything that is in them, and recognize that God did not make them out of things that existed. And in the same way the human race came into being. Do not fear this butcher, but prove worthy of your brothers. Accept death, so that in God's mercy I may get you back again along with your brothers.

2 Maccabees 7.27–29

O God,
too many people have died witnessing to
their faith and identity.
As we remember the courage of the woman
and her seven sons
who stood firm against the cruelty of King
Antiochus,
renew our commitment to our way in Christ,
so that it could stand firm against any threat
and hold on to the hope of new life and
vindication
in Jesus, our martyred, risen Saviour.

৪০ ೞ

It seems appropriate to end this chapter with the Maccabaean martyrs and heroes, for with them we are at the very fountainhead of the cult of the saints. In 2 Maccabees Judas Maccabaeus recounts a dream to encourage his troops: he had seen Onias, a former High Priest, and also the prophet Jeremiah. 'And Onias spoke, saying, "This is a man who loves the family of Israel and prays much for the people and the holy city – Jeremiah, the prophet of God" ' (2 Maccabees 15.14). The next generations celebrated the newer heroes of the Maccabaean times, as well as the older prophets. They were already a 'cloud of witnesses' supporting and praying for God's people in their ongoing pilgrimage and struggle.

In these three characters from the Hebrew scriptures, we have travelled a great part of the journey of God's ancient people, from the springtime of success with King David, through the miseries of 'structural sin' and retribution in the time of Jeremiah and on to the beginning of deeper hopes that God could vindicate his righteousness even in the face of evil and death itself. In, and between, the lines of the Old Testament and the Apocrypha we glimpse real flesh-and-blood human beings choosing and acting on their vision of truth and of God.

⁎ ∾

Yahweh, Lord of Hosts,
your Word has always been sowing insight
in the hearts of men and women.
We praise you for the great cloud of
witnesses
in your ancient people, the Jews,
and we pray that we may never belittle
their achievements of wisdom and courage.
Give us their encouragement,
for we ask in the name of Jesus,
your Word made flesh.

Chapter 2

Those who 'gave counsel because they were intelligent'
The 'heretics'

The Greek word *hairesis* (heresy) originally meant a choice for a particular philosophical view and had no connotation of a wrong or unorthodox choice. In the history of the Church this changed quite quickly: 'heresy' very soon took on negative connotations. Those who sought to think through theological matters, especially the relationship of Father, Son and Spirit in the godhead, and the relationship of humanity and divinity in the person of Jesus Christ, in ways not approved in the central counsels – and councils – of the Church, were attacked and rejected as misguided heretics. Of course, centralized power structures of an 'official' Church came into being only after Constantine embraced the faith in the fourth century. Thereafter popes and councils, usually backed up by the secular arm, could pursue and marginalize those whose views did not fit.

Nevertheless the early centuries of the Church reveal a ferment of ideas, in which there was a strong encounter with the culture, politics and philosophy of the Greek and Roman world and in which the mainly unsystematic texts of the Bible were gradually placed within a theological superstructure. The historic creeds are one of the principal fruits of the process of argument and discussion that went on in those early times, as well as the many writings of the Fathers (the great Christian apologists and teachers of that period), and there came into being an accumulating body of 'Christian doctrine'. But this was real and fierce argument and discussion, and those who eventually ended up losing and being hounded as heretics actually played a vital role in the process.

In 1996, Maurice Wiles wrote:

> The study of early Christian doctrine has been
> transformed by a change in attitude towards
> heresy and the heresiarchs. Gone is the
> picture of the gradual flowering of a single,
> consistent vision of Christian truth,
> developing only in the sense of receiving an
> increasing precision of expression, something
> forced on the church by the need to combat
> perversions of that truth deliberately
> introduced by malevolent heretics. In its place
> has come a picture of the Christian church
> seeking to discover what the truth might be in
> the context of always changing conditions and
> new problems. In that revised picture the
> roles of 'father' and 'heretic' are much less
> sharply contrasted. Pelagius and Nestorius are
> not seen as men of evil will; they are seen
> rather as Christians determined to defend
> some aspect of Christian truth that was
> genuinely at risk in the teaching of St
> Augustine or of St Cyril. Even if their overall
> presentation of the faith be judged less
> satisfactory than that of their ultimately
> canonized opponents, they were standing out
> for important Christian insights to which their
> orthodox Christian opponents did not do full
> justice.[1]

I believe, therefore, that it is right and worthwhile to
have a second look at the outstanding 'minority
spokesmen', not only of the early centuries but right
through to recent times. They may have been condemned
and excommunicated as heretics, but they saw themselves
as defenders and exponents of the faith and yet were often
shabbily treated by the Church. Pelagius led a movement
seeking to set a very high standard of Christian life and
morality at a time when Christianity had become the

'default religion' in the Roman Empire and there were a lot of pretty sloppy, nominal Christians around. If, in his desire to affirm human free will and the possibility of achieving great goodness, he ultimately put too much emphasis on will and effort and not enough on the freely given grace of God enabling faith and righteousness, did that make it right that his name and writings should be totally blackened and then almost expunged from the record? I don't think so, and I believe that it is right that what Pelagius positively achieved should now be rescued from its fifth-century suppression (as indeed it is being in specialist circles) and celebrated. Of course, 'It is romantic tosh to suppose that heretics are necessarily creative theological heroes persecuted for being ahead of their time,' as Paul Bagshaw wrote recently.[2] I agree with that, and there is no reason why a rehabilitation of Pelagius need ignore the negative aspects of his theology and turn him into some kind of perfect resistance hero. A martyr of theological suppression, perhaps, but ultimately a lesser figure beside Augustine or Jerome.

We must add here, however, as a painful supplement to the above point, that a positive remembrance of some of the 'heretics' of all ages can be an act of atonement for the harsh and inhuman treatment meted out by the Church on so many of them. In the later Middle Ages, in particular, the violent repression of dissident groups, the failure of councils and inquisitions to deal fairly with those who criticized an often corrupt Church, and the summary execution of those found 'guilty' are a permanent and shameful stain on the history of the Church. The fifteenth-century Bohemian martyr, Jan Hus, believed that he was helping the Church to reform itself by exposing the unworthiness and secular power and wealth of so many priests and monks; he seems genuinely to have believed that his 'whistle-blowing' would be welcomed by the church hierarchy; it wasn't – Hus was burnt at the stake in 1415. To celebrate the courage of Hus – without losing a sense of the historical complexity that brought him to his fate – is a small act of apology for a Church too often motivated by its power structures rather than the honest search for gospel values and truth. The Church of England's Liturgical Commission expressed the opinion, in its commentary on the Common Worship Calendar of 2000, that commemorations of saints could witness to past and even continuing rifts and divisions within the community of faith and be an opportunity for prayer that they might be overcome. What I am proposing seems very much in line with that view.

The 'heretics' are worth celebrating because they have often been the 'grit in the oyster', raising awkward questions, perhaps in an extreme form, and forcing everyone to do some hard thinking, with the hope that the end result would be a 'pearl of great price', that is, God's reality and God's kingdom explained and proclaimed in ever greater subtlety. Sometimes, it is true, the theological shouting matches that went on, for example in the fourth century about the relation of human and divine in Jesus Christ, seem to us now pointless and pedantic – and very unchristian in the sheer harshness and unwillingness of opponents to go a small way towards each other; but that was the culture of their world, there *could* be only one right opinion, and the final result *was* a greater precision and subtlety of Christian doctrine. Origen did a great deal of work on ways of interpreting the Bible at different levels of meaning, and he constantly engaged with Greek philosophy in striving to put together a complete theological system, but he was working less than 200 years after the time of Jesus and many issues of Christian doctrine had hardly yet been aired. Some of his speculations were later condemned as opposed to Christianity, and his work too was ruthlessly and wickedly suppressed, but it is quite clear that the Church owed him a huge debt as a teacher and raiser of questions.

And yesterday's heretic may become tomorrow's pioneer. Because the nineteenth-century Anglican Bishop of Natal, John William Colenso, was ruthlessly honest about the legendary unhistorical character of much of the material in the first six books of the Bible, the church in South Africa tried to deprive him of his position and he was vilified by mainstream Christians. Today many of his ideas have not in fact proved durable, and yet his basic critical approach to the Bible is taken for granted in theological study and across the churches. And, furthermore, Colenso was willing to do his radical thinking at grassroots level – in Africa, with his Christian converts – and not just hidden away in an ivory tower. For his brave pioneering work in that and other fields he deserves to be remembered and celebrated.

It is interesting to reflect how many of the same heresies turn up again and again through Christian history (some might say, 'like bad pennies'), but we are surely now in a position to see that, because religious thought needs renewing in every generation, it constantly needs challenges, and even bad or extreme ideas put forward as challenges to orthodoxy can produce the needed renewal. Ideas about the subordinate status of Christ, or even his pure humanity, recur from Arius onwards, requiring subtlety of response in formulating the way in which we can say he is God and also fully human. The tendency to speak of the death of Christ as exemplary or inspiring rather than as sacrificial and atoning perhaps finds its origin in Peter Abelard, and is increasingly popular among today's liberal Christians. The freedom of the human will and its basic potentiality for good (as well as evil), affirmed by Pelagius, was swept away by Augustine's profound reflections on the ineradicability of human sin and its absolute dependency upon the grace, and choice, of God in Christ, and yet Pelagianism keeps popping up as something like a necessary pole of the argument (human freedom over against the 'remorseless providence' of God) and it retains its appeal to modern people. As for Augustine's and Calvin's view of the 'invincible' quality of God's prevenient grace – the doctrine of 'double predestination' – it finds expression again and again down the centuries. It might be thought somewhat impertinent to call Calvinism heretical, but it all depends which way you look at the question. It may all depend, more than we would care to wish, on where the political centre of gravity of the Church is at any given time. At all events, remembering the heretics helps each one of us to decide where we stand, what makes sense and what doesn't make sense, how we truly view what the Church teaches.

What is increasingly different about the modern world in contrast to the old one (one may say, the post-Reformation as opposed to the pre-Reformation world) is that now different theologies, and indeed all parts of the theological spectrum, are alive and well, believed and lived by, in different parts of the worldwide Church. There is live-and-let-live instead of war to the death, with the losers consigned to the outer darkness of excommunication or worse. Of course, each denomination still has its 'non-negotiable' articles of doctrine; there may be quarrels and mutual anathemas within churches on specific issues; and far too many Christians still play the game of living in a pre-modern world in which there is only one truth and everyone else is wrong; but *deep down* most Christians know that if they were forced by theological conviction to leave a particular denomination, they would quickly find another one occupying the right bit of the spectrum for them. Modern America is a deeply Christian nation, and you can find any Christian flavour you want, including some groups well beyond the normal 'tuning dial' in both directions existing alongside each other.

Increasingly, as the pressure to conform to social and theological norms fades, even the mainstream churches will find people sitting in their pews whose individual convictions are not quite at one with the 'official line' in that denomination, and perhaps rather idiosyncratic and indeed 'heretical' in the old sense. And we should heed Gill Evans' warning:

> There is no longer a widespread respect for a body of authoritative tradition against which disputes can be readily tested. Too much is in the melting pot. Too much freedom of choice for the individual, at least in western societies, makes people unwilling to bend to rulings. They argue. They think for themselves, sometimes with insufficient evidence. They take positions, sometimes without the training to use language exactly or the knowledge to see that the position is in fact a classic heresy.[3]

The study of the heretics in their very specific historical and biographical context will help people to know whether they *really* want to stand with 'a classic heresy'.

Healthy Christian theology demands that 'this point is balanced against that point' in a dialectic that allows the greatness and uncontainable otherness of God to be felt and experienced, with a knowing and an 'unknowing' that rightly subsists in a very few absolutely central credal statements but can never rest in simplistic ideas. And that is why the celebration of former 'heretics' can be so profoundly helpful and a source of wisdom. They are not wholly right; they may be substantially wrong (mainly through one-sidedness); many of them had a certain 'bolshiness' or arrogance which meant they would not compromise; but they stand 'in another place on the dial', and it is refreshing and enlightening to tune into them now and then, and see how God, the world and our faith look from that point of view.

Origen
c. 185–c. 254

> The man who went down [from Jerusalem to Jericho] is Adam; Jerusalem means Paradise; Jericho, the world; the robbers, the enemy powers; the Priest stands for the Law; the Levite for the Prophets; the Samaritan for Christ. The wounds stand for our disobedience; the beast, the body of the Lord. The common house, that is the inn, which receives all who wish to enter it, is interpreted as the Church. Furthermore the two denarii are understood to mean the Father and the Son; the innkeeper, the Head of the Church, to whom the plan of redemption and its means have been entrusted. And concerning that which the Samaritan promises at his return, this was a figure of the Second Coming of the Saviour.
>
> Origen[4]

'Origen is a great theologian, Augustine and Aquinas his only peers in Christian history.'[5] That's the opinion of Henri Crouzel, one of the foremost authorities on Origen. It was shared by St Jerome (c. AD 342–420), who for most of his life thought that Origen was the greatest teacher of the Early Church after the apostles. And yet after his death Origen was accused of all kinds of heresies, his teaching was condemned by ecumenical councils in Constantinople in the sixth century, and he is not found in any liturgical calendar.

Has a serious injustice been committed?

It seems more than likely that a serious injustice has been committed, for several reasons. Firstly, Origen's name was dragged into various theological squabbles from the time after his death in the middle of the third century, but these arguments were often more about personalities and politics than about what he had actually said or meant. Secondly, most of the great theologians in the 150 years after Origen's death followed and deeply respected him. Thirdly, Origen was judged, inappropriately, by the later standards of theology, when matters of Christian doctrine had been laid down more precisely and given legal force. Finally, his critics failed to appreciate the way in which he might sometimes be writing in exploratory, speculative mode, rather than giving systematic teaching; if they had been willing to compare 'difficult passages' of Origen with things he said elsewhere, they would have been less able to cry 'Heresy!' (One can't help thinking of David Jenkins, the former and controversial Bishop of Durham, whose exuberant, speculative, verbally inventive style was easily twisted, by convenient editing, into heresy or nonsense.)

The greatest sin against Origen must be the deliberate pulping of his works by those who thought they were wrong. Origen wrote in Greek, and most of what he wrote, apart from a few fragments and Latin translations, has been destroyed. For someone who was a brilliant biblical scholar, a famed teacher, an unstoppable preacher and a deeply spiritual man, whose words were often taken down verbatim by an army of stenographers, the loss of so many of his words is a massive tragedy. The polemical anti-Origenists were not above misquoting Origen or ascribing to him the words of later followers. But then all's fair in love, war and theology.

And yet, Origen can be retrieved from the rubbish heap to which later Christianity tried to consign him. He was born (about AD 185) and lived the first part of his life in Alexandria. As an extremely committed Christian (he would have been happy to achieve martyrdom), he lived in a world in which the growing Church lived side by side with the Judaism from which it had separated itself, in which the power of the pagan Roman Empire was still likely to break out in persecution of Christians at any time, and in which Greek culture and philosophy played an important role. Origen's father, Leonides, who had taught him, was beheaded in the persecution under Emperor Septimus Severus when Origen was still a teenager, but Origen continued his studies and opened a school of grammar to support his family when he was only 18. Demetrius, the Bishop of Alexandria, entrusted the teaching of the catechumens (trainee Christians) to Origen, but it wasn't long before he was studying and teaching at a much more advanced level. He was well known for living a life of 'strenuous asceticism', and his chastity gave rise to a later story, which may or may not be true, that he had actually castrated himself to remove all fear of temptation in instructing female catechumens. His studies in pagan and sacred literature, in theology and philosophy soon bore fruit in a massive output of writings, most of them based on the Bible. A wealthy Christian called Ambrose provided Origen with shorthand writers to facilitate his extraordinary production of Bible commentaries, treatises and homilies.

Origen made a number of journeys from Alexandria in the early part of the third century – to Rome and Arabia, to Asia Minor and Palestine, to Antioch and Greece – to teach, preach, discuss heresies or even to escape the persecutions under Emperor Caracalla in 215, but he had to leave his home city for good in 231, following a dispute with his bishop about his ordination as priest by another bishop in Palestine. He settled in Caesarea, and continued to teach and also to travel for that purpose. There was more persecution of Christians under Emperor Decius, and in 250 Origen was imprisoned and tortured, being cruelly kept alive so that he might be forced to apostasize, but on the death of the emperor he was set free. His health was broken, and he died at the age of 69 at Tyre, in about 254.

The three great achievements of Origen's teaching and writing were: as a pioneer in the detailed, scholarly study of the Bible; as an interpreter of the Bible; and as a theologian expounding and explaining Christian faith in relation to the very best philosophical (mainly Neoplatonic and Stoic) wisdom that existed at the time.

1. Throughout his life Origen worked on a massive project known as the *Hexapla*. In this he set out the Old Testament in six columns. The first column had the Hebrew text; the second column had the Hebrew words in Greek transliterations; and the third, fourth, fifth and sixth columns contained four different Greek translations. He then added a seventh, eighth and ninth column for some parts of the Old Testament, when there were some other versions. Little marks and signs showed where the versions differed from each other. The point of all this was to provide a sound basis for interpretation of the meaning of the Bible, and to facilitate arguments about the Old Testament between Jews and Christians, who shared these scriptures but differed considerably about their interpretation.

One must portray the meaning of the sacred writings in a threefold way upon one's own soul, so that the simple man may be edified by what we call the flesh of the scripture, this name being given to the obvious interpretation; while the man who has made some progress may be edified by its soul, as it were; and the man who is perfect and like those mentioned by the apostle ('We speak wisdom among the perfect ...'), this man may be edified by the spiritual law, which has a 'shadow of the good things to come.' For just as a man consists of body, soul and spirit, so in the same way does the scripture, which has been prepared by God to be given for man's salvation.

Origen[6]

---

2. Origen was, first and foremost, an exegete, that is, his writings expound the meaning of both the Old and New Testaments. He is famed for his moral and spiritual (allegorical) interpretations of the Bible but he always began with a clear analysis of the text and its literal (verbal) meaning. Origen believed passionately that the whole Bible was inspired by God and that all of it found its true meaning and climax in Christ, and that meant that even in its apparently most obscure, time-bound and rebarbative parts some deep spiritual and Christian meaning could be found. We would find many of Origen's exegeses extremely strained, even bizarre; and Bible commentators today pay strict attention to the historical and religious context of the human creators of the Bible's text, as Origen does not do, before moving to more universal meanings; and yet Origen was only continuing the New Testament's practice of seeing previous scripture as pointing to Christ. He interpreted Sarah following Abraham as flesh following reason; Pharaoh's daughter finding the baby Moses as the Church discovering the meaning of the law; and the female lover in the Song of Songs as the Church or the Christian soul longing for Christ the bridegroom. Whatever the quality of Origen's own individual interpretations, he reminds us of two things: that a Bible text can have more than one meaning; and that preachers of all traditions sell their hearers short if they do not prepare with *thorough* exegesis of their texts.

For as the different strings of the psaltery or lyre are regarded by the unmusical person ... as unharmonious by reason of the dissimilarity of their sounds; even so they who know not how to hear God's harmony in his holy scriptures think there is a discord between the Old and the New [Testaments], or between the Prophets and the Law, or between the different Gospels, or that the Apostle [Paul] is out of harmony either with the Gospel or with himself, or with the other apostles. But

> when the man trained in the music of God arrives, a man of skill in deed and word ... he shall produce the sound of God's music, knowing from his art how to strike the strings in time, now the strings of the Law, now harmoniously with them the strings of the Gospel, now the strings of Prophecy, and when occasion demands the Apostolic strings that harmonize with them or similarly with the Gospel. For he knows that all scripture is the one perfect and attuned instrument of God, producing from its various notes a single sound of salvation for those who are willing to learn.
>
> Origen[7]

3. Origen also put forward many ideas of a speculative theological and philosophical character. The briefest summary of his thought might run like this: God in overflowing love created rational and spiritual beings through the Word, who is the Son, eternally generated by the Father (and, with the Holy Spirit, one with God). The rational beings, however, neglected to adore God and fell, but they fell to different depths, some to be angels, some to be human beings, some to be demons. All previously had ethereal bodies, but those who became human received corporeal forms and a terrestrial existence, a place of testing and an opportunity to be redeemed and rise, returning to the primal state of blessedness. One soul had not fallen but had remained in adoring union with the Father, and the Word united himself with this soul and became incarnate in a body derived from the Virgin Mary. By his human life and death, his descent to deliver the captive souls in hell, Christ, the eternal Word, reveals that each human being has a divine origin and relationship and can be redeemed from the sin which has defaced and obscured them. Each soul is the bride of the eternal Word, and the Church is the great 'school of souls' in which erring pupils are disciplined and made ready to be reunited with the Word. The atoning and sanctifying

process does not stop at death, but continues in the world to come, where there will be resurrection bodies for all, Origen anticipating the doctrine of purgatory. It seems that he believed that eventually all the rational beings, even those who had become devils, would be drawn back up to unity in the Trinity.

We see therefore that men have a kind of blood relationship with God; and since God knows all things and not a single intellectual truth can escape his notice – for God the Father, with his only-begotten Son and the Holy Spirit, stands alone in his knowledge not only of the things he has created but also of himself – it is possible that a rational mind also, by advancing from a knowledge of small to a knowledge of greater things and from things visible to things invisible, may attain to an increasingly perfect understanding. For it has been placed in a body and of necessity advances from things of sense, which are bodily, to things beyond sense perception, which are incorporeal and intellectual.

Origen[8]

Those who attacked Origen accused him of:

- making the Son subordinate to the Father, as in later Arianism;
- turning the idea of the resurrection of the body into something that sounded pretty spiritual;
- denying the doctrine of hell, because ultimately all – even the devil himself – would be saved;
- speculating about the pre-existence of souls and the possibility of everlasting cycles of fall and redemption;
- and, through the endlessly allegorical interpretation of scripture, losing sight of the way in which real history was God's instrument of salvation.

It is hard to say whether Origen was truly guilty of any of these charges, because his posthumous enemies have destroyed so much of the vital evidence. It is certainly ironic that, although he was famous for his doughty defence of Christianity when it was intellectually and physically under threat, he ended by being regarded as a dangerous heretic. Origen lived in a very different world from ours, in which no one thought that two people could speculate in opposite directions and both be right in some ways. Perhaps Origen's mistake was to write too much and to write too freely in exploring possibilities of meaning. In our world of instant communication and endless interactive discussion, he would have been in his element. And, wherever his voice was heard, people would have been aware that the Christian faith was a spiritual and intellectual force to be reckoned with.

What would the Church be without its thinkers and its mystics, who believe that those who seek the pearl of great price will be led by the Holy Spirit into all truth? Even their errors are more instructive than the docile orthodoxy of those who say they believe whatever the Bible says, or what the Holy Church teaches. To disparage reason is blasphemy against the Holy Spirit, whose gifts are wisdom and understanding, counsel and might, knowledge and the fear of the Lord. In this faith Origen lived, worked, suffered and died.

Dean Inge[9]

Eternal and loving God,
your Word and Wisdom, Jesus Christ,
became incarnate
to draw all souls in all times and all places up
to your divinity.
Give us the intellectual energy, with your
great exponent, Origen,

to read the scriptures so thoroughly and
so deeply that we are drawn up to the vision
of your truth,
Father, Son and Holy Spirit.

ଚ୍ଚ ଔ

Jan Hus
c. 1370–1415

I, Jan Hus, in hope a priest of Jesus Christ, fearing to offend God, and fearing to fall into perjury, do hereby profess my unwillingness to abjure all or any of the articles produced against me by false witnesses. For God is my witness that I neither preached, affirmed, nor defended them, though they say that I did. Moreover, concerning the articles that they have extracted from my books, I say that I detest any false interpretation which any of them bears. But inasmuch as I fear to offend against the truth, or to gainsay the opinion of the doctors of the Church, I cannot abjure any of them. And if it were possible that my voice could now reach the whole world, as at the Day of Judgement every lie and every sin that I have committed will be made manifest, then would I gladly abjure before all the world every falsehood and error which I either had thought of saying or actually said. I say I write this of my own free will and choice. Written with my own hand, on this first day of July.

Jan Hus[10]

It was in July 1415 that Jan Hus wrote this final denial that he was in any sense a heretic. Five days later he was burned at the stake by the Catholic Church. He was a player and a victim in the ecclesiastical politics of his day. His condemnation and death were a tragedy, both for himself and for the Church of his day, revealing its deep failings.

Nearly 600 years later, in 1999, at an international consultation of historians on Jan Hus, Pope John Paul II said:

> Today, on the threshold of the millennium, I feel that it is my duty to express my deep regret for the hideous death of Jan Hus and for the resulting injuries, source of conflicts and divisions which were torn in the spirit and hearts of the Bohemian people because of it.[11]

Jan Hus was born of poor parents in Husinec in southern Bohemia about 1370. About 1390 he enrolled in the University of Prague and some seven years later received his master's degree and began teaching at the university. He was ordained priest in 1400 and a year later became Dean of the Philosophical Faculty in the University. In 1402 Hus was appointed preacher at the Bethlehem Chapel in Prague.

This chapel, which can be seen today in Prague, rebuilt, was created by pupils of Jan Milic of Kromeriz in 1391 as part of a new movement of national reform. The main feature of its interior was the square pulpit elevated on a stout pillar, which the priest entered directly from his residential quarters behind. Here Hus preached in Czech rather than Latin, and became the leader of the reform movement, the essence of which was expressed in his powerful vernacular preaching (during the 12 years of his ministry there Hus preached something like 3,000 sermons) and in some of the wall decorations, one part of which showed the pope astride a large horse resplendent in his papal pomp next to a picture of Christ in all his poverty carrying his cross. This was, then, an early movement for the reform of the Catholic Church, taking much inspiration from the works of the English theologian, John Wyclif (c. 1320–1384), protesting against the corrupting wealth and power of the popes and prelates and the low standards of many priests, seeking a return to the simplicity of the Early Church, and attempting to create a vernacular Czech national church.

Reform of the Church was badly needed. The clerical estate owned about one half of all the land in Bohemia, and the great wealth and simoniacal practices of the higher clergy aroused jealousy and resentment among the poor priests. The Bohemian peasantry resented the Church as one of the heaviest land taxers. All this was at a time when the papacy itself was discredited because of the Great Schism (1378–1417), when there were rival popes in Avignon and Rome. In 1402 Zbynek Zajíc was appointed Archbishop of Prague, although he was only 25 years old and had mainly courtly and military experience; his principal qualification was that he was willing to pay the pope 2,800 gulden for his appointment plus 1,480 gulden for his predecessors' arrears. In spite of this, Zbynek was initially advised by Hus and was a supporter of the reform movement.

I know not how well the pope or bishop could read (the story of Jesus' humble entry into Jerusalem), although perhaps he could. For many have been popes, archbishops, cardinals, bishops, canons and priests who could not read books. How could he read it, since it all contradicts him? Christ on a little ass, he on a large white horse or warhorse, which is accoutred with gold-studded bridle, the breast strap and the stirrups covered with precious stones, the coloured hat tassels reaching to the ground, and the coverings of the horses dragging on the ground. They drive before him a she-ass or a mule carrying God's body, while she is cropping the grass along the road. They pay no attention to her or to Christ's body, but kneel before the pope, calling him the most holy, while he rides under a baldachin. They push themselves forward begging for

> benefices, and kiss his feet, if the guards permit it. For they beat back with silver cudgels the poor from his feet. The pope, sitting on that war horse and laughing at it, enjoys such high praise. And our dear silent and humble Saviour rides with great weeping on a little ass!
>
> Jan Hus[12]

In the University of Prague there was bitter rivalry between the German and the Czech masters, the latter being largely in favour of Church reform. In 1403 a German master, Johann Hübner, drew up a list of 45 articles, selected from Wyclif's writings, and had them condemned as heretical, the German masters outvoting the Czechs. The articles included the following 'heresies':

- that the bread and wine in communion remain unchanged, although the body and blood of Christ are 'sacramentally' present in it;
- that sacraments performed by a priest or bishop while in mortal sin are invalid;
- that a priest should possess no property;
- that it is permissible for a deacon or priest to preach without authorization of the pope or bishop;
- that delinquent clerics may be deprived by secular lords of their possessions;
- that tithes are only alms and cannot be enforced;
- that monks are not Christian;
- that Pope Sylvester and Emperor Constantine erred in endowing the Church;
- that it is not necessary for salvation to believe that the Roman Church is supreme over all other churches;
- that to believe in papal or episcopal indulgences is vain.

These articles were to haunt Jan Hus and led to his death. Without doubt they represent a fundamental threat to the late medieval Roman Catholic Church and the early dawn of the Reformation of the following century; without doubt, too, Jan Hus, although he believed many of these articles, was actually more Catholic than Wyclif, and tried in his written works to give a moderate and nuanced account of the reforms that were demanded; nevertheless, once the association between the articles and Hus as the leader of the reform movement had been made by the Catholic conservatives, it stuck, and he was lost.

> I exhort you for the sake of the most kind Jesus himself that you love one another, root out schisms, and promote the honour of God before all else. Remember that I have always sought the advancement of the university to the honour of God, that I grieved over your discords and excesses, and wished to unite our illustrious nation into one ... Moreover, dearly beloved in Christ Jesus, stand in the truth you have learned, for it conquers all and is mighty to eternity ... I said that I detest whatever false sense exists in any of the articles, and commit it to the correction of the Lord Jesus Christ, who knows my sincere intention and does not interpret it in a wrong sense which I do not intend.
>
> Jan Hus[13]

In 1409 a Council of the Roman Catholic Church was called at Pisa to dethrone the two rival popes, declare a new single pope and reform the Church. Hus now quarrelled with Archbishop Zbynek who opposed the Council. The German masters in the university supported the archbishop, but then had their voting majority taken away from them by King Wenceslas, so that the Czech masters triumphed. There was now a mass emigration of Germans from Prague to several German universities, and

Jan Hus was elected rector of the now Czech-dominated university. The Council of Pisa, meanwhile, had achieved the magnificent outcome of *three* popes: they had elected Alexander V in place of the two existing popes, but *they* hadn't gone quietly. Archbishop Zbynek died in 1411, having sought from Alexander a papal Bull against Wyclif's writings and Hus's preaching, but he failed to stop Hus preaching in the Bethlehem Chapel and teaching in the university of Prague. Hus had even been excommunicated by Zbynek and summoned to appear before the pope to answer the charges of Wyclifite heresy, but he sent representatives to plead his cause.

In 1412 one of the rival popes, John XXIII, Alexander V's successor, began to sell indulgences to finance his campaign against Ladislaus of Naples who was supporting a rival pope, Gregory XII. King Wenceslas, who got a cut of the profits, supported this, but when Hus and Jerome of Prague protested, arousing both the university and the populace against the papal commission which was selling the indulgences, Hus fatally lost the support of the king. Hus's enemies in Rome then renewed the trial against him in the Curia, and he was declared under major excommunication for refusing to appear, and an interdict was pronounced over Prague or any other place where Hus might reside. In order to spare the city from deprivation of the sacraments, Hus voluntarily left Prague in October 1412 and found refuge mostly in southern Bohemia in the castles of nobles friendly to him. During the next two years he wrote a great deal, answering his opponents' charges in a vigorous polemical style. The most important of his treatises was *De Ecclesia* (*On the Church*). He also wrote a large number of treatises in Czech and a collection of sermons entitled *Postilla*.

[He who preaches] that priests are gods, God's creators, and that they have the power both to save or condemn whomever they want; that no-one can be saved without them; that no-one ought to punish them; and that they should eat, drink, and wear nothing but the best – he who preaches thus is a reverend preacher and should preach; but whoever preaches that priests should not commit adultery, rob people by avarice and simony, leave other men's wives alone, and be content with one benefice ... him they immediately dub a slanderer of the holy priesthood, a destroyer of the holy Church, and a heretic who should not be allowed to preach. They drive him [to court] and condemn him. And when that devil's net does not suffice, they stop the services.

Jan Hus[14]

The beginning of the end, both for the great papal schism and for Jan Hus's life, came in November 1414. King Sigismund of Hungary, King Wenceslas's half-brother, newly elected as king of the Romans, saw the opportunity of gaining prestige as the restorer of the Church's unity. He forced John XXIII to call the Council of Constance to find a final solution of the Schism and to put an end to the heresies, and he invited Hus to attend the Council to explain his views, promising a safe-conduct, whatever should be the outcome. King Wenceslas also supported the Council, keen to put an end to the suspicion that his country harboured heresy. Hus was at first reluctant to travel, fearing for his life, but, relying on the offer of the safe-conduct, he set off. Shortly after arriving in Constance, he was arrested and kept in close confinement. Sigismund was at first incensed at the defiance of his safe-conduct, but then realized that the success of the Council and the ending of the Schism depended on dealing strictly with Hus. Hus was held from December 1414 to March 1415 in a Dominican monastery on an island in Lake Constance, then transferred to Gottlieben, the castle of the Bishop of Constance on the Rhine, where he was kept in bonds during the day and chained by one hand to the wall during the night. Early in his captivity, in an examination by three judges, Hus had strongly denied that he had ever held 33 of the 45 Wyclif heretical articles and the remaining 12 he had only believed in a modified sense. Finally, from 5–8 June a hearing was held in the Franciscan monastery in Constance before the distinguished prelates of the Council and in the presence of King Sigismund; many charges were made against Hus, but his attempts to defend himself were ignored. On 18 June Hus received a final list of 30 charges against him, to which he was only able to give written answers. In every case except one he was able to say that the charges were erroneously formulated and his understanding of them deliberately misinterpreted. He could not abjure, therefore, things which he had never believed. Several attempts were now made by members of the Council to persuade Hus to renounce the 30 articles, never mind their precise meaning, to save his life, but Hus refused, and on 1 July made his final declaration to the Council, quoted above.

After one final unsuccessful attempt to persuade him to recant, Hus was taken before the Council in Constance Cathedral on 6 July, and the full charges against him were read out. He loudly protested against their injustice, but was not allowed to speak. Finally he fell on his knees and prayed, asking that his enemies might be forgiven. Thereupon he was dressed in the vestments required for the celebration of the mass, and the bishops then proceeded with the ritual of his degradation from the office of priest, starting with the removal of the chalice, continuing with all the robes, and ending with the obliteration of the tonsure with scissors, in each case uttering an appropriate curse. Finally they placed on his head a tall paper crown on which were painted three devils fighting for the possession of a soul and the inscription,

'This is a heresiarch', and handed him over to the executioners with the words, 'We commit your soul to the devil!' Hus responded, 'And I commit it to the most merciful Lord Jesus Christ.'

Hus was now taken to the place of execution in a procession accompanied by most of the inhabitants of Constance. On the way they passed the cemetery, where Hus's books were being burned. When they reached the place, Hus knelt and prayed that God might have mercy on him. They disrobed him down to his shirt and tied him, with his hands behind his back, to the stake. He faced east, to which some bystanders objected, so he was turned to the west. When bound by the neck to the stake with a rusty chain, he commented with a smile that his Saviour had been bound with a heavier chain. The executioners placed wood interspersed with straw about his body up to the chin. After one final exhortation to recant, the fire was lit. Hus began to sing, 'Christ, thou Son of the living God, have mercy on us'; and then, 'Christ, thou Son of the living God, have mercy on me'; and then, 'Thou who art born of Mary ...'; but he did not finish, because the wind then blew the flame into his face. He then continued to pray silently until he died shortly afterwards.

Therefore, faithful Christian, seek the truth, hear the truth, learn the truth, love the truth, speak the truth, adhere to the truth, defend the truth to death; for truth will make you free from sin, the devil, the death of the soul, and finally from eternal death.

Jan Hus[15]

God of truth,
in all the tragedy of doctrines fought over
and a Church corrupted by wealth and
power,
we thank you for those like Jan Hus,
who put truth above personal safety.
We thank you, too, for the perspectives of
history,
and we pray that your Church may learn
the lessons of its wayward youth.
We ask our prayer in the name of the one
who is our truth,
Jesus Christ.

ℬ ℭ

John William Colenso
1814–83

In the book *Christianity Rediscovered*, published in 1978, Vincent Donovan wrote of his attempt to move beyond the Catholic mission compound, to live as a simple companion and conversation partner with the Masai people of East Africa, with the purpose of 'rediscovering Christianity' as he shared it with the people but also allowed it to be re-expressed through the culture and thought-forms of the Masai. In moving out into vulnerable companionship, Donovan was adopting a church-planting approach in the manner of St Paul: now the Masai were respected as those among whom the Spirit of God had already been at work for centuries, and they could be invited, if they wished, to work out a Christianity true to their own vision of God and the community.

It's fascinating to think that, more than a hundred years before Donovan, another Christian priest was beginning to grope his way towards real respect for the culture and language of Africans, and desperately trying to present a Christianity that was not just a colonialists' trump card. He was John William Colenso.

Nothing is more plain in the New Testament than that the sum and substance of it, as of the Old, is not a system of religious worship, not a summary of many things to be believed or done, so that 'whosoever shall not believe or do them, without doubt he shall perish everlastingly', but a revelation of God and of our relation to him, as that of children to a loving Father.

John William Colenso[16]

In 1853, approaching his fortieth birthday, Colenso was consecrated the first missionary bishop of Natal, the new and unsettled British colony in Southern Africa carved out from the Zulu kingdom by traders, adventurers and Dutch trekkers. He had been born into an impoverished nonconformist family in Cornwall, but he graduated in mathematics at St John's College, Cambridge and later became a fellow at the college, becoming ordained in the Church of England. He was a brilliant mathematician and published several maths textbooks. Through the influence of his wife, Frances, he became strongly attached to the Broad Church movement centred round F.D. Maurice, believing that the Church must come to terms with modern scientific ideas and more radical demands for social justice. In the years prior to his appointment to Natal, he was vicar of Forncett St Mary in Norfolk.

Once arrived in his diocese, the new bishop deliberately put himself alongside the Zulu people in the daily life of the mission station. He soon earned criticism from the church in Britain for his leniency in not insisting on the divorce of the wives of polygamists on their baptism. But his engagement with the Zulu language was legendary.

Less than three months after his party's arrival in the Colony Colenso advertised in the colonial press a Zulu–English Dictionary, a Zulu Grammar and a revised version (in Zulu) of St Matthew's Gospel. This very zealous and bustling man achieved an astonishing amount in the linguistic field in the first seven years of his episcopate, and this in addition to establishing a new mission and administering a Diocese ... He had translated the entire New Testament, and the books of Genesis, Exodus and Samuel in the Old. He had published, with financial aid from the Government, a dictionary of 522 pages, various Zulu reading books, a Zulu liturgy, a tract on the Decalogue, and readers in Geography, Geology, History and Astronomy, apart from sundry Grammars – a truly Herculean labour.[17]

Colenso had learned Zulu by endless conversations with the young men at his school, and one of the Zulu publications was of the diaries of his three Zulu companions when he and they made an expedition to visit the Zulu king Mpande and his heir Cetshwayo in 1859. This was the first indigenous Zulu literature. The effect of such long-term exposure to native language and culture was profound, reinforcing and bringing to expression the liberal views that Bishop Colenso had long held. The missionary, apologetic situation in which he now found himself did not make him retreat into traditional formulations of doctrine. Quite the contrary. He had to be honest with his Zulu conversation partners as they asked him ever more searching questions about Christian faith.

Here ... as I have said, amidst my work in this land, I have been brought face to face with the very questions which I then put by [in parish work]. While translating the story of the Flood, I have had a simple-minded, but intelligent, native – one with the docility of a child, but the reasoning powers of mature age – look up and ask, 'Is all that true? Do you really believe that all this happened thus – that all the beasts, and birds, and creeping things, upon the earth, large and small, from hot countries and cold, came thus by pairs, and entered into the ark with Noah? And did Noah gather food for them all, for the beasts and birds of prey, as well as the rest?' My heart answered in the words of the Prophet, 'Shall a man speak lies in the Name of the Lord?' (Zechariah 13.3) I dared not do so.

John William Colenso[18]

This was not quite, of course, the equal conversation that Vincent Donovan aspired to have with the Masai in the 1960s, but it is at least a respect for the Zulu hearer that wishes to be 'honest to God'. Colenso published two biblical commentaries, on Romans in 1861 and on the Pentateuch and Joshua from 1862 to 1879. Both arose from his desire to be honest to the faith as he grasped it, as a modern person and as he felt it needed to be explicated in a missionary situation.

His ideas about Romans arose from his horror at what he saw as the negative, threatening preaching of many of his fellow-missionaries. He believed that it was wrong to say that only those who had specifically put their faith in what Jesus had done on the cross – bearing the just punishment of a righteous God on human sin in our stead – would be saved. He knew that many colonists found in their baptism, their 'election' as Christians, a ground for feelings of superiority over the native people, even a legitimization for their seizure of the land from the Zulu, whom they believed to be depraved and primitive. He also realized that to speak of baptism in exclusive terms was deeply counterproductive in a Zulu culture, in which the ancestors are honoured and constantly brought into a relationship of community with the living as a guarantee of cultural identity and morality. How could a Zulu become a Christian, if that meant consigning all their forebears to hell-fire?

So Colenso expounded Romans as a message of hope and grace for all humankind.

> But now, irrespective of law, the righteousness of God has been disclosed, and is attested by the law and the prophets, the righteousness of God through faith in Jesus Christ for all who believe. For there is no distinction, since all have sinned and fall short of the glory of God; they are now justified by his grace as a gift, through the redemption that is in Christ Jesus (3.21–24).

This righteousness, says Colenso, has come to all without distinction, Jew or Greek, colonist or native – whether or not they know it – but in fact all can know it, even outside direct faith in Jesus. The task of the missionary is to bring to specific awareness what God has done in Christ, to move faith and trust in God, where they already exist, into the full light of expression through the Church's faith and sacraments.

He himself, the Father of Spirits, is everywhere enlightening and quickening the spirits of men. Every good thought, which has ever stirred within a heathen's mind, is a token of that work which God's good Spirit is working within him, as one of the great Human Family, redeemed by the love of God in Christ Jesus, and related to the Second Adam by a second spiritual birth (of which Baptism is the express sign and seal to the Christian) as they are by their natural birth to the first Adam.

John William Colenso[19]

As for Colenso's *The Pentateuch and the Book of Joshua Critically Examined*, this, too arose from his attempt honestly to answer the question of Zulu converts, 'Is it true?' His awareness of contemporary geology and the sheer logistical impossibility of many of the stories from Genesis onward compelled him to confess that the stories could not be by Moses and could not be historically true.

The truth in the present instance ... is this, that the Pentateuch, as a whole, was not written by Moses, and that, with respect to some, at least, of the chief portions of the story, it cannot be regarded as historically true. It does not, therefore, cease to 'contain the true Word of God', with 'all things necessary for salvation', to be 'profitable for doctrine, reproof, correction, instruction in righteousness'. It still remains an integral portion of that Book, which, whatever intermixture it may show of human elements – of error, infirmity, passion, and ignorance, – has yet, through God's Providence and the special working of His Spirit on the minds of its writers, been the means of revealing to us His True Name, the Name of the only living and true God, and has all along been, and, as far as we know, will never cease to be, the mightiest instrument in the hands of the Divine Teacher, for awakening in our minds just conceptions of His Character, and of His gracious and merciful dealings with the children of men.

John William Colenso[20]

The seven parts of *The Pentateuch* eventually ran to 3,500 pages, and Colenso's skills as a mathematician were incidentally put to good use in exposing the unbelievable numbers claimed for the people of Israel in the desert. John Rogerson, writing on Old Testament criticism in the nineteenth century, sums up Colenso's achievement:

Colenso was far more than a mathematician dabbling with biblical figures and dimensions. By unremitting labour in the midst of an incredibly demanding life as a missionary, he mastered as probably no English scholar had before him, the technicalities of Old Testament criticism. Many of his observations are now commonplace in Old Testament scholarship, and anyone who cares to read through all seven parts of 'The Pentateuch' will be confronted with problems which cannot be overlooked today, even if not all of Colenso's answers remain valid.[21]

Nevertheless, whether valid or not, Colenso's ideas were then regarded by most church people as dangerous heresy. He even lost the friendship of the liberal F.D. Maurice because of them. Bishop Gray of Cape Town convened an ecclesiastical court and had Colenso excommunicated and deposed in 1863. Colenso appealed to the Judicial Committee of the Privy Council in London, and they declared that Gray and the church in South Africa had no right to depose him as a bishop of the Church of England. The very first Lambeth Conference of Bishops of the Anglican Communion was called in 1867 in part to discuss the issues raised by the Colenso case. Colenso remained in Natal until his death in 1883, but the Anglican Church set up alternative diocesan structures there, and Colenso was not recognized. He was subjected to a great deal of personal vituperation, and the hymn 'The Church's one foundation' by Samuel J. Stone was written at this time, containing thinly veiled criticism of Colenso: 'Though with a scornful wonder men see her [the Church] sore opprest, by schisms rent asunder, by heresies distrest ...' etc. (This hymn is never sung at Colenso's old college, St John's College, Cambridge.)

> A bishop there was of Natal
> Who took a Zulu for a pal.
> Said the African, 'Look 'ere,
> Ain't the Pentateuch queer?'
> And converted my Lord of Natal.
>
> Contemporary limerick[22]

Colenso and his family spent his later years fighting on behalf of the Zulu people, and he often came into conflict with the settlers as he exposed cases of injustice. In 1879, when the British suffered a major defeat in their war against the Zulus, Colenso was asked to preach on a day of 'Humiliation and Prayer', but to the surprise of the congregation his sermon was mostly devoted to exposing the injustice of the campaign. On his death he was mourned by the Zulu people, to whom he was and remains today 'Sobantu' ('Father of the People'). He is buried in St Peter's Cathedral, Natal. The schism in Natal, with a 'Colenso church' existing alongside the official Church of England, was not finally healed until 1912, when the Bishop of Natal recovered the endowments of which Colenso had been registered proprietor. By the end of the twentieth century there were moves within the South African Church and in the mission society, USPG, to rehabilitate Colenso and celebrate his achievements.

Today liberal Christians can honour John William Colenso for being a pioneer of honesty in reading the Bible and of opposition to harshly exclusivist presentations of the faith (Christianity rediscovered 'outside the mission compound'); while even conservative Christians can praise him for his attempts to bring a truly Zulu Christianity into being and to stand alongside them in the name of Christ in vulnerable companionship.

Most men who call themselves Christians would say that they believed the Bible, not knowing what they meant, never having attempted ... to separate historical record from inspired teaching. But when a liberal-minded clergyman does come among us ... as our pastor, we feel not unnaturally a desire to know what it is, at any rate, that he disbelieves ... It is soon manifest to us that he has accepted the teaching of the rocks and stones, and that we may give up the actual six days, and give up also the deluge as a drowning of all the world. Indeed, we had almost come to fancy that even the old rector had become hazy on these points. And gradually there leak out to us, as to the falling of manna from heaven, and as to the position of Jonah within the whale, and as to the speaking of Balaam's ass, certain doubts, not expressed indeed, but which are made manifest to us as existing by the absence of expressions of belief ... And lastly, there comes out a subscription list for Bishop Colenso, and we find our new rector's name down for a five-pound note! That we regard as the sign, to be recognized by us as the most certain of all things, that he has cut the rope which bound his barque to the old shore, and that he is going out to sea in quest of a better land. Shall we go with him, or shall we stay where we are?

Anthony Trollope[23]

Merciful Father,
in the completed life of your Son you offer
acceptance and forgiveness to all people
everywhere.
As he taught the Zulu people of your
unconditional love,
so may we learn from John William Colenso
to be vulnerable and honest
as we communicate the hope of our faith
in Jesus Christ our Saviour.

℘ ℅

> If, as Schleiermacher suggests, the distinctive essence of Christianity consists in the fact that God has redeemed us through Jesus Christ, and through no one else and in no other way, it must follow that the Christian understanding of God, Jesus Christ, and human nature should be consistent with this understanding of redemption ... Heresy is not a form of unbelief; it is something that arises within the context of faith itself. For Schleiermacher, heresy is fundamentally *an inadequate or inauthentic form of Christian faith.*[24]

If Alistair McGrath is right in thus agreeing with Schleiermacher, we can certainly acquit our three candidates on the charge of heresy. They all had an overwhelmingly strong sense of the redemption wrought in Jesus Christ, and you could almost say an excess of enthusiasm for presenting the Christian claims in a thorough, rational way, and from a reformed and chastened Church, true to the example of Jesus. This would be true of many of the 'heretics'. Of course, they had a lop sided, partisan, subjective view, as we all do; we are all prisoners of our age and our culture. There will also be views which are nearly 'off the end of the spectrum' and can hardly with justice be called Christian at all. Nevertheless the Church only has a chance of pointing towards God's truth if it allows *all the perspectives*, including those that seem wrong and 'heretical', into the dynamic of conversation.

℘ ℅

God of wisdom and love,
you have promised redemption in the gospel
entrusted to your people,
and your Spirit continually leads the Church
into more truth.
Forgive the violence and intransigence
of those who drew sharp lines round
revelation,
and help us to learn also from those whose
idealism was unwelcome
and whose perspectives were suppressed by
the powerful.
Continue to refresh us with insights from
unlikely sources,
and take from us that certainty which is no
better than irreverence.
We ask this prayer in the name of Jesus
Christ, your Word, our Hope.

Chapter 3

Those who 'composed musical tunes'
The servants of St Cecilia

'Church' and 'music' seem to us almost an item. The western Church was the seedbed for a glorious tradition of music: without the liturgy and patronage of the Church there could have been no western classical music as we know it. Go into any English cathedral for a service, and you will hear choral music and performance style which are the heir of an unbroken tradition going back hundreds of years into the Middle Ages. Methodism, according to the 1933 *Methodist Hymn Book*, was 'born in song'. It would be unthinkable to most contemporary Christian worshippers to go to church on a Sunday morning and not sing. The very level of conflict and misery caused within many a church congregation over differences about which music is appropriate for worship is a powerful sign of its significance in people's approach to God.

Singing and music go back to the earliest times of Christian corporate worship. The letter to the Ephesians asks the believers to 'be filled with the Spirit, addressing one another in psalms and hymns and spiritual songs, singing and making melody to the Lord with all your heart',[1] and it is clear that when they gathered in each other's homes for worship, they sang psalms and New Testament canticles. We have evidence of Christian hymns from the third century, and by the fourth century singing was already a fundamental feature of the Eucharist. From there developed plainsong, whose codification was attributed to Pope Gregory the Great (d. 604), and from about the ninth century singing different lines of music at once (polyphony) began to be developed, at first in the monasteries and later in the cathedrals and parish churches. The late medieval mass was a musical feast with introits, hymns, antiphons, graduals and the ordinary of the mass (Kyrie, Gloria, Credo, Sanctus, Benedictus and

Agnus Dei), following each other in glorious succession. Musical instruments were added, culminating in the orchestral masses of Mozart, Haydn, Beethoven, Schubert and Bruckner.

With such massive works as (the Lutheran) Bach's Mass in B Minor or (the nominally Catholic) Beethoven's *Missa Solemnis,* liturgical use finally became impractical, and from the eighteenth century much religious music (Handel's oratorios, for example) emigrated from the church building to the concert hall. In the last two centuries church music has tended to become much simpler, relying heavily upon the organ and beginning to take into account the need for wider congregational participation beyond the music for a trained choir. The great Protestant contribution was metrical psalms and hymns. As high art music took possession of the concert hall, the music of the Church flirted ever more daringly with popular music styles. The Salvation Army bands, for example, sought to reclaim some of the 'best tunes' from the 'devil'.

The *Catechism of the Catholic Church* could hardly be more positive about the role of music: 'The musical tradition of the universal Church is a treasure of inestimable value, greater even than that of any other art,' it says, quoting from one of the Vatican II documents.[2] While reminding the reader that it essentially belongs in the celebration of the liturgy, it goes on to quote from St Augustine in his *Confessions*, speaking about the period during which he was baptized:

> The tears flowed from me when I heard your hymns and canticles, for the sweet singing of your church moved me deeply. The music surged in my ears, truth seeped into my heart, and my feelings of devotion overflowed, so that the tears streamed down. But they were tears of gladness.[3]

But General Booth's talk of 'the devil' in relation to music reveals an undercurrent of anxiety in the Church's attitude to music. Augustine, a little later in the *Confessions,* expresses this anxiety perfectly:

> Sometimes I feel that I treat it [music] with more honour than it deserves. I realise that when they are sung these sacred words stir my mind to greater religious fervour and kindle in me a more ardent flame of piety than they would if they were not sung; and I also know that there are particular modes in song and in the voice, corresponding to my various emotions and able to stimulate them because of some mysterious relationship between the two. But I ought not to allow my mind to be paralysed by the gratification of my senses, which often leads it astray. For the senses are not content to take second place. Simply because I allow them their due, as adjuncts to reason, they attempt to take precedence and forge ahead of it, with the result that I sometimes sin in this way but am not aware of it until later.[4]

He ends up, however, feeling that his own failings are not a strong enough reason for banning music, and says that he is 'inclined to approve of the custom of singing in church, in order that by indulging the ears weaker spirits may be inspired with feelings of devotion'.[5]

Two problems clearly emerge here. One is the problem that music is too overpowering in worship, leading the mind's focus away from the meaning of the liturgy. The other is that music has a sensual quality which may arouse urges and instincts quite inimical to sobriety and reverence.

As regards the first of these, we have the classic conflict of priest and musician. A cathedral canon may have structured his or her proposed liturgy to allow a deep meaning and logical progress to unfold, only to find that the choirmaster has already planned and begun rehearsing a long and complicated motet for that service, a musical item which will inevitably interrupt the flow and integrity of what the canon had planned. Who will blink first? Complaints from clerics about the over-dominance or over-complexity of music echo down the centuries. The twelfth-century abbot of Rievaulx, Aelred, attacked music in worship because it was too complex and actually obscured the words of the liturgy, and the Cistercian houses did not use polyphony. Pope John XXII issued a bull in the fourteenth century forbidding complexity in church music for the same reason as Aelred. By the late Middle Ages, however, polyphony was often elaborate and complicated, and it was abandoned at the time of the Reformation in the sixteenth century, both Catholic and Protestant writers speaking against it. When Archbishop Thomas Cranmer published the first English Book of Common Prayer in 1549, he engaged John Merbecke to provide music for the parts of the service that were to be sung, but insisted that there should be no fancy ornamentation, but rather 'for every syllable a note'. The Council of Trent (1545–63) ordered that masses be sung 'clearly and at the right speed', and that singing 'be constituted not to give empty pleasure to the ear, but in such a way that the words may be clearly understood by all'. In the middle of the eighteenth century the pope issued an edict curtailing the use of trumpets and timpani in church services, and the Austro-Hungarian monarchs, Maria Theresa and Joseph II, sought to cut back extravagant musical performances at religious services in the same period. Perhaps they had reason to do so:

> Taken as a whole, the musical ambition and flamboyance of sacred music by Haydn and his contemporaries encouraged more than one commentator to note that going to the church was like going to a concert.[6]

As for the sensual quality of music, Christian commentators have always had their doubts. For the early Christian writers the use of music at banquets, in the theatre and in taverns or in relation to pagan mythology in the wider world was enough to give it a bad name. Augustine's anxieties about music's sensual, purely emotional effects are echoed from the time of the Reformation onwards by Puritan rejection of music as the source of hedonistic and trivial pastimes or the evangelical desire to 'reclaim' popular music for spiritual use. 'Sex, drugs and rock 'n' roll' are not just a late twentieth-century phenomenon, nor indeed the use of pop tunes in sacred contexts. But the anxiety remains that the music outside the control of the Church may induce longings very different from those of the saint kneeling before the crucifix.

These doubts may go some way towards explaining why the Church has almost no composers in its lists of saints. Even its famed patron saint of music, the third-century martyr Cecilia, turns out to be almost certainly legendary; even her legend is only tenuously linked to music. We should not, of course, forget that composer abbess, Hildegard of Bingen; and perhaps even Philip Neri ought to be mentioned, as the founder of the musical oratorio. It is very clear here, though, that, for sainthood, other criteria than 'mere musical genius' have been applied: you get noticed not for being a composer but for being a notable religious and teacher or a great mystic and helper of the poor. Composers, it seems, were either humble servants of the Church and of its liturgy, whose essential duty was *not* to be noticed, not to obtrude their powerful emotions and cleverness too much on the meaning of the words; or else, in the post-Reformation era, they were increasingly dangerous free agents whose true sphere was perhaps the decadent pagan world beyond the reach of the Church.

And yet, after all is said on the negative side, for 2,000 years the Church has welcomed the use of music as a gift of God and a vehicle for God's praise. Theologians followed earlier philosophers in speaking about the harmony of music reflecting the harmony of the spheres, the mathematical harmony of the universe itself, and it remains true that the structure of a Bach fugue or a late Beethoven piano sonata speaks deeply and satisfyingly to the mind – even without overt religious text or references – of ultimate meaning and order and hope in the universe, of starting from somewhere, travelling and arriving and 'knowing the place for the first time'[7]. In recent years Jeremy Begbie has demonstrated the value of music as an analogy and way of experiencing the quality and richness of events and meanings in time, and even of seeking to grasp the life of God as Trinity – as a powerful chord or even as three-part polyphony. Above all, how much harder it would be for us to praise God affectively – with all our heart and soul – without the use of music. Yes, of course there are the dangers of mere emotionalism or the deadly effects of the over-polished choir performing for a passive 'congregation', but – in spite of the Quakers – we would be lost without music in worship. In his book on Mozart, Hans Küng wrote:

> 'When I hear great music, I believe that I know that what this music says cannot be untrue.' So conceded the theological musicologist Theodor W. Adorno, who as is well known was more than reserved towards traditional religion. He was taking part in a discussion about revelation and autonomous reason. As an example Adorno gave Bach's *St Matthew Passion*; he could equally well have given Mozart's *Requiem*. I think that music which speaks the truth is not just limited, say, to vocal music or explicitly religious music; it also includes purely instrumental music ... An abstract masterpiece can speak the truth in

the pure language of sound. Indeed tones, sounds, can speak and in the end say something inexpressible, unspeakable: in the midst of music the 'ineffable mystery'.[8]

The three composers I have chosen to focus on come from different centuries, and I chose them because each was a conscious and committed believer for whom music was certainly a theological expression. I could have chosen many others, and there would be good ground also for celebrating some of the great Christian *performers* of music, choir directors and organists, singers and instrumentalists. With William Byrd, Anton Bruckner and Olivier Messiaen, however, there is no shadow of suspicion that they were merely institutional adherents writing music at the behest of a dominant ecclesiastical establishment. Let them stand for all who have 'spoken the truth in the pure language of sound' and expressed something of the 'ineffable mystery' of God.

William Byrd
c. 1542–1623

You are born in the last years of the reign of Henry VIII, the king who threw off the pope's control of the Church in England; you are a young child during the six years of Edward VI's reign, when Archbishop Thomas Cranmer was imposing a much stricter Protestantism on his country, with the 1549 and 1552 Books of Common Prayer; you are hardly yet a teenager when Queen Mary turns everything back to the Catholic status quo and institutes her reign of terror; and you live your adult life through the whole reign of Queen Elizabeth and a good part of that of James I, as the Church of England establishes its reality and power at the expense of Catholics and Puritans. Not a comfortable time to be alive, especially when you have spent your whole life in unconcealed loyalty to the pope and the service of the old

Latin liturgy, and can write in your last will and testament that you may 'live and dye a true and perfect member of the Holy Catholike Churche withoute which I believe there is noe salvacon for me'. Those are the words of the composer, William Byrd, whom a clerk at the Chapel Royal on his death called 'A Father of Musicke'.

But just how uncomfortable was his life?

Life for Catholics under the reigns of Elizabeth (1558–1603) and James (1603–1625) was a strangely mixed and unpredictable affair. Both monarchs tried to give Catholics a certain amount of practical toleration, but were forced by Catholic plots and rebellions and by threats from Catholic powers overseas to apply harsher sanctions. Once Pope Pius V had proclaimed his bull *Regnans in Excelsis* in 1570, excommunicating Elizabeth from the Church, it was very much more difficult to be both a good Catholic and loyal to the English crown. There were three sorts of sanctions applied by the Penal Code passed by Elizabeth's parliaments: Catholics were excluded from any post in national or local government and could not travel more than five miles from their homes without a special licence; they were fined for not attending worship in their local (Church of England) parish church, and were then known as 'recusants'; and priests who celebrated the old Latin mass were condemned to death as traitors. In practice, however, these laws were implemented in a patchy way. Many Catholic non-church attenders were never registered; the travelling rule was seldom enforced; and in many remoter parts of the country (north of the Trent and west of the Avon) and in the homes of wealthy Catholics the old religious practices continued in secret.

Although enforcement may have been haphazard, the threat was always there. Catholic priests, trained on the Continent, and later Jesuit missionaries, had to be smuggled into the country and live a secret life as laymen, or living in a secret roof chamber in a great house; mass was celebrated in secret. And both priests and laypeople were executed, sometimes because they were suspected of involvement in plots (like the Gunpowder Plot of 1605), and sometimes just for saying mass or hiding a priest. The Roman Catholic Church today celebrates Forty Martyrs of England and Wales – a 'focus group' for some 357 believed to have been martyred between 1535 and 1680. They include Edmund Campion, Margaret Clitherow, Cuthbert Mayne and Robert Southwell.

This was William Byrd's world. It seems likely that he was a child chorister at the Chapel Royal during Mary's reign, for he is described as a pupil and protégé of the composer Thomas Tallis. His first musical appointment (1563) was as organist of Lincoln Cathedral. He was not much more than 20 years old and he stayed almost ten years. In 1572 Byrd was appointed organist at the Chapel Royal, together with his teacher, Tallis, and in 1575 Queen Elizabeth granted the two of them a monopoly of music publishing for 25 years. Byrd lived with his first wife and children in Harlington, Middlesex, for 15 years, before retiring about 1592 (he was about 50) to Stondon Massey in Essex, where he lived with his second wife until his death in 1623.

Reasons briefly set down by th' auctor, to perswade every one to learne to sing.

First, it is a knowledge easely taught, and quickly learned, where there is a good Master, and an apt Scoller.

2. The exercise of singing is delightfull to Nature & good to preserue the health of Man.

3. It doth strengthen all the parts of the brest, & doth open the pipes.

4. It is a singuler good remedie for a stutting & stammering in the speech.

---

5. It is the best meanes to procure a perfect pronunciation, & to make a good Orator.

6. It is the onely way to know where Nature hath bestowed the benefit of a good voyce: which guift is so rare, as there is not one among a thousand, that hath it: and in many, that excellent guift is lost, because they want Art to expresse Nature.

7. There is not any Musicke of Instruments whatsoever, comparable to that which is made of the voyces of Men, where the voices are good, and the same well sorted and ordered.

8. The better the voyce is, the meeter it is to honour and serue God there-with: and the voyce of man is chiefly to be employed to that ende.

> Omnis Spiritus Laudet Dominum
> Since singing is so good a thing,
> I wish all men would learne to sing.
>
> William Byrd[9]

It is remarkable how openly William Byrd lived as a Catholic near the centre of a society which officially persecuted and suppressed Catholicism. He regularly appeared, with both his wives, before the County Sessions as a recusant and he was closely associated with Jesuits. In the late 1570s seminary priests from abroad had begun to arrive, and in 1581 Edmund Campion and two other Jesuits were executed, beginning a grim period of Elizabethan persecutions. In 1588 Byrd published a setting of the banned poem by Father Henry Walpole 'Why do I use my paper, incke and pen' which celebrated Campion's martyrdom; the words were changed so that it could appear to be about the Protestant martyrs under Mary, but Government spies were not fooled. In 1586 Byrd attended a clandestine week-long meeting at a country house to welcome two of the most prominent Jesuit missionaries, Robert Southwell and Henry Garnet, and in 1605 he is known to have played the organ at another gathering at which Garnet was present. It seems likely that he harboured Jesuits and other Catholic fugitives in his home, and he may even have supplied financial support.

> Why do I use my paper, incke and pen
>   And call my wits to counsel what to saie?
> Such memories were made for mortall men:
>   I speak of Saints whose names cannot decaye.
> An Angels' trump were fitted for to sound
> Their glorious death, if such on earth were found.
>
> Henry Walpole[10]

William Byrd gave covert musical support to the Catholic cause mainly through his continual composition of Latin motets. There was, of course, little outlet for such works in Protestant England, and they would have been performed mainly in Catholic houses. Like artists in many periods of political oppression, Byrd found a way of writing in code, choosing unexceptionable biblical texts which nevertheless had a deeper significance for fellow recusants. Some of the motets, for example, lament for Jerusalem during the Babylonian captivity; others pray that the congregation may be liberated; many use texts that corresponded with the last words of Catholic martyrs on the gallows or with texts used in contemporary Jesuit controversial literature. The motet 'Deus, venerunt gentes', which laments the bodies of martyrs thrown to the birds and the beasts, clearly refers to Campion; 'Circumspice, Jerusalem' celebrating sons returning from the East in the service of God was very likely Byrd's offering at the welcome for Southwell and Garnet.

On one occasion Philippe de Monte, Kapellmeister to the Holy Roman Emperor, sent Byrd a motet, 'Super flumina Babylonis', with words from Psalm 137, 'By the waters of Babylon, there we sat down, yea we wept'. Byrd responded by sending back his own motet on the same psalm, 'Quomodo cantabimus', 'How shall we sing the Lord's song in a strange land? If I forget thee, O Jerusalem, let my right hand forget her cunning.' For 'Jerusalem', read 'Rome'; and to show that his right hand had lost none of its cunning, Byrd included in his motet a three-part canon by inversion, that is, music like a round, in which each successive voice sings the opposite of the opening voice, going down by the same intervals that the first voice went up, and vice versa. In the 1590s Byrd published three Latin masses, and although the printer left the composer's name off the title pages, it is there on every other page of the music. These were to be the last composed in England until the twentieth century. But just listen to the defiant, assertive way he sets 'et in unam sanctam catholicam ecclesiam' (I believe in one holy Catholic Church) in the Mass for Four Voices.

How did he get away with it? Probably by being simply too brilliant a composer. Elizabeth would have been mad to get rid of such a wonderful ornament to her Chapel Royal, and it seems that she granted him some kind of remission from his recusancy. And although Byrd was an open and avowed Catholic, he somehow managed to 'square the circle' of the pope's bull by simultaneously maintaining his loyalty to the crown. One suspects, though, that the simple religious honesty and conviction which he did not attempt to hide were his best protection.

Since, relying on divine mercy, I have reached such a span of years that I have seen many of my pupils in the realm of music – men most excellently equipped in that art – pass from life while I survive; and since in my own life I consider that the richness of divine bounty has been conferred and indeed showered upon me; my mind is afire, remembering my faith, my duty, and my devotion to God, to leave behind me for future generations, in however small a measure, some public testimony of a heart that is grateful. And so, at this advanced age, I have tried, however unworthy and inadequate I may be, to put notes, as a crown, to certain holy praises in the Christian service. And, since from your household – which is most friendly to me and mine – these travails in music have for the most part sprung, and have from that kindly warmth brought forth richer fruit; so accept, most generous lord, these little flowers, gathered, almost, from your own garden and due to be given to you as tithe; and let it not be a burden to you to guard these last works of mine, so that they may go forth into the world to the glory of the most glorious and mighty God, to the magnifying of your own renown, and to the delight of all who worship the muses.

William Byrd, Dedication of the Second Book of *Gradualia* to Baron Petre of Writtle[11]

Many people have a very close friend whose political or religious views are anathema to them; it's one of the paradoxical things about a good relationship, that it can transcend mere opinions. Perhaps there is an analogy here with the way early Protestant England could happily contain – and celebrate – a great Catholic composer. Perhaps our awareness of the political and religious intolerance, intrigues and conflicts of the sixteenth and seventeenth centuries has too effectively hidden those cases where English people, divided by religion, may nevertheless have lived, worked, eaten and drunk together with mutual affection and respect.

We cannot know how much of this was true, but we do know for certain that William Byrd wrote great music – songs, music for keyboard and for viol consort, and so much sacred music, expressing his profound faith – and we can be thankful that that sacred music is still heard today – in Latin and in English – in both Catholic and Anglican worship, transcending yesterday's quarrels.

We celebrate the single-mindedness, and quite possibly at times the sheer stubbornness, of William Byrd – devoted musician and devoted believer.

> *God, whom the angels praise in harmony and*
> *song, you gave to William Byrd his glorious*
> *gift as a composer and the grace of a steady*
> *faith in troubled times.*
> *Help each one of us, in integrity and*
> *faithfulness,*
> *so to grasp hold of what you have given,*
> *that through the richness of many skills*
> *the world may come at last to the perfect*
> *cadence and resolution of your love*
> *in Jesus our Lord.*

ᛞ ᛃ

Anton Bruckner
1824–96

Anton Bruckner's life represents a set of contradictions. First there is the 'country bumpkin' who was finally honoured in sophisticated Vienna. Then there is the composer of inconsequential small-scale pieces in a conservative style for local performers who around the age of 40 started writing massive symphonies instead. There is the anxious, indecisive character, always looking for guidance and reassurance from his friends or those with influence, who nevertheless wrote masterpiece after masterpiece with few performances and little recognition in sight. There is the deeply religious Roman Catholic who wrote the last of his mass settings at the age of 43 and thereafter little but symphonies for the remaining 28 years of his life. Finally there is the composer whose symphonies have been called 'cathedrals in sound' who in his final work gave expression to a deep anguish and uncertainty.

> He had the reputation of being a rather simple man. I remember my father telling me how he went to see the composer one day when he was working on the [eighth] symphony in our house. He could hear Bruckner trying out a theme on the piano, and so he didn't disturb him. Instead, my father noted down the theme and went to try it out on the church organ. After a while Bruckner came into the church and heard what was being played. Of course he got into a terrible state. 'Where did you hear that?' he said. My father wanted to tease him, and replied, 'Oh, somewhere in Vienna; I don't know – perhaps a band played it in the park.' Bruckner then fell on his knees before the altar, crying out, 'God forgive me! I have stolen another man's music without knowing it!'
>
> Then naturally my father had to put him out of his misery and told him the truth. 'You scoundrel!' shouted the composer in his broad Upper-Austrian dialect. 'But never mind. Let's go and have a glass of Pilsner together. I forgive you.'
>
> Julius Bayer[12]

Bruckner never lost the character and attitudes that were formed by his upbringing in the countryside of Upper Austria. He was born in 1824 in the small village of Ansfelden near Linz, the eldest child of the village schoolmaster and church organist. When he was only four he was already playing some of the church hymns on his little violin, and by the age of ten he was able to deputize for his father on the organ. He was only thirteen when his father died, and his mother sent him to be a choir boy at the nearby Augustinian monastery of St Florian. He trained and worked as a school teacher, returning to St Florian as teacher in the parish school in 1845, where he stayed for some ten years, becoming the organist in 1848. The seat of the splendid organ at St Florian was without doubt Bruckner's spiritual home, and he returned to it often, as a source of peace and inspiration.

To the end Bruckner retained his rural accent, a provincial politeness and deferral to authority, unsophisticated clothes (the white shirt with the very big collar, the generously cut black suit, the short trousers to facilitate organ pedalling, and the wide-brimmed black slouch hat) and a very hearty appetite for simple and substantial dishes in Austrian inns. With his corpulent person in the baggy black suit and topped by the great rough round head and massive hooked nose, he looked every inch the Austrian peasant, up to town for the day. After a successful rehearsal of one of his symphonies he actually gave the great conductor Hans Richter a tip, to buy himself a drink. Once when the emperor asked if there were anything he could do for him, Bruckner asked him if he could stop the music critic Eduard Hanslick saying such nasty things about his music. Yet this was the Professor of Harmony and Counterpoint at the Vienna Conservatory from 1868 to 1891. This was the lecturer in the same subjects at Vienna University, where he was granted an honorary doctorate in 1891. This was the well-known organist at the Court Chapel in Vienna. This was the composer who gathered an ever-growing group of conductors and younger composers as his friends and supporters, whose seventh symphony received a triumphant premiere in Leipzig in 1884 and whose fame began to spread around the world.

In 1855 Bruckner became the organist at Linz Cathedral, and in 1863 he wrote his first symphony and began the series of eleven symphonies (two trial efforts and the nine numbered ones), the three great mass settings and other works that have made his reputation. He had become the organist at Linz Cathedral in 1855, and, in spite of being an experienced composer by this time, had embarked on two periods of further study, with Simon Sechter for harmony and counterpoint and with

Otto Kitzler for musical form and orchestration. He was such an assiduous pupil that on one occasion, when he sent Sechter seventeen notebooks full of exercises, the latter had to plead with him to relax a bit. It is no exaggeration to say that if Bruckner had died in 1863, when he was already 39, he would barely have troubled the pages of *Groves Dictionary of Music and Musicians*. What made the difference was the music of Richard Wagner. Bruckner's teacher, Kitzler, was doing a performance of Wagner's *Tannhäuser* in Linz and together they studied the score. So a genius could break all Sechter's rules and create music of deep power and passion! It was a revelation, but it was almost as though Bruckner had always known it. From now on Wagner was the 'Meister aller Meister' (the master of all masters). In 1865 Bruckner met Wagner, in Munich, but did not have the courage to show him his First Symphony which he had taken along. Eight years later at Bayreuth Wagner graciously acceded to the composer's request to dedicate his Third Symphony to him. For many years after Bruckner moved to Vienna in 1868 to take up his post at the Conservatory it did him no good at all to be viewed as a disciple of Wagner. Eduard Hanslick, the influential critic and champion of Brahms as the true heir of the Viennese classical tradition, rubbished Bruckner year after year, and even Brahms himself was not above the odd nasty dig at him. When Wagner died in 1883 Bruckner was in the middle of the slow movement of his Seventh Symphony; he added a solemn coda using four Wagner tubas in memory of his revered mentor. The simple, religious countryman was a very different man from the complex, worldly, egomaniacal Wagner, and he wrote very different music; and yet it is unlikely that Bruckner would have begun writing his symphonies without Wagner's inspiration.

Bruckner has been described as nervous, indecisive, even a victim of life. Certainly he had to be pushed to further his career. When the auditions for the role of organist at Linz Cathedral were taking place in 1855 Bruckner had to be more or less dragged along by one of his old teachers – and then blew them all away with his improvisation and got the job. Both when he moved from St Florian to Linz and later when he moved to Vienna, he asked his old employer to keep the job open in case things didn't work out. His indecisiveness seems to be conclusively proved by the endless revisions he made to his symphonies. There were two periods in the Vienna years when new composition almost came to a standstill because he was too busy going back over the works he had already done, improving them. It was, of course, very difficult for Bruckner to get his huge pieces performed or published in 1870s Vienna. There was the constant sniping of the Brahms faction, and the few performances that happened were either disastrous or very qualified successes. Well-meaning friends and supporters made suggestions and criticisms of his music, trying to make it more 'accessible' (for example, by means of major cuts, or by making it sound more like Wagner), and Bruckner got down to the work of revision. The First, Second, Third, Fourth and Eighth Symphonies all had major subsequent surgery and today exist in several different versions. When the conductor Herman Levi said he could not understand the massive Eighth Symphony, Bruckner spent several years redoing it – which meant that he ran out of time for the Ninth, dying before he could complete the last of the four movements. And yet, in spite of all this, Bruckner still had the inner certainty to keep writing music and simply started writing number Five even though no one had heard number Four. His revisions can be seen in the light of an artistic perfectionism quite as much as caving in to well-intentioned friends. Towards the end of his life he had all the original manuscripts of his major works wrapped up, ready for presentation to the Vienna Court Library after his death: the real Bruckner made available, as he said, 'for a later time'. Above all, there was Bruckner's sovereign decisiveness in improvisations on the organ, of which he was a unique master. This is exemplified by the story of his examination in 1861 for a diploma to teach harmony and counterpoint in Vienna.

He [Bruckner] often told us, in wickedly ironic terms, about his so-called 'examination', in which he was called upon to give proof of his 'theoretical capability'. It took place in the Piaristenkirche. Professor Sechter wrote out a four-bar theme which – after Dessoff had refused to do it – Herbeck extended to eight bars. The theme was given to Bruckner. He stared, undecided, at the paper for a long time, and the 'examination committee' began to grow suspicious. Then he sat calmly at the organ and worked the theme up into a tremendous fugue, which overflowed into an even longer free fantasy. The members of the committee broke up and went their separate ways. As Herbeck was leaving he was heard to say, 'He should have examined us'.

Carl Hruby[13]

Why did this very devout Catholic write the last of his seven mass settings in 1867–68 and thereafter very little overtly religious music? That Bruckner was very devout throughout his life is beyond question. His pupils often realized that he was praying in the middle of a lesson, and his preparation for an organ improvisation was always deep prayer. Nevertheless two good reasons can be given for his turning away from specifically religious compositions in the Vienna years: the lack of invitation and opportunity; and the inner recognition that the wordless symphony was now to be his means of praise to 'the dear God', to whom he thus dedicated his last symphony. Bruckner did set Psalm 150 and the *Te Deum* in his latter years, triumphant shouts of praise to God, and one of his great admirers, the composer Gustav Mahler, crossed out in his score the list of instrumental parts and wrote in, 'For the tongues of angels, heaven-blest, chastened hearts and souls purified by fire.' In 1885–86 the painter Fritz von Uhde painted *The Last Supper*; not without good reason he painted a portrait of Bruckner as one of the disciples round the table.

A performance of Bruckner's Mass in D minor conducted by Franz Bayer with Bruckner himself at the organ in Steyr parish church on Easter Sunday 1893

The Credo began. The D minor Mass is an Easter Mass in the truest sense of the word; this Credo can be compared to no other, because it portrays the death and ascension of the Redeemer in such a masterful way. 'Et sepultus est' – 'and he was buried'. A solo organ accompanies the body of Christ to the grave in indescribably moving tones ...

Bayer had prepared a surprise for Bruckner at the aforementioned organ solo. On several occasions the Master had stated that the solo ought to be played from the high altar. Perhaps he hoped to achieve a special effect from the distance, or did he also picture the high altar as the grave of Christ? He never explained any further.

Now, because it was Holy Week, a harmonium had been placed in the presbytery. Bayer had ordered that it be positioned behind the altar, together with a player who had been specially instructed as to what to do.

The bellows-operator at the great organ had been told not to allow any air to pass through the instrument in this particular part of the Mass.

The moment arrived. The orchestra faded away and Bruckner pressed the keys, about to say his musical prayer to the Lord. But – what happened? The organ made no sound. But, as if from far away in the distance,

---

> the wonderful chords sounded from the high altar above in a gentle *piano*.
>
> That was too much for the Master. For a moment his face seemed frozen, and then large tears began to roll down over his cheeks.
>
> Julia Bayer[14]

And so we come to the final contradiction: why so much anguish in the last, the ninth Symphony? As Stephen Johnson writes:

> Nowhere else in Bruckner's output does one encounter such disturbingly ambiguous harmonies and tortured melodic lines – the opening theme of the Adagio, with its upward 'missed octave' leap, is as pained as anything in Mahler ... The pounding rhythms and grinding dissonances of the central Scherzo have invited comparison with Bartok, Prokofiev or Shostakovitch ... There are moments of radiance [in the Adagio] amid the anguished crescendos and long wintry melodies. But the final climax contains the most anguished music in the whole symphony, with trombones, tuba and the other bass instruments bellowing out the Adagio's 'missed octave' violin theme *fff*. The culminating discord is left hanging in the air, unresolved.[15]

So we see deeply here the reality that the jolly, peasantlike professor cracking jokes with his gang of students in the Viennese inn is also the very private, very lonely man, who in spite of his faith, knows that he is travelling alone into the unknown, into death.

Bruckner knew a good deal of pain and anguish in his life. He lost his father when he was barely a teenager; his mother's death in 1860 left him deeply bereft; he kept falling in love with young girls, but was so strait-laced that he asked them to marry him before any relationship had been established, and was rejected over and over again; his worth as a composer was not recognized by the wider world until he was 60 years old; he had known periods of depression and paranoia, and even one period in a sanatorium for a 'cold cure', at which time he developed an obsessive counting mania; he had something of an obsession with death, on occasion going out of his way to view corpses. But Bruckner's symphonies are not really autobiographical; they transmute whatever he knew of pain and hope into universal statements of the human condition under God. Each one is a human journey towards the light, and whatever struggles there may have been on the way, all of them end in glory.

Religion was a primary force in the life of this great creative genius. He prayed regularly, and if his devotions sometimes took strange forms, they were still sincerely offered and deeply felt. It was impossible to disturb him when he knelt at prayer before his great crucifix, and so I often had the opportunity to hear what he said as I stood quietly with him in the room. There would be several 'Our Father's and 'Hail Mary's, and he would often conclude with a free prayer, for example, 'Dear God, let me soon be well again; you see, I need my health so that I can finish the Ninth', and so on. This last request was uttered somewhat impatiently; it was concluded with a threefold Amen, and on a few occasions, on the third Amen, he would slap his thighs with both hands, as if to say, 'If the dear Lord doesn't hear me, then it's not my fault!'

Richard Heller (Bruckner's doctor in the last two years of his life)[16]

Bruckner desperately prayed that he might live to complete the Ninth Symphony, but he did not; only sketches remain, impossible to piece together. The hope, the glory, the triumph over despair that he had so often achieved and incarnated in his music was now, at the point where he had pictured humanity's deepest doubt and grief, denied to him – in art. 'For now we see in a mirror dimly, but then face to face. Now I know in part; then I shall understand fully, even as I have been fully understood.'[17] Bruckner's music takes us almost as far as we can go, now. The rest we must leave in the hands of 'our dear God'.

Once he went on a trip to Kirchdorf ... The trip took in the fortress at Altpernstein ... When they came to the dungeons, Bruckner crawled – or rather squeezed – his way inside through a narrow hole in the wall. But when it came to getting back out again, all his efforts were in vain. No one knew what to do. The fearful Bruckner relived all the torments of the prisoners of olden times. And while he was experiencing these terrifying fantasies, he composed a *resurrexit*, until at last they were able to get his voluminous frame free.

Linda Schönbeck[18]

Dear God,
for whose glory the music of Anton Bruckner
was created,
give us too the faithfulness in prayer
and the determination of our inner gifts,
to struggle through the deep valleys of grief
and frustration
and to improvise our journey to the peak of
the mountain,
where you are fully known, Father, Son and
Spirit, for ever.

&ο ᴄ୫

Olivier Messiaen
1908–92

In all the horrors of twentieth-century wars, music played a vital role in human experience and survival: from 'It's a long way to Tipperary' to 'We'll meet again', from the deep sadness of Elgar's 1918 Cello Concerto to the hope-out-of-struggle of Tippett's *A Child of our Time* (1944). Even in the concentration camps music was played, sounds representing human hope and faith in the face of ultimate evil and despair.

One of the most extraordinary premières of the Second World War was Olivier Messiaen's *Quatuor pour la Fin du Temps*. It was given in January 1941 at the Stalag VIIIA prisoner-of-war camp at Görlitz in Silesia (now part of Poland), where Messiaen, aged 32, was a prisoner of war. He had been called up at the beginning of the war, but owing to his poor eyesight he had become a medical auxiliary, instead of joining the army. He was captured by the Germans when they invaded France and taken to Görlitz with 'a haversack containing all my treasures, i.e. a little library of scores ... going from the Brandenburg Concertos of Bach to the Lyric Suite of Berg'. In the camp he came across a violinist, a clarinettist and a cellist, and he wrote a trio which they performed in the washrooms. After this he added seven more movements to the trio, incorporating his own instrument, the piano, and this became the hour-long *Quartet for the End of Time*. Only when the work was completed did the Germans find a piano for them; it was hardly an ideal instrument – an upright piano, out of tune, with many of its keys not working properly – but on this Messiaen, with his three fellow prisoners, gave the first performance of his new work. The concert was given in freezing conditions and the audience consisted of some 5,000 people in the camp – people from all walks of life, including workers, intellectuals, doctors and priests. 'Never have I been listened to with such attention and understanding,' said Messiaen afterwards.

One might well imagine that for many in a prisoner-of-war camp anything was better than nothing to combat the longueurs of passive prison life, but it is fascinating to note the parallels of that experience with the theme of Messiaen's work. For the quartet was a meditation on the end of time, pictured in the Revelation of John: 'Then the angel that I had seen, standing on the sea and the land, raised his right hand to heaven, and swore by him who lives for ever and ever, and made heaven and all that it contains, and earth and all it contains, and the sea and all it contains: "The time of waiting is over, at the time when the seventh angel is heard sounding his trumpet, the mystery of God will be fulfilled, just as he announced in the gospel to his servants the prophets".'[19] Through many different techniques in the Quartet Messiaen seeks to convey both 'the end of time' and to write a music of contemplation in which there often seems to be no more forward movement or development. In the first movement, for example, the cello and piano have two quite independent rhythmic phrases, based on the rhythms of Indian music and phrases that are palindromes (the same forwards as backwards), while the violin and clarinet have quite separate birdsongs above these – the piano and cello could in theory keep repeating their music for ever. In another movement there is the instruction that it is to be played 'infinitely slowly'. This combination of a static and ecstatic music of contemplation and Messiaen's preoccupation with God, eternity, time and the central events of the Christian creed is the key to most of his work as a composer.

> Certainly, like St Paul, I see in nature a manifestation of one of the aspects of divinity, but it's equally certain that God's creations are not God himself. Moreover, all God's creations are enclosed in Time, and Time is one of God's strangest creatures because it is totally opposed to Him who is Eternal by nature, to Him who is without beginning, end or succession.
>
> Olivier Messiaen[20]

Messiaen was born in December 1908 at Avignon. His father was an English teacher and his mother a poet. When his father was called up in the First World War, the family moved to Grenoble, and after the war to Nantes. Olivier always rejoiced in mountains, remembering them from his childhood in Grenoble. He also remembered declaiming the whole of Shakespeare at the age of eight. He taught himself to play the piano, and between the ages of seven and ten he asked for and received complete scores of operas as Christmas presents, which he would play and sing through. From the age of eight he began composing. When his father gained a teaching post in Paris in 1919, Messiaen entered the Conservatoire there at the age of 11. His career there was brilliant; he won many prizes, and, after showing wonderful improvisation skills on the keyboard, he was introduced to Marcel Dupré and began to study the organ with him. In 1931 he was appointed organist at the Église de la Sainte Trinité in Paris, a post he was to hold for over 60 years.

> On account of the succession of different priests-in-charge at the Trinité, my services were rather wisely shared out: for the High Mass on Sunday, I played only plainsong ...; for the eleven o'clock Mass on Sundays, classical and romantic music; for the Mass at noon ... I was allowed to play my own music; and finally, for the five o'clock Vespers, I was obliged to improvise because

the verses were too short to allow for the playing of pieces between the Psalms and during the Magnificat.

Claude Samuel: Weren't the various priests-in-charge ... a bit startled by the introduction into their church of music as daring as that of the Livre d'orgue?

They weren't startled because the truths I express, the Truths of the Faith are startling; they are fairytales, in turn mysterious, harrowing, glorious and sometimes terrifying, always based on a luminous, unchanging Reality. I am perforce a hundred thousand degrees below each Truth. No, the priests weren't startled, but the parishioners were, because they don't always know the texts they hear.

Olivier Messiaen[21]

Messiaen was released from Görlitz in May 1941 and appointed a Professor of Harmony at the Paris Conservatoire, where he continued to teach until his retirement in 1978. He married a fellow-composer and violinist Claire Delbos in 1932, and after her death in 1959, married the brilliant pianist Yvonne Loriod, for whom he wrote, and with whom he played, many of his pieces.

Claude Samuel: What impressions do you want to communicate to your listeners?

The first idea that I wished to express – and the most important, because it stands above them all – is the existence of the truths of the Catholic faith. I've the good fortune to be a Catholic. I was born a believer, and it happens that the Scriptures struck me even as a child. So a number of my works are intended to bring out the theological truths of the Catholic faith. That is the first aspect of my work, the noblest and, doubtless, the most useful and valuable; perhaps the only one which I won't regret at the hour of my death. But I'm a human being and, like all human beings, I'm sensitive to human love. I've tried to express this in three of my works through the medium of the greatest myth of human love, that of Tristan and Isolde. Finally, I have a profound love for nature. I think that nature infinitely surpasses us, and I've always sought lessons from it. By preference, I've loved birds, so I've examined birdsong especially: I've studied ornithology. There is in my music this juxtaposition of Catholic faith, the Tristan and Isolde myth and a highly developed use of birdsong.

Olivier Messiaen[22]

Messiaen's celebration of human love is found in works created at the end of the 1940s, by far the best known being the Turangalila Symphony, in 10 movements, for piano, ondes martenot (an electronic instrument) and orchestra. As for birdsong, Messiaen became a knowledgeable ornithologist and wrote down in precise notation the songs of birds on several continents, incorporating them into many of his compositions, especially from the 1950s onwards. Throughout his composing career, however, the themes of Christian story and theology inspired his works: *L'Ascension, La Nativité du Seigneur, Et Expecto Resurrectionem Mortuorum, La Transfiguration.* He wrote little for actual liturgical performance, although many of his organ works can be played before, after or during a service, and churchgoers may well have heard the 'Transport de Joie' from *L'Ascension* or 'Dieu Parmi Nous' from *La Nativité.* In 1943 he wrote *Visions de l'Amen* for two pianos.

'Amen' has four different meanings:

Amen, so be it! The creative act.

Amen, I submit, I accept. Thy will be done!

> Amen, the wish, the desire, that this may be, that you would give to me and I to you.
>
> Amen, that is, all is fixed for ever, consummated in Paradise.
>
> Adding to these the life of creatures that say 'Amen' by the very fact that they exist, I have tried to express the varied richness of the Amen in seven musical visions.
>
> Olivier Messiaen[23]

Messiaen's music lends itself perfectly to the expression of timeless or symbolic ideas. It is often slow to the point where movement seems almost to cease. It does not 'develop' as most western classical music did until the beginning of the twentieth century. It uses phrases that can only be transposed to a few other keys and irregular palindromic rhythms that fold back on themselves and do not keep moving regularly onwards. It uses massive hieratic chords (Messiaen had a form of synaesthesia which meant that he always 'saw' colours associated with different keys and chords) and employs many exotic tuned percussion instruments (Messiaen was fascinated by the music of Bali, Java and Japan). At times there is the ecstasy of the mystic, but the music more often seeks to express a sense of sheer intellectual awe at the full reality of supernatural truths. In a century when much classical music became completely secularized or at best agnostic, and when religious music was often 'dumbed down' Olivier Messiaen has offered a Christian music of inspiration and of theological and musical rigour which speaks across the limits of Christianity. In a review of Melvyn Tan's performance of *Vingt Regards sur l'Enfant Jésus* at the Spitalfields Festival in June 2005, Tim Ashley wrote:

> Tan unfolded its vast architecture with complete coherence from the opening, in which swaying chords summon up a vision of

God's timeless majesty, to the final pages, in which the same theme returns in jubilant splendour as Messiaen celebrates the intersection of the human and the divine. In between came jubilant cacophonies of praise and moments of piercing beauty, as the music seemed to go beyond time to offer us glimpses into eternity.[24]

In 1975 Messiaen was commissioned by the Paris Opera to write an opera based on Saint Francis. He completed the four-hour score of *Saint François d'Assise* in 1983: in eight scenes, it requires an orchestra of 120, including very large wind and percussion sections and three ondes martenot with a choir of 150. Saint Francis was a natural choice for Messiaen: he was the saint who 'most resembled Christ', and, of course, he could incorporate his favourite birdsong, as Francis preached to the birds. He desired that the saint should have the appearance of the Cimabue portrait and the gestures of Giotto's representation of him in the Assisi frescoes. The angel who appears had to resemble the Gabriel of Fra Angelico's *Annunciation* in Florence. In the third scene of what Messiaen liked to call a 'spectacle' rather than an opera we see a leper in rags, his body covered with black spots and blood (like the lepers in Grünewald's Isenheim Altar). Francis enters and, overcoming his disgust, he speaks with the leper about offering his suffering in patience to God, but the leper wants bodily healing. The angel appears, to the sound of birdsong, and sings to the leper, 'Leper, your heart condemns you, but God is greater than your heart. He is love. He knows all.' Francis now recognizes that the fault is his in not loving the man enough. He embraces the leper, who is miraculously transformed and does a dance of triumph. Both men then become aware of their unworthiness, but the chorus concludes the scene singing that those who greatly love will be pardoned. At the very end of the opera Francis, dying, sings, 'Music and poetry have led me towards you:

by image, by symbol and by want of truth ... Deliver me, intoxicate me, dazzle me forever by your excess of truth.' After the saint's body has been removed, there remains an intense light on the place where it lay, which becomes more dazzling as the chorus sings a huge resurrection chorale ending in C major with the whole orchestra.

Messiaen himself died in April 1992.

> *Eternal Word of God, Jesus our Lord,*
> *revealed in time but now risen,*
> *ascended, glorified,*
> *we praise you that in the music of Olivier*
> *Messiaen we may contemplate your truth*
> *in the sound of stillness and in the ecstasy*
> *of love,*
> *and recognize too that we cannot yet fully*
> *apprehend your being,*
> *which is the being of God.*
> *We ask this prayer in your name.*

಄ ಬ

One of the requirements of canonization in the Roman Catholic Church is that the would-be saint should be the source of miracles, either in their lifetime or posthumously. I would suggest that the great composers become sources of miracles for all time. As human individuals they are fallible and imperfect, but in the music they write they leave behind something that can transfigure the hearer. For those who perform or hear a piece like Handel's *Messiah* or who sing a great hymn tune may well not emerge from this experience quite the same people. As they have the spiritual experience of the music, they recognize and partake in the beauty and truth that were in the mind and heart of its creator.

಄ ಬ

God, maker of sound and silence,
you share your creativity with all who write
and make music.
We rejoice in the miracles created by
composers of faith and genius,
who speak the truth in the pure language of
sound,
and in many tones bring us nearer to your
inexpressible unity,
Father, Son and Holy Spirit.

Chapter 4

Those who 'put verses in writing'
Christian poets, novelists and playwrights

Why are there so few poets, dramatists and novelists inscribed in the calendars of the Church's saints?

No one can deny Christianity's fundamental influence in the development of European and western literature, nor its key role in passing on to the modern world the treasures of Greek and Roman classical literature. It is impossible seriously to study our literature up to the twentieth century without knowing the classical background, but above all the Hebrew scriptures of the Old Testament and the Greek New Testament. David Lyle Jeffrey wrote, 'To understand something of the Bible, and of its transmission in and through English literature, is to reckon sympathetically with the development of English cultural consciousness in its richest and most coherent levels of expression.'[1]

The Bible contains many different kinds of literary material, but certainly a great deal of poetry and story. In the first century after the resurrection Christians produced that unique genre of storytelling, mingling history, symbolic narrative and theological proclamation, that we know as the gospels (both the canonical and the apocryphal ones). Through 2,000 years since the time of the Bible, there have been Christian works of literature in many different forms: translations of the Bible itself; commentaries on books of the Bible (many of an allegorical, mystical and poetic quality); works of theology, philosophy, history and science; letters, polemics and sermons; liturgy, hymns and mystical writing; autobiography (as in Augustine's *Confessions*) and hagiography (the lives of the saints); poetry, drama and parable. Many Christian writers are canonized and listed in calendars of remembrance, especially the great teachers and defenders of the faith; they are honoured as bearers of the Word.

It remains true, however, that very few Christian writers are honoured purely for their literary creations, and certainly not just for being a poet or a biographer or a dramatist. (It is of course an anachronism for most of the Christian centuries to think of poetry, biography or drama divorced from the primary service of the Church and of Christian doctrine; and the novel only emerged in the seventeenth century.) Augustine is honoured for his powerful and creative defence of what was to be Christian orthodoxy rather than as the author of a unique spiritual autobiography. The seventh-century bishop of Poitiers, Venantius Fortunatus, is celebrated for his kindly pastoral ministry as well as his brilliant hymns and lives of the saints. The fact that Sir Thomas More wrote an extremely clever work of science fiction, *Utopia*, probably did not materially influence the decision to canonize him. Can one think of even one official saint whose sole claim to fame was that he or she wrote verse, drama or fiction? Perhaps Julian of Norwich is the nearest we can get to such a phenomenon; her *Showings*, of course, was a mystical work of theology, not a poem, play or novel, but it has a strongly poetic element. Nothing else is known about Julian except that she was an anchoress and wrote of what was revealed to her, so she at least is honoured purely as a writer.

Has the Church then had some problems with the 'literary sphere'? In spite of Christianity's absolutely central role in the history of western literature, it *has* had one or two problems here. At the very beginning, as the Church expanded mainly into the Gentile world of the Roman Empire, it had to come to terms with the literature and culture of Greece and Rome. For some of the Fathers, this was a source of embarrassment, as they looked at the very poor literary quality of the *koine* Greek of the New Testament in comparison with some of the great works of

Hellenistic culture, and wondered how they could account for the Holy Spirit's rather poor taste in inspiring such literature. In the third century, however, Tertullian reacted in the opposite direction, completely rejecting Greek culture as having anything to do with Christianity: 'What has Athens to do with Jerusalem?' he asked. 'We must seek the Lord in purity of heart ... Since Christ Jesus, there is no need for further curiosity, since the gospel, no need for further research.'[2] In the end, Christianity accepted the Greek philosophers, Plato and Aristotle and their later successors, and struggled to bring their thought into line with their own direct Hebrew heritage, while remaining for the time being somewhat suspicious of the poetic and dramatic culture of the Greco-Roman world. Greek drama and poetry were steeped in the myths and language of polytheism, and there was no way that the early Christians could be involved in that without fatal compromise. Roman theatrical *spectacula* (shows) were completely unacceptable to Christians for at least four reasons: the implicit pagan polytheism; the hateful violence of the gladiatorial and other spectacular shows; the crude obscenity of many of the comedies; and the hedonistic indulgence of those who liked the shows, which was quite opposed to the desirable quality of Christian asceticism.

Nevertheless classical literature of all kinds, not just philosophy, was a major influence on Latin writers of the Middle Ages. It was interpreted allegorically, in very much the same way as the Bible itself, and much imitated. The fourth-century Spanish poet Juvencus, for instance, turned part of the Bible into Latin verse. Virgil's *Aeneid* was interpreted symbolically as the story of the soul's journey through life to paradise (Rome). Many poets produced Christian epic poems. In addition to hymns and religious poetry, there was also secular poetry (such as *Carmina Burana*, the thirteenth-century collection which includes moral and satirical verse, love poetry, drinking songs and liturgical dramas by many different poets). And of course eventually there was Christian drama, emerging from the liturgical celebration of the Christian story. In the ninth century the Saxon nun, Hrosvit, wrote some edifying 'comedies' in the manner of the Roman playwright Terence, and in the same century the English monk Ethelwold described the 'praiseworthy custom' of celebrating the death and resurrection of Christ by a representation, with mime and dialogue, to be performed in church during or after the liturgical rites. The mystery plays were now developing: plays performed increasingly outside the church by members of craft guilds or professional actors and dealing with both biblical and apocryphal stories, allegorical debates, saints' lives and posthumous miracles, and miracles of the sacrament. These plays reached their zenith in the fifteenth and sixteenth centuries, but had more or less disappeared by the seventeenth century. It is perhaps surprising how much farcical and bawdy material could be included in the mystery plays; and alongside them there was a great development of purely secular drama in the Middle Ages.

The mystery plays were written in the vernacular. It was perhaps Dante's great achievement in the fourteenth century to show that poetry in the vernacular could equal or even surpass the languages of the classical and biblical past, and in the *Divine Comedy* to make a Christian work of art which was not just a rehash of the Bible and traditional piety, but, incorporating also the world of pagan classical literature, was a truly new autonomous poetic creation. The freedom of the Christian artist was thus asserted.

And as the modern world dawns with the Renaissance and then the Reformation, the Church adopts an ambivalent but not truly repressive attitude to the growing freedoms. There are certainly examples of the medieval Church being intolerant of stage plays, and many of the Puritans took a very low view of the theatre, but the broad movement was towards an acceptance of literary and artistic freedom. Some Protestants, such as the sixteenth-century Calvinist theologian Theodore Beza, even wrote religious drama. The Oberammergau passion play began about this period. That notable Puritan, John Milton, achieved immortality with the great epic of fall and redemption, *Paradise Lost* and *Paradise Regained*, incorporating a great amount of later apocryphal tradition, 'rationalised imagination' and classical allusion into the paradise garden and the wilderness of the temptation. In the post-Renaissance world poetry came to be viewed as the natural language of religion, in which prophetic and spiritual awareness could be expressed through allusion, image and symbol. The novel too, which began to develop as a form in the post-Reformation world, was seen, especially from the nineteenth century onwards, as an ideal medium for expressing the pilgrimage of the human soul through the conflicts and temptations of life, and for showing the real meaning of good and evil in concrete human situations. Some of the nineteenth–century lives of Jesus - such as that by Ernest Renan (1863) – approach the form of a novel at times, and this interest in understanding the history, the theology and the psychology of Jesus in literary form really took off in the twentieth century, with a flood of novels, plays, musicals and films. From a British point of view after the end of the mystery plays, it was for many years forbidden to present Jesus Christ directly on stage, and many Christians would have concurred with this ban, but since Dorothy Sayers broke the taboo in her radio play, *The Man Born to be King*, just after the Second World War, there have been many presentations of Jesus on stage, not least modern revivals of the medieval mystery plays.

The issue of the acceptability of the religious poet, the dramatist or the novelist becomes, then, a calculus between, on the one hand, the new spiritual insights and ways of approaching the mystery of God that they may provide, and, on the other hand, the danger of the freedom of the modern autonomous writer, perhaps too infected by the way of the world and no longer directly accountable to the councils of the Church. Did Milton become seduced by his own creation, Satan, that arrogant yet heroic figure of evil and despair? Was Dostoyevsky too keen to put the full panoply of human sin and misery and the objections to Christianity and the Church on display? How comfortable should we be with the way Dorothy Sayers rated John's Gospel as the most historical gospel and then blended the other gospels in a single storyline heavily based on John? Those Christians who give away tickets for Mel Gibson's *The Passion of the Christ* are the same ones who stand in protest outside *The Last Temptation of Christ* or *Monty Python's Life of Brian*. For such Christians the first is like the poetry of the early Middle Ages: it simply re-presents the truths declared in the Bible; the other two are, for them, illegitimate extensions of the facts and mockeries of the truth.

Related to this is the well-known and troubling question of the gap between the life of the artist and his or her literary claim on our attention. The author may have written 'like an angel' but lived as a human being somewhat lower than the angels. Does Milton's achievement in *Paradise Lost* lose out to our awareness that he was often horrible to his daughters or subscribed to 'heretical' views about the divinity of Jesus?

It seems that the Church as an official body has taken the negative side on these issues. That not even Dante is honoured by the Catholic Church speaks volumes for this choice. 'I still have many things to say to you, but you cannot bear them now. When the Spirit of truth comes, he will guide you into all the truth.'[3] Thus Jesus in John's Gospel. Does the Church not trust that the Spirit may still be speaking through the 'unacknowledged legislators' of the world?

In the end, and in a world where Christendom is no more and the Church can no longer dictate what people think and write (and certainly in a situation where the

Church appears to refuse to 'endorse' great writers), each Christian will have to make their own judgement on the spiritual value of each writer. My own view is that the creative urge of the writer is indeed inspired by the Spirit of God and is done in the image of the creator God. That urge may, of course, become perverted or trivialized, but even in a disordered and troubled soul like that of Dostoyevsky there remain an irresistible love of God and love of humanity which are absolutely unmistakeable in his writing and which qualify such a human being *as a writer* to be held in everlasting honour by Christians and indeed people of any faith or idealism at all.

John Milton
1608–74

In Shakespeare's play *Julius Caesar,* after the murder of Caesar and the brilliant oratory of Mark Antony's 'Friends, Romans, countrymen', there is a horrific scene of mindless political violence as the mob sets upon the poet Cinna just because he has the same name as one of the conspirators against Caesar. He protests that he is Cinna the poet, not Cinna the conspirator, but the crowd's bloodlust is up, and they cry, 'Tear him for his bad verses, tear him for his bad verses.' Any excuse for a bit of therapeutic thuggery.

In 1660, at the restoration of the monarchy, John Milton, poet *and* politician, ran a similar, and perhaps more justified, risk of political vengeance. For 20 years he had been one of the outstanding and effective propaganda mouthpieces of the Puritan revolution that had seen the overthrow and execution of King Charles I, he had been an admirer of the Protector Oliver Cromwell and had taken office in the government of the Commonwealth. For 20 years he had deliberately put his poetic ambitions – he longed to write a great epic poem – on to the back burner, in order to do his sacred duty of removing for ever all unaccountable tyrants from oppressing the British people. Even in March and April 1660, when plans for bringing Charles II back as king were far advanced, Milton, with a sort of naive and obstinate courage, was publishing his last political pamphlet, *The Readie and Easie Way to Establish a Free Commonwealth*. This was something like the literary equivalent of standing in front of a tank in Tiananmen Square, and the historians have not found a clear answer to the question why Milton survived when other leaders of the Commonwealth were executed. It's possible that friends pleaded his case; or it may be that, at the age of 51 and already blind for almost a decade, he was no longer seen as any threat. At all events, he was kept in hiding by his friends, and after the Act of Oblivion which pardoned most of the Commonwealth supporters in August, he was kept in protective custody until December, and then released into private life. Some of his most offensive pamphlets were publicly burned, but Milton's period in custody probably saved him from Cinna the poet's fate on the London streets.

Milton had 14 more years to live. If he *had* been executed or torn to pieces by a royalist mob in 1660, he would have died deeply disappointed in all his political and ecclesiastical ideas, and deprived of the great poetical work he intended still to do. Nevertheless, the world would certainly have remembered him.

> Let us with a gladsom mind
> Praise the Lord, for he is kind,
> For his mercies ay endure,
> Ever faithfull, ever sure.
>
> Let us blaze his Name abroad,
> For of gods he is the God;
> For, &c.

> O let us his praises tell,
> That doth the wrathfull tyrants quell
> For, &c.
>
> That with his miracles doth make
> Amazed Heaven and Earth to shake.
> For, &c.
>
> That by his wisdom did create
> The painted Heav'ns so full of state.
> For, &c.
>
> That did the solid Earth ordain
> To rise above the watry plain.
> For, &c.
>
> John Milton (aged 15), *Psalm 136*[4]

We would have remembered his brilliance as a scholar, above all in Latin, but also in Hebrew, Greek and Modern Languages. The son of a prosperous scrivener and moneylender, Milton went to St Paul's School in London and, from 1625 to 1632, attended Christ's College, Cambridge, eventually attaining his MA. He wrote poetry in Latin as well as English, and for a time believed he was heading for ordination in the Church of England. But this vision quickly faded for the young Puritan-minded scholar when William Laud, Bishop of London and later Archbishop of Canterbury, re-established the many pre-Reformation practices in the Church and repressed the Puritans. The first of Milton's tracts after 1640 were attacks on episcopal hierarchy and the ritualistic use of the Book of Common Prayer. Milton believed that British Christians should be free and independent, living under the guidance of scripture and the Holy Spirit, not under the thumb of prelates still half sympathetic to Rome. Later, in *Paradise Lost,* he was to describe the tragic corruption of the Church by worldly power. The archangel

Michael describes the future course of human salvation to Adam, and tells him that, after the time of Christ and the great apostles, 'grievous Wolves' will become the Church's leaders:

> Who all the sacred mysteries of Heav'n
> To their own vile advantages shall turne
> Of lucre and ambition, and the truth
> With superstitions and traditions taint ...
> Then shall they seek to avail themselves of names,
> Places and titles, and with these to joine
> Secular power, though feigning still to act
> By spiritual, to themselves appropriating
> The Spirit of God.[5]

And Michael predicts 'heavier persecution' 'on all who in the worship persevere of Spirit and Truth', while the majority of Christians misguidedly 'will deem in outward Rites and specious formes Religion satisfi'd'. Little wonder, then, if the 27-year-old Milton decided not to 'subscribe slave' in a Church of England governed by prelacy, and spent the years from 1632 first at his father's house in Hammersmith and then at Horton near Windsor studying the Greek and Latin classics, mathematics, music and cosmography, deepening his liberal ideas and writing poetry, and then, in 1638–39 on a tour of Italy (during which he met the old astronomer Galileo Galilei).

A Milton dead in 1660 we would have remembered, of course, for poetry, even though he had written so little in the previous 20 years – poetry of grace and charm, but also poetry of earnest ideas and morality, such as *On the Morning of Christ's Nativity*, *L'Allegro* and *Il Penseroso*, the masque *Comus*, the elegy *Lycidas*, sonnets and many Latin verses. The sixteenth Sonnet is about his own blindness.

When I consider how my light is spent,
  E're half my days, in this dark world and wide,
  And that one Talent which is death to hide,
  Lodg'd with me useless, though my soul more bent
To serve therewith my Maker, and present
  My true account, least he returning chide,
  Doth God exact day-labour, light deny'd,
  I fondly ask; But patience to prevent
That murmur, soon replies, God doth not need
  Either man's work or his own gifts, who best
  Bear his mild yoak, they serve him best, his State
Is Kingly. Thousands at his bidding speed
  And post o're Land and Ocean without rest:
  They also serve who only stand and waite.

John Milton, *Sonnet XVI*[6]

But Milton constantly did considerably more than 'stand and waite'. He played a political and religious role in the turbulent years leading to the Civil War, the execution of the king and Cromwell's Commonwealth. He cut short his tour of Italy because of rumours of political tension in England, took up residence in London, and from 1641–60 devoted a great amount of his time and energy to pamphleteering in the cause of political and religious liberty.

He promoted the complete disestablishment of the Church, wrote about the best education for boys, defended the freedom of the press and civil liberties, suggested that incompatibility in marriage would be a better ground for divorce than adultery, and affirmed that a monarch governs only by the will of the people.

It has been assumed that he came to his views about divorce as a result of his marriage in 1642 to Mary Powell, the daughter of a royalist squire. They were ill matched in almost every way. After staying with him only a few weeks, she returned to her family, but then they were reunited in

1645 and lived together until her death in 1652 soon after giving birth to their third daughter. Milton subsequently married Catherine Woodstock late in 1656, but she was dead within 15 months, having given birth to a daughter who also died. Finally, in 1663 he married 24-year-old Elizabeth Minshull, 30 years his junior; she outlived him.

Milton's published views on the power of the people drew him to Cromwell's attention, and after the execution of Charles I in 1649 Milton became 'secretary for foreign languages' to Cromwell's Council of State. In this role he had to write to foreign governments and translate documents, usually in Latin, and he was expected to continue to be a 'spin doctor' for the regime. Milton handsomely obliged with many tracts in defence of the Commonwealth.

Even if Milton had died in 1660 we should still know what his theology was. *A Treatise on Christian Doctrine* was only published in 1825, but it seems to have been finished before the Restoration. It seems to show Milton 'thinking outside the box' on matters of Christian theology: arguing that Christ was subordinate to God the Father; promoting divorce – and polygamy; denying the efficacy of all sacraments; maintaining the corporeality and the mortality of the human soul; even wondering about the importance of the Atonement. He had been brought up an Anglican, and had later supported the idea of presbyterian church government and worked with the Puritans running the Commonwealth, but by the end of his life Milton had moved even beyond the Independent churches and was attached to no church, with an individual faith, worked out for himself.

And so, even if John Milton had perished in 1660 like Cinna the poet, we should have much to remember him for. We might also have a stumpy torso of an epic poem *Paradise Lost*, for it is likely that Milton began it before 1660. It was finished by 1665 and published, in ten books, in 1667. In 1671 a second epic poem in four books,

Paradise Regain'd, and *Samson Agonistes,* a 'closet tragedy' (that is, one for reading rather than performing), were published. To produce these massive epics the blind Milton composed sections in his head, and, when he was ready to be 'milked', he would dictate to one of his daughters or another relative or amanuensis.

Milton is remembered mainly for these late poems. *Paradise Lost* tells the story of the fall of Satan and the rebellious angels from heaven, God's creation of the world in reparation for that loss to heaven, Satan's tempting of Eve in the paradise garden, the 'fall' of humankind, and the ejection of Adam and Eve from Paradise. It is scarcely an exaggeration to say that Milton's epic has fixed in the consciousness of subsequent Christians the atmosphere and details of a story, some of which is barely hinted at in the Bible: the thrilling cosmic scale of heaven and earth and hell (surely the parent of many a twentieth-century fantasy novel); the magnificently complex figure of Satan, heroic and lonely, the negative image of Christ himself, with bitter self-knowledge of his own fatal choice to reject God's supremacy, but always renewing his will to spoil everything that is lovely and good as long as ever he can; the overwhelming sense of delight in the created order, and yet of so much future ill which Eve and Adam's choice sets in train. But the story ends with glimpses of hope, and in *Paradise Regain'd* the fate of tempted and fallen Eve is reversed as Christ resists all the temptations of Satan in the desert.

> Now thou hast aveng'd
> Supplanted Adam, and by vanquishing
> Temptation, hast regain'd lost Paradise,
> And frustrated the conquest fraudulent:
> He never more henceforth will dare set foot
> In Paradise to tempt; his snares are broke:
> For though that seat of earthly bliss be fail'd,
> A fairer Paradise is founded now

> For Adam and his chosen Sons, whom thou
> A Saviour art come down to re-install,
> Where they shall dwell secure, when time shall be
> Of Tempter and Temptation without fear.
>
> John Milton, *Paradise Regain'd*[7]

It its not hard to see in these last great poems Milton's reflection on all his efforts to bring in a new kind of world in the thrilling years of the Puritan Commonwealth. What cosmic, eschatological hopes there had been; what deep disillusion in the end. In *Paradise Regain'd* Milton pictures the disciples' hopes that the Messiah will free his people from all that oppresses them, and he extends Jesus' second temptation so that Satan shows him both potential political power in the Roman Empire and the wisdom of Greek culture. Milton himself, like many of his idealistic contemporaries, had hoped, by intellectual wisdom and engagement in politics, to bring in the kingdom. But now he puts all these hopes as temptations in Satan's mouth and shows Christ rejecting them, and instead, through the power of the Spirit, given at his baptism, sacrificing his own will in inner obedience to God. The angels finally sing of Christ's victory, overcoming temptation and regaining the lost Paradise. From now on it will be possible for all to vanquish temptation, in the power of the newly given Spirit.

In *Samson Agonistes* Milton virtually draws a picture of himself in old age as Samson in Philistine captivity – blind, shut in, defeated in all his campaigns, looking back on the foolishness of his attempt to serve his God in action, and still being tempted by others to follow his own limited desires, but finally able to feel 'some rouzing motions' of thought, which is the will of God in him, and to do his final deed.

Milton's final deeds were these epic poems, offering hope in a world horribly disfigured and destroyed by human pride and sin. At the end of *Paradise Lost* Adam, now fallen and about to be thrown out of Paradise, nevertheless responds to the archangel Michael with a pledge of faith.

> Henceforth I learne, that to obey is best,
> and love with feare the onely God, to walk
> As in his presence, ever to observe
> His providence, and on him sole depend,
> Merciful over all his works, with good
> Still overcoming evil, and by small
> Accomplishing great things, by things deemd weak
> Subverting worldly strong, and worldly wise
> By simply meek.
>
> John Milton, *Paradise Lost*[8]

Michael tells them that, though they must leave Paradise, their obedience will give them 'a Paradise within thee, happier farr'. Humankind has failed, but that is not the last word in the story. Adam and Eve must leave Paradise, but everything is still to play for.

> They looking back, all th' Eastern side beheld
> Of Paradise, so late their happie seat,
> Wav'd over by that flaming Brand, the Gate
> With dreadful Faces throng'd and fierie Armes:
> Som natural tears they drop'd, but wip'd them soon;
> The World was all before them, where to choose
> Thir place of rest, and Providence thir guide:
> They hand in hand with wandring steps and slow
> Through Eden took their solitarie way.
>
> John Milton, *Paradise Lost*[9]

God, supreme being,
giving the wonderful earth and sovereign
freedom to the sons and daughters made in
your image,
giving time for the fatal fall of sin to be
repaired by the obedience of your Son,
giving your Holy Spirit to help all your
children back to inner paradise:
show us, guided by your son John Milton,
how we also may 'justify your ways' and live
in hope.

ᘓ ᘔ

Fyodor Dostoyevsky
1821–81

If the sufferings of children go to make up the sum of sufferings which is necessary for the purchase of truth, then I say beforehand that the entire truth is not worth such a price ... I do not want a mother to embrace the torturer who had her child torn to pieces by his dogs! She has no right to forgive him! If she likes, she can forgive him for herself, she can forgive the torturer for the immeasurable suffering he has inflicted upon her as a mother; but she has no right to forgive him for the sufferings of her tortured child. She has no right to forgive the torturer for that, even if her child were to forgive him! And if that is so, if they have no right to forgive him, what becomes of the harmony? Is there in the whole world a being who could or would have the right to forgive? I don't want harmony. I don't want it, out of the love I bear to mankind. I want to remain with my suffering unavenged. I'd rather remain with my suffering unavenged and my indignation unappeased, even if I were wrong. Besides, too high a price has been placed on harmony. We cannot afford to pay so much for admission. And therefore I hasten to return my

> ticket of admission. And indeed, if I am an honest man, I'm bound to hand it back as soon as possible. This I am doing. It is not God that I do not accept, Alyosha. I merely most respectfully return him the ticket.
>
> Dostoyevsky, *The Brothers Karamazov*[10]

It is Dostoyevsky's ability to plumb the lowest depths of the evil and suffering that human beings inflict and experience, with all the seemingly unanswerable challenges they pose to the idea of a good creator and of ultimate salvation, and to 'stay with the questions', refusing to leap to easy rational, social or theological solutions, that make him one of the greatest Christian novelists. Of course, there's a kind of mad, even arrogant, perversity in Ivan Karamazov's speech from Dostoyevsky's last novel: as though he would continue to stand out against God, even after all the evil and suffering of the world had somehow finally been made right. And yet overwhelmingly, there is in him the audacious dignity of Job, asserting his human sense of what is right, maintaining his integrity in the face of those who would too smoothly, too quickly, justify the ways of God to humanity. You could say that Ivan and Job insist on appealing past the gatekeepers to the sovereign beyond. They live in a world – our world – in which there are few answers to so much apparently pointless suffering, but they are not easily fobbed off. They prefer to stay with their protests and their questions.

Fyodor Dostoyevsky first read the book of Job at the age of eight. For all his many moral failures, his political and religious extremisms, and the truly disastrous and disordered quality of much of his life, he ultimately achieved, above all in his last novels, the kind of human dignity that has stared into the abyss and yet can still say, 'There is love. There is community. There is hope in God.' The only 'proof' of that is the dignity, the protests, the compassion, the Christ-like actions of the human being *who cannot demonstrate the righteousness of God.* Dostoyevsky finally approached that dignity.

> The work of Dostoyevsky is the climax of Russian literature and it is the finest expression of its earnest, religious, tormented character; its path of sorrow led to Dostoyevsky, and all the shadows of Russian life and history were gathered together in him. But there was a glimmer of light, shining through a crack in the old world. The tragedy of Dostoyevsky, like all true tragedy, involves purification and release, though those who are held by it in unescapable [*sic*] darkness, who accept only its misery, do not understand this. There is a freeing of the spirit and joy to be had from reading Dostoyevsky, the joy that one gets from suffering. It is the path the Christian has to tread ... [Dostoyevsky] gave up the humanitarian belief in man and believed in him in the Christian way, deepening and strengthening that faith. For that very reason Dostoyevsky could not be a pessimistic and despairing writer; there is always light in his darkness, and it is the light of Christ.
>
> Nicholas Berdyaev[11]

But it had been a hard, hard road to the triumph in 1880 of *The Brothers Karamazov,* and by the following year he was dead at the age of 59. Like the Beirut hostage Brian Keenan, Dostoyevsky's life was cut in half by traumatic imprisonment; he was always a writer and thinker, and from start to finish there was a headlong, 'unrevised' quality to his life and his writing, but the writer and thinker who emerged from his 'evil cradling' was very different from the one who went into it.

In the late 1840s, in his late twenties, Dostoyevsky appeared very much the radical atheist and socialist; his main motivation was the desire to end serfdom in Russia.

He had grown up in the old-fashioned piety of the family of a retired military surgeon who had served as a doctor at the Mariinsky Hospital for the Poor in Moscow and then, on becoming ennobled, had bought a country estate. After school, Fyodor spent six years at the Academy of Military Engineering in St Petersburg, but resigned as a military engineer and sub-lieutenant in 1843, soon after completing his degree. He and his elder brother Mikhail had always devoured literature, and Fyodor was now determined to live as a writer. Within three years he had success with his novella *Poor Folk,* showing deep understanding of the psychological effects of poverty. Years later Dostoyevsky recalled how he was woken up at 4 a.m. by two fellow-writers to whom he had shown the manuscript of the book; they had to tell him straightaway how brilliant they thought it. The leading critic Belinsky hailed the book as the first Russian social novel, but in the years that immediately followed Dostoyevsky's stories and novellas showed more interest in individual psychology, madness and moral disintegration than in social critique, and this, together with his own extreme shyness and touchy vanity, tended to alienate those supporters who had favoured the social concerns of his first novel. Nevertheless in 1847 he joined the Petrashevsky Circle, a group of intellectuals who discussed utopian socialism and planned pamphlets against the government, and in 1849 he was arrested and sentenced to death for this.

After eight months in prison, Dostoyevsky and other prisoners were led out into Semyonovsky Square, offered last rites and told they were about to be shot. At the very last minute a 'messenger' arrived to say that Tsar Nicholas I had deigned to spare their lives. This mock execution was part of the punishment. Its effect on Dostoyevsky may be imagined; it was immensely to increase his sense of life as a gift and of the vital freedom and responsibility of the individual. He now faced four years in a Siberian prison labour camp followed by a further five years as a soldier in a Siberian garrison. He did not return to St Petersburg until 1859.

He returned a very different man from the one who had mixed with the radical liberals and western-influenced aristocratic intellectuals before 1849. He had faced as a daily reality the lives of the lowest and the lost: the brutality of the prison guards and the callousness of criminals who had murdered children without remorse, the deep hatred that the lowest classes felt for the land-owners, but, in the midst of all the filth and degradation, the existence of decent, honest souls. He wrote of it directly in *The House of the Dead* (1861–62), and the experience coloured all his later writing. The New Testament was the only book the prisoners were allowed to read; its study had a profound effect on Dostoyevsky. He came to reject the 'top-down' socialism of the intellectuals, which would impose a rational system on society but not improve the freedom and sense of belonging of the lowest classes. He came to believe in the dignity and fundamental goodness of common people, and became increasingly attached to the Russian Orthodox faith as the faith of those common people. Equally he had seen at first hand how fundamentally flawed and irrational people are and realized that there could be no redemption or social salvation without suffering, the acceptance of personal guilt, and the working together of all classes within the Church. Dostoyevsky went to Siberia as a (recovering) socialist atheist, and returned as a conservative believer. From now on the traditional patriarchal family in equal relations with other families under the sacred canopy of the Orthodox Church were to be his remedy for the bitter divisions and mad conflicts of the Russian people: it was to be a 'return to the soil', a 'universal communion in the name of Christ'.

In spite of this programme and in spite of Dostoyevsky's renewed faith, he could never give up probing the questions which stood against the faith of the Church. Perhaps his most characteristic remark was in a letter to the woman who had given him a copy of the New Testament when on his way to Siberia.

I am a child of unbelief and doubt even now and (as I well know) I shall be to the grave. What fearful suffering this desire to believe has caused me and still causes me as it increases in strength in my soul as the contrary proofs multiply! However, God sends me at other times many minutes during which I am entirely at peace: ... and during such minutes I have composed for myself a confession of faith ...; this is it: to believe that there is nothing more beautiful, more profound, more sympathetic, more reasonable, more manly and perfect than Christ, and not only nothing like Him exists, but I say to myself with jealous love, that it even cannot exist. And even more: if someone were to prove to me that Christ is not the truth, I would rather remain with Christ than with the truth.

Fyodor Dostoyevsky[12]

From 1859 Dostoyevsky resumed his life as a full-time writer, but now for more than a decade disorder followed disaster in his life. From the 1840s he suffered from epilepsy. In 1857 he married a widow, Mariya Isaeva, but the seven years of their marriage until her death in 1864 were unhappy. He started two journals in the 1860s, one of which was closed by the government, and the other closed when his brother and collaborator, Mikhail, died. He never had enough money, and his extensive travels around western Europe during the 1860s were made partly to escape his creditors. On these journeys he became increasingly addicted to gambling. He also had an affair with the writer Appolinariya Suslova.

In 1866 Dostoyevsky concluded a desperate deal with an unscrupulous publisher, agreeing to deliver to them a new novel with a very tight deadline in return for their advance payment; if he failed to meet the deadline, the publisher would have free rights over all his works for nine years. He hired a stenographer, with less than a month remaining, and dictated *The Gambler,* finishing just in time. The following year he married his stenographer, Anna Snitkina, and with her help began to put his life on an even keel; they had four children, two of whom survived to adulthood. During the next four years they continued to travel around Europe, Dostoyevsky writing novels, and they returned to St Petersburg in 1871. Anna finally managed to wean Fyodor away from his gambling addiction. So began his final decade, with relative stability and growing fame, as the late novels appeared and as he communicated his stories, memories, reportage, hopes and dreams in the *Diary of a Writer* (1875–77). Increasingly he presented himself as a prophet of healing and reconciliation for Russia, and increasingly he developed a dialogue with his readers, who recognized the lived reality at the base of all he wrote.

Dostoyevsky's greatest novels belong to the period after his Siberian exile. The best known are *Notes from the Underground* (1864), *Crime and Punishment* (1866), *The Idiot* (1868–69), *The Possessed* (1872) and *The Brothers Karamazov* (1879–80). In these novels he shows how human beings can be corrupted with pride and wrong ideas, yet in some cases find salvation. In both *The Idiot* (Prince Myshkin) and *The Brothers Karamazov* (Alyosha) he draws portraits of a Christ-like figure. As Konstantin Mochulsky said of the latter book, 'Never in all world literature has Christianity been advanced with such striking force as the religion of spiritual freedom.'[13]

Dostoyevsky put into the mouth of his *Underground* man these words:

> As for myself, in my life I have pushed to the extreme what you yourselves have never dared to take even half way. Because you have constantly mistaken your cowardice for

> prudence and have constantly deceived
> yourselves with comforting reflections. The
> truth is that I have been more *alive* than
> you.[14]

These words seem to be true, too, of Fyodor Dostoyevsky the man, who had lived through the torments of Russian society and re-presented them to his readers in unflinching close-up. They are true also of the way, even within his last, most Christian novel, *The Brothers Karamazov*, he does not 'deceive us with comforting reflections', but gives utterance to the toughest objections to the faith and role of the Church.

The Catholic theologian, Yves Congar, once said that his fellow theologians ought to read the chapter called 'The Grand Inquisitor', in *The Brothers Karamazov*, once a year. In it Ivan Karamazov imagines Christ returning to earth in the middle of the Spanish Inquisition. One hundred heretics have just been consigned to the flames. The Grand Inquisitor, an old, old cardinal, has Christ thrown into jail, then comes to see him. At first he threatens him with the heretics' flames, but later allows him to go – as long as he truly goes and no longer seeks to meddle in the work he has committed to the Church. Before this he delivers a massive monologue to the silent Christ. He reminds him of the three temptations which the devil put before him in the wilderness, and says that in each case he made the *wrong* choice. If instead he had offered the world guaranteed freedom from hunger (turning stones into bread), miraculous, mysterious power from on high that could not be questioned (throwing himself from the pinnacle of the Temple) and absolute political power in his own hands (albeit the gift of the devil), he could have saved humanity from the unbearable burden of its own freedom, which only leads to conflict and chaos, because humans are weak and sinful. In rejecting the temptations and allowing humanity freely to choose or ignore his way of love and faith, Christ had effectively created a way that was for the spiritual elite alone, those few who could cope with their own freedom and make good choices of love and selflessness. The rest he had in effect abandoned to their own hopeless, selfish, animal strivings, completely overestimating their potential freely to follow his way. And so, the Grand Inquisitor says, the Catholic Church had come to realize that only by offering people total security, a totalitarian package of loaves, rules and meaning, based on *miracle, mystery and authority,* could they satisfy and help the mass of humankind. They had taken away the burden of freedom from them, and so *corrected* Christ's work, *in his name.*

'How does your poem end?' [Alyosha] asked suddenly, his eyes fixed on the ground. 'Or was that the end?'

'I intended to finish it as follows: when the Inquisitor finished speaking, he waited for some time for the Prisoner's reply. His silence distressed him. He saw that the Prisoner had been listening intently to him all the time, looking gently into his face and evidently not wishing to say anything in reply. The old man would have liked him to say something, however bitter and terrible. But he suddenly approached the old man and kissed him gently on his bloodless, aged lips. That was all his answer.'

Dostoyevsky, *The Brothers Karamazov*[15]

Fyodor Dostoyevsky had experienced at first hand and powerfully presented all the chaotic weakness of humanity; he had offered a devastating analysis of totalitarian solutions, whether Catholic or socialist; finally, in the figure of Father Zossima, Alyosha Karamazov's mentor, he had offered the only hope for the world, the simple effort to love the earth, to love one's neighbour, actively and indefatigably. The Prisoner Christ had replied to the Inquisitor not with argument and power, but with love. After the death of Zossima, Alyosha begins to find the way of hope.

After he has tasted the bitter anguish of death and decay Alyosha is blinded by the dazzling truth of the religion of the resurrection; he no longer sees the staretz Zossima in his coffin, the breath of corruption is blown away: he is called to the marriage-feast. 'The little withered old man, his face covered with wrinkles, came towards him, laughing softly and happily. The coffin was gone, and he was dressed as he had been yesterday when he was sitting with them and the guests all around. His face was uncovered, his eyes shining. He, too, then was bidden to the feast, the wedding at Cana in Galilee.' And when the old man says to him, 'We are drinking the new wine, the wine of new and great gladness,' resurrection is victorious over death in the soul of Alyosha and he is born again. 'His enraptured soul was craving for freedom, space, openness ... The silence of earth seemed to melt in the silence of the heavens, the mystery of the world was joined with the mystery of the stars ... Alyosha stood gazing, and suddenly, as though his legs had given way, he threw himself to the ground. He did not know why he kissed it, why he had such an irresistible desire to embrace the whole of it. But kiss it he did, weeping and sobbing, watering it with his tears, passionately vowing to love it for ever.'

Nicholas Berdyaev[16]

By the end of his life Dostoyevsky had achieved both a personal peace and understanding and also a public role as the unifier of Russian society. But there can be no doubt that, had he lived longer, he would have gone on asking difficult questions of God.

> *Mysterious God,*
> *you have entrusted the privilege and burden*
> *of freedom to creatures who hideously misuse*
> *it.*
> *As we thank you now for the unflinching gaze*
> *of Fyodor Dostoyevsky,*
> *we ask you to save us from bland and callous*
> *optimism.*
> *Help us rather to take small, practical steps*
> *of love across a fractured world,*
> *in the spirit of Jesus Christ, your gift of hope.*

ᘒ ᘓ

Dorothy L. Sayers
1893–1957

Dorothy Sayers died very suddenly in December 1957. She was 64, and had pushed herself hard in a writing career of more than 40 years, often working late into the night. She was then in the middle of translating the *Paradiso* of Dante's *The Divine Comedy*. She had completed work on the *Inferno* and *Purgatorio* and almost two-thirds of the *Paradiso,* but the last thirteen cantos had to be completed by another scholar. So Sayers moved without warning into a closer experience of the wider reality of Dante's imaginative poem, the afterlife which might include the experience of hell, purgatory or heaven, but was essentially about the truth and judgement of God, that truth which she had always trusted in and spent a good portion of her literary life affirming and defending.

Since I cannot come at God through intuition, or through my emotions, or through my 'inner light' ... there is only the intellect left. And that is a very different matter. You said that I ... gave people the impression of caring only for a dogmatic pattern. That is quite true. I remember once saying to Charles Williams: 'I do not know whether I believe in Christ or whether I am only in love with the pattern.' And Charles said, with his usual prompt understanding, that he had exactly the same doubts about himself. But this you must try to accept: when we say 'in love with the pattern', we mean *in love* ... The thing is, however, that where the intellect is dominant it becomes the channel of all the other feelings. The passionate intellect is really passionate. It is the only point at which ecstasy can enter. I do not know whether we can be saved through the intellect, but I do know that I can be saved by nothing else. I know that, if there is judgement, I shall have to be able to say: 'This alone, Lord, in Thee and in me, have I never betrayed, and may it suffice to know and love and choose Thee after this manner, for I have no other love, or knowledge, or choice in me.'

Dorothy L. Sayers[17]

There was a tough, very Catholic, intellectual logic about Dorothy Sayers' faith; she stood firmly against all the trends that sought to water Christianity down or push God out as an unnecessary hypothesis. She reflected on the problems of a modern, purely humanist world and of a 'woolly' Church in many of her essays.

Dorothy Sayers lived her life in the first half of the twentieth century well balanced between the best culture and wisdom of elite British society and the teaching of the Church. She was unwavering in her belief that the very best human culture and achievement were deeply incomplete without the embracing pattern of Christian faith and doctrine, and her own literary career saw a progress from culture as 'mere entertainment' towards writing in the service of Christianity. She remained deeply critical of the quality of modern society, believing that it had lost its way because it had lost God, and deeply sceptical of the quality of many Christians, accusing them of 'sentimentalism and slipshod thinking'. Was there something of the elitist fogey about her? Yes, certainly, for she had a brilliant intellect and total conviction in her faith, and she had little patience with the foibles and failings of the world and the Church. C.S. Lewis said of her, 'I liked her ... for the extraordinary zest and edge of her conversation.' She remains a bracing and challenging personality, someone to whom we still need to listen.

Jesus Christ is unique – unique among gods and men. There have been incarnate gods aplenty, and slain-and-resurrected gods not a few; but He is the only God who has a date in history. And plenty of founders of religions have had dates, and some of them have been prophets or avatars of the Divine; but only this one was personally God. There is no more astonishing collocation of phrases than that which, in the Nicene Creed, sets these two statements flatly side by side: 'Very God of very God ... He suffered under Pontius Pilate'. All over the world, thousands of times a day, Christians recite the name of a rather undistinguished Roman pro-consul – not in execration ... but merely because that name fixes within a few years the date of the death of God.

Dorothy L. Sayers[18]

Dorothy Sayers was the only daughter of the Revd Henry Sayers, headmaster of Christ Church Cathedral School, Oxford, and later rector of Bluntisham in Cambridgeshire. Dorothy was educated at Godolphin School, Salisbury, and Somerville College, Oxford, graduating with a First in Medieval Literature. In her early twenties she worked as a teacher and also, for a time, as a reader for Blackwell's publishers, and between 1916 and 1919, she published two collections of poetry. In *Catholic Tales and Christian Songs,* her second collection, is a poem entitled 'The Mocking of Christ: A Mystery'. It pictures the soon-to-be-crucified Christ being mocked by the soldiers and then by a host of other symbolic figures. At the head of the piece is a misquote from Genesis: 'So man made God in his own image', and the mockers all wish to claim Christ in their own image. Thus an emperor gives Christ a 'temporal crown, sword and sceptre', a king and a pope both put their insignia on Christ and fight over him, a 'patriot' puts a helmet on Christ's head and then fights with 'a patriot of another nationality' who tries to put a different helmet on him, and representatives of other religions and philosophies, such as the Buddha, a 'green person' or Plato all try to claim him. In the middle of this Sayers has a bit of fun at the expense of the Church of England, with a bishop, a cathedral organist, a couple of curates, a 'respectable gentleman' and 'a sentimental person'.

The first curate 'setteth a tea-cup in Christ's hand' and says:

'Gossip and tea! Gossip and tea!
Communicants' class at a quarter-past-three.
Oh dear! Mrs Kidgup smells strongly of gin,
And this is God's house ... no, she must not come in!
Magdalen? Yes, yes, but that's in the Bible,
And quite a special case ... if it wasn't a libel.'

The second curate 'giveth Christ a cricket-bat and pads, and beateth Him boisterously upon the back' and says:

'Here we are again, hurray!
Keep your shoulders square and play!
That's the way that heaven is won ...
Well hit my lad! Again, Sir ... run!'

The 'sentimental person' arrives to say:

> 'Gentle Jesus mild and meek
> Smooth Your hair down neat and sleek;
> I am sure You did not say:
> "Tasteless salt is cast away" ...
> Jesus, that would never do,
> Or what would become of You?'

He parts Christ's hair in the middle.

Dorothy L. Sayers, 'The Mocking of Christ: A Mystery'[19]

At the end Christ is left alone, and 'they put on Him his own robe'.

Sayers, all her life the Anglo-Catholic Anglican with a deep commitment to the person of Christ, who would later be known for her deep and subtle presentation of Christian doctrine and ethics, nevertheless went through a period in her twenties when she lived rather differently. She fell in love with a member of a motorcycling gang, Bill White; they had a son, Anthony, who was brought up by Dorothy's cousin, Ivy Shrimpton. There was also an unhappy love affair with the Russian-born novelist, John Cournos. From 1922 she worked for seven years as a copywriter for Benson's advertising agency in London. Later she was to write with wit and acerbity about the ethics of this profession. In the essay *Why Work?* she sharply attacked 'advertisements imploring and exhorting and cajoling and menacing and bullying us to glut ourselves with things we do not want, in the name of snobbery and idleness and sex-appeal'. In the novel *Murder Must Advertise* she has a copywriter say:

> How should anything be sacred to an advertiser? We spend our whole time asking intimate questions of perfect strangers and it naturally blunts our finer feelings: 'Mother, Has Your Child Learnt Regular Habits?'; 'Are

> You Troubled with Fulness After Eating?'; 'Do
> You Suffer from Superfluous Hair?' ... Upon
> my soul, I sometimes wonder why the long-
> suffering public doesn't rise up and slay us.[20]

In 1926 Sayers married a divorced man, Captain
Oswald Atherton Fleming, a war correspondent and
veteran of World War I. He died in 1950.

Meanwhile Sayers had begun to write her detective
novels, most of them featuring the aristocratic amateur
sleuth, Lord Peter Wimsey. The first was *Whose Body?*
published in 1923, and the last, *Thrones, Dominations,*
was put aside half finished in 1938 (and recently
completed by Jill Paton Walsh). Her achievement in this
kind of writing was considerable:

> She raised this literary genre to a notable
> level, creating a glittering ambience and local
> colour, drawing her characters with
> psychological depth, critically analysing the
> social setting, often with irony and humour,
> and viewing crime also from an ethical and
> theological perspective.[21]

Despite her fame and commercial success in detective
fiction, Sayers put it aside, and in the last 20 years of her
life concentrated on literary and theological work. In 1937
she was asked to write a religious drama for the
Canterbury Festival. The festival had been started by
George Bell when he was dean, and a recent commission
had been T.S. Eliot's *Murder in the Cathedral.* Sayers'
play, *The Zeal of Thy House,* was about the twelfth-
century French architect, William of Sens, who rebuilt the
burnt-out choir of the cathedral. Very much like William
Golding's *The Spire,* it is a story of self-possessed
arrogance, but the builder's pride is brought low with a
dramatic fall to earth and he has to recognize that he must
leave his work to others, just as Christ did. The final
chorus of the play says,

> Children of men, lift up your hearts. Laud and magnify God, the everlasting Wisdom, the holy, undivided and adorable Trinity. Praise Him that He hath made man in His own image, a maker and craftsman like Himself, a little mirror of His Triune Majesty. For every work of creation is threefold, an earthly trinity to match the heavenly.[22]

Sayers further explored this idea in a book, *The Mind of the Maker,* published in 1941. In it she compared God as Trinity with the creative artist's process of creation, focusing on the threefold aspects of Idea, Energy and Power. This was her great strength: to put the great Christian doctrines into human-scale analogies and relevant, challenging examples. In her essay *The Other Six Deadly Sins* she shows how easy it is for both Church and society to duck the reality of sin: the Church, for example, by being quicker to condemn sexual immorality than financial chicanery; society by promoting avarice under the name of enterprise or envy under the principle of egalitarianism.

Dorothy Sayers was a tough critic of the Church (although she was careful also to say 'the Church is you and me') for trying to uphold standards of morality while simultaneously divesting itself of the theological dogmas which were their rational foundations. That neglect was at the root of its failure to influence modern society. She scorned a Christianity that fostered a mild 'gentle Jesus sentimentality' with vaguely humanistic ethics. 'We cannot blink the fact,' she wrote, 'that gentle Jesus, meek and mild, was so stiff in His opinions and so inflammatory in His language, that He was thrown out of church, stoned, hunted from place to place, and finally gibbetted as a firebrand and a public danger.'[23]

The people who hanged Christ never, to do them justice, accused Him of being a bore – on the contrary; they thought Him too dynamic to be safe. It has been left for later generations to muffle up that shattering personality and surround Him with an atmosphere of tedium ... We have very efficiently pared the claws of the Lion of Judah, turning Him into a household pet for pale curates and pious old ladies. To those who knew Him, however, He in no way suggested a milk-and-water person; they objected to Him as a dangerous firebrand. True, He was tender to the unfortunate, patient with honest enquirers and humble before Heaven; but He insulted respectable clergymen by calling them hypocrites; He referrred to King Herod as 'that fox'; He went to parties in disreputable company and was looked upon as a 'gluttonous man and a wine-bibber, a friend of publicans and sinners'; He assaulted indignant tradesmen and threw them and their belongings out of the Temple; He drove a coach-and-horses through a number of sacrosanct and hoary regulations; He cured diseases by any means that came handy, with a shocking casualness in the matter of other people's pigs and property; He showed no proper deference for wealth or social position; when confronted with neat, dialectical traps, He displayed a paradoxical humour that affronted serious-minded people, and He retorted by asking disagreeably searching questions that could not be answered by rule of thumb. He was emphatically not a dull man in His human lifetime, and if He was God, there can be nothing dull about God either.

Dorothy Sayers[24]

Sayers did her best to give back Jesus his fire and his challenge in her pioneering dramatic creation, the 12 plays on the life of Jesus, *The Man Born To Be King,* which she wrote for BBC Radio and which were broadcast to great acclaim in 1942. This acclaim soon drowned the protests from some conservative Christian groups at the modern, non-Authorised-Version way Jesus and all the other characters were made to speak, not to mention that *Jesus was portrayed in a dramatic work not in a church*. One published objection read:

> A sinful man presuming to impersonate the Sinless One! It detracts from the honour due to the Divine Majesty. In the present instance the man chosen to impersonate the Eternal Son of God – attributing to Him some words our Divine Saviour never uttered – is a professional actor. Could anything be more distressful to reverent-minded Christians?[25]

Sayers' aim in the plays was twofold – to present good biblical theology, and to make abundantly clear that these were real historical events in the real world, not some other-worldly tableau. In this she succeeds magnificently, partly by following John's Gospel closely, but mainly by the sheer imaginative energy of the characterization and the narrative thrust. Her 'helpful hints' to the radio producer and actors before each play also give us a glimpse of the energy and drive of the woman. In the introduction to the play of Jesus' trial, for example, she suddenly writes:

> And let us, my darlings, have no reservations or inhibitions, but a good, big, thundering piece of theatre in the grand manner – not too loud till we get to the final outburst – but with pace, pace, pace and passion.[26]

The creator of Lord Peter Wimsey, the translator of *The Divine Comedy*, the robust Anglo-Catholic defender of Christian truth and righteousness, the excoriater of modern society, gave, in *The Man Born To Be King*, her supreme account of the faith that was in her.

Let us, in Heaven's name, drag out the Divine Drama from under the dreadful accumulation of slipshod thinking and trashy sentiment heaped upon it, and set it on an open stage to startle the world into some sort of vigorous reaction. If the pious are the first to be shocked, so much the worse for the pious – others will pass into the Kingdom of Heaven before them. If all men are offended because of Christ, let them be offended; but where is the sense of their being offended at something that is not Christ and is nothing like Him? We do Him singularly little honour by watering down His personality till it could not offend a fly. Surely it is not the business of the Church to adapt Christ to men, but to adapt men to Christ.

It is the dogma that is the drama – not beautiful phrases, nor comforting sentiments, nor vague aspirations to loving-kindness and uplift, nor the promise of something nice after death – but the terrifying assertion that the same God who made the world lived in the world and passed through the grave and gate of death. Show that to the heathen, and they may not believe it; but at least they may realize that here is something that a man might be glad to believe.

Dorothy Sayers[27]

God the Maker,
you who entrust to us the role of creators in
your image,
give us the courage to receive the truths of
which we are heirs
and to do the work that is given us with
integrity as in your sight,
after the example of your daughter,
Dorothy Sayers,
for whose clarity and faith we give you
thanks today,
Father, Son and Holy Spirit.

ℬ ℭ

After this brief glimpse into the lives and work of three Christian creative writers, we can see that, even though their lives were less than perfect, they have extended and deepened our understanding of evil and redemption, of meaninglessness opening into purpose and hope, and of fresh ways to apprehend the Bible's revelation. Could we ask for more?

When the Bible itself is so full of poetry and storytelling, when Jesus himself was such a brilliant and compulsive storyteller, when Christianity itself is a 'history of salvation', it is right that we should celebrate the outstanding story-makers of our faith.

ℬ ℭ

All praise to you,
Word made flesh,
story-maker who became the story told,
for you have inspired many
to celebrate you in poetry and narrative,
and to deepen our apprehension of your
incarnate truth.
Continue to reveal yourself,
as we may bear it,
in the words of faithful and determined
explorers.
We ask this of your Holy Spirit.

Chapter 5

Those who 'set their heart on painting a lifelike image'
The artists who 'saw salvation'

Fra Angelico may well be the only Christian artist on his way to canonization in the western Church (long called *Il Beato,* he was officially beatified by the Roman Catholic Church in 1982). Many of the artists from the early Christian centuries and in the Middle Ages are unknown by name, like the creators of the mystery plays, but even when we come to the Renaissance and the modern period, it is not possible to find any painters or sculptors or architects in the calendars of the saints. Even Fra Angelico will probably 'get in' as much for his role as a monk and his supposed saintly nature as for his artistic work. What is the cause of this? Is it, as with the Church's great musicians, that the artists were seen merely as humble servants of the Church? Is it because Christianity is fundamentally a religion of the word (the Word), established in holy books and set forward in many great writings? Is it that the great Christian writers and teachers are duly honoured (although poetry and storytelling lose out to doctrine and philosophy), but the artists and composers are put on a lower rung? Or is the neglect of artists another aspect of the Church's anxiety with the post-Renaissance autonomous creator whose work is no longer simply a medium for spirituality but an independent art object for secular aesthetic appreciation?

It is, I believe, all of these, but behind them lies a deeper question. It is the question of the very legitimacy of visual art in the practice of religious faith.

Of the three 'Abrahamic faiths', both Judaism and Islam have proclaimed prohibition on the making of images – 'of anything that is in heaven above, or that is in the earth beneath, or that is in the water under the earth'[1]

– in conformity with the second of the Ten Commandments, which also forbids the bowing down in worship to such 'idols'. Surrounded as they were by peoples who created personified images of gods in animal or human shape, the Hebrew people stood out against that in the name of the one true God, who was beyond being seen or pictured.

The first Christians were Jews, and yet astonishingly they did not feel that their monotheism was being compromised when they came to believe that in Jesus Christ they had seen their God in human form. The doctrine of the incarnation inevitably allowed the development of Christian iconography.

> In effect the West of today has the genius of images because two thousand years ago the first Christians were possessed of the genius of mediation. Through the learned argument of 'Christology', they asserted Christ as a middle term, an intermediary between God and man, and applied this principle to imagery. As the reasoning developed, both Christ and images were held to be at the cross roads of the spiritual and the corporeal, and to mediate between the bipolar opposites – Creator: creature; Spirit: matter – in precisely the same ways. If we assume that the Word became incarnate in man who was fully man, it logically follows that a material as thick as pigment or coloured paste can become 'the tabernacle of the Holy Spirit'; if the Son is the visible image of the Father, who is the invisible image of the Son, and that God did not deem it impious to assume the form of a material and human body, it should not be impious for man to produce material and human images of God.[2]

Judaism and Islam have in fact in different cultural periods occasionally wavered from their prohibition on images, and of course both Hebrew and Greek scriptures have provided rich material for art within the Christian tradition.

> Here is a remarkable paradox: the book that prohibits images has become a treasury of images, the great storehouse of them for the western eye. The book recording the first ban on making and worshipping idols ... has become our prime visual reference.[3]

The earliest Christian art is known from burial places, the Roman catacombs in the second century. The imagery tends to be symbolic or typological. A fish stands for Christ, bread and wine for the Eucharist, a ship for the Church, the story of Jonah and the whale for death and resurrection. Jesus appears as the good shepherd or like a classical figure such as Orpheus. The earliest depicted gospel scenes are the miracles, not the passion story. When Christianity arrived as a permitted religion at the beginning of the fourth century, church art developed at a pace. New basilicas were built, and in them were found mosaics and wall paintings, sarcophagi with sculptured reliefs, ivory carvings and decorated books. In the Byzantine churches the massive Christ Pantocrator dominated the apse or the dome. If you visit the church of Santa Maria Maggiore in Rome, you can see the extensive mosaics portraying scenes from the Old and New Testaments; they were begun in 432.

In the eastern part of the Roman Empire painting developed in a symbolic and didactic way, the stylized icon painting with which we are still familiar soon emerging. In the West there was greater freedom, although the Church dictated the manner and content of the decoration of its great cathedrals and churches. The medieval cathedral, with its paintings, stained-glass, sculpture and textiles, was a sort of visual encyclopedia of theology, history, hagiography, natural history, science, morality and the trades and crafts: the whole ordered world was depicted, providing instruction even for the many who could not read. As the Renaissance arrived, Christian art in the West rapidly developed, with greater realism, more overt emotionalism, a greater focus on humanity without the supernatural trappings of the three-decker universe, and of course the celebration of the human body itself. John Drury[4] has drawn attention, for example, to the way that Velazquez at the beginning of the seventeenth century subtly distances himself from – without denying – scripture stories and ecclesiastical doctrines, bringing the human perceiving subject into the foreground. Asked to paint the Immaculate Conception, he paints Mary without the cherubs and most of the heavenly impedimenta; and he paints John on Patmos having his revelation of the woman clothed with the sun at equal size with Mary. The story of Jesus rebuking Martha for fussing about domestic details instead of listening to him like Mary is placed right in the background of a picture showing two domestic servants in the kitchen (in other words, when will *they* ever have time to sit at Jesus' feet?).

Does there, then, need to be any doubt about the value of the artist in the Christian faith? In both East and West there has been the abundant creation of magnificent places of worship decorated with all kind of art objects, whose role and purpose have been to lead the faithful Christian to a deeper understanding of their faith and into an attitude of praise, penitence and prayer. Works of art in all their materiality effectively connect the believer with the sources of faith in the actual human events of history, but also have the power to be vehicles of transcendence, by story and symbol, and by loving attention to humanity and the created order, drawing the viewer out into the wider realm of the Spirit. If the traditional stylized poses and rich decoration of the eastern icon affirm the holy otherness of those depicted and the supernatural power at work in their lives, the western Renaissance artist glories in our humanity and in the emotions of joy, grief, penitence and praise that the events of salvation history draw from us.

And yet Christian art has not had a history of uncontroversial plain sailing. In both East and West there has been trouble about images. This began first of all in the East, when, near the beginning of the eighth century, the Byzantine emperor banned the use of icons of Jesus, Mary and the saints; many of the icons were destroyed and their defenders faced martyrdom. What came to be called the iconoclastic controversy continued, with a short break, until well into the ninth century, with the monasteries forming the main defence of icons, and, when the use of icons was finally fully restored in 843, this was proclaimed as the 'triumph of Orthodoxy', and is still celebrated as such. The arguments of the iconoclasts included the following: icons were a clear breach of the second commandment; if you believed, as many did then, that the full being of God dwelt in Jesus (monophysitism), then it was sacrilege to depict him; and if you wanted an object for worship that was completely consubstantial with Christ – which an icon plainly wasn't – then you had it in the Eucharist. On the other side, the iconodules (or iconophiles), including notably John of Damascus, argued that even the Old Testament actually allowed figurative art, and the fact that God had joined his divinity to a true humanity (matter) in Jesus anyway justified the use of material imagery; and their *coup de grâce* was the clear affirmation that those who venerated images were not worshipping the image but what the image depicted. Sadly, the iconoclastic controversy played a role in the developing schism between the eastern and western Church which came to a final break in 1054. At this stage the western Church did not take such an intense attitude to religious imagery (either for or against) and it was becoming allergic to pronouncements from eastern councils and emperors (both for and against).

It was at the Reformation that the western Church came up against its own form of iconoclasm. The Protestant reformers did not like the way religious images were used in the church. In the Anglican world, Article 22 of the Thirty Nine Articles[5] rejected 'Worshipping and Adoration, as well of Images as of Reliques' together with Purgatory, Pardons and the invocation of Saints, as 'a fond thing vainly invented, and grounded upon no warranty of scripture, but rather repugnant to the Word of God'. In *The Praise of Folly* Erasmus mocked those

> that have gotten a foolish but pleasant persuasion that if they can but see a wooden or painted Polypheme Christopher, they shall not die that day; or do but salute a carved Barbara, in the usual set form, that he shall return safe from battle.[6]

As well as the Roman Catholic Church's encouragement of superstition and the clear defiance of the second Commandment, the reformers objected to the way pilgrimages to places with cultic images and relics were associated with the traffic in indulgences and also to the way in which opulent new paintings and sculptures proclaimed the wealth and ostentation of the donor quite as much as the glory of God. And so many statues and stained-glass windows were smashed, crucifixes were burned, painted walls in churches were whitewashed throughout the lands of the Reformation, and much medieval art was lost for ever. Nevertheless the Reformation iconoclasts did not have the last word. Attacks on church decoration were sporadic and incomplete. Luther himself held back the more fanatical image-smashers and preferred to retain some church decoration, including the crucifix. Calvin and Zwingli objected to the religious use of art, but not to art with religious subjects as such. Reformation artists like Dürer and Rembrandt focus on the 'image of God' in ordinary humanity. And Christian art continues to the present day, even if it sometimes looks as though it might drown in kitsch and mediocrity.

Have the doubts sown by the iconoclasts subtly influenced the downgrading of the artist and sculptor, the architect and craftsman, as not quite worthy to be honoured for what they gave to their fellow-Christians? I think it is important to reassert that the iconoclasts decisively lost the argument. It was in the flesh-and-blood reality of Jesus Christ that the first Christians saw God and saw salvation. In the gospels they gave us four different perspectives on that historical reality, not saying that one was more true than the others. The artists have given us many more perspectives on Jesus, the human being, and on those who believed in him. We should celebrate the wonder of their skill and intelligence, their seeing that opens *our* eyes. I think, too, that it is important for us to celebrate not only the artists as a category, not only individual works of art which speak to us, but also the artists themselves, whose faith *was* their artistic creation.

Fra Angelico
1387–1455

Fra Giovanni was a simple man and most holy in his habits ... He was most gentle and temperate, living chastely, removed from the cares of the world. He would often say that whoever practised art needed a quiet life and freedom from care, and that he who occupied himself with the things of Christ ought always to be with Christ ... I cannot bestow too much praise on this holy father, who was so humble and modest in all his works and conversation, so fluent and devout in his painting, the saints by his hand being more like those blessed beings than those of any other. He never retouched or repaired any of his pictures, always leaving them in the condition in which they were first seen, believing, so he said, that this was the will of God.

> Some say that Fra Giovanni never took up his brush without first making a prayer. He never made a Crucifix when the tears did not course down his cheeks, while the goodness of his sincere and great soul in religion may be seen from the attitudes of his figures.
>
> Vasari[7]

Do you need to be a good Christian to produce good Christian art? The violent career of a Caravaggio proves the opposite, but in Fra Angelico we find, nevertheless, a great artist who happened also, by all accounts, to be an exceptionally good and devout Christian. In fact, he was a priest and a monk in the Dominican order. We do not know a great deal about him, and there is something appropriate about the way he let his painting do the talking, faithfully serving the Church and drawing attention to the great events, symbols and doctrines of the Christian faith.

He was born Guido di Pietro near Castello di Vicchio in Tuscany in 1387. He entered the Dominican convent at Fiesole near Florence in 1407, and his first work in art there was illuminating manuscripts. He was now named Fra (Brother) Angelico Giovanni da Fiesole. Between 1409 and 1418 he moved to the community house at Foligno and then to Cortona, before returning to Fiesole. This was caused by the struggle of three rival popes (from Rome, Pisa and Avignon) for supremacy during the Great Schism. In 1436 Fra Angelico was invited to Florence to decorate the new convent of San Marco which had just been allotted to the Dominican order, and in 1445 Pope Eugenius IV invited him to Rome, where he painted the frescoes of two chapels. Eugenius is said to have invited Fra Angelico to be the Archbishop of Florence, but he declined in order not to be taken away from the full devotion to his art. He did, however, become Prior of the Dominican convent in Fiesole in 1450. At Rome he also executed some beautiful miniatures for choral books. He died in Rome in 1455, and he is buried in the church of Santa Maria sopra Minerva there.

Fra Angelico speaks to us through his art, and to a great degree with the communal vision and faith of the Dominican order of the Catholic Church, the Friars Preachers, of which he was a lifelong member. Founded by Dominic in 1215, the order was notable for two things: it was devoted above all to the preaching of the word, and this meant that it cultivated learning and maintained good libraries in its convents; and, within their general Rule, individual convents had a certain autonomy, and could, for example, choose whether to follow a more austere Observant discipline or not. The movement of Dominican Observance had begun at the end of the fourteenth century at the instigation of Raymond of Capua, its great preacher being Raymond's disciple, Giovanni Dominici.

Dominici's most important work, the *Lucula Noctis*, is a defence of traditional spirituality against the onslaughts of the humanists. Let the Christian cultivate the earth rather than study heathen books; let him read not the poetry of antiquity but the 'Holy Writ, in which the Lord has laid out the true poetry of wisdom, and the true eloquence of the spirit of truth'. Let those who have charge of the young remember that 'Christ is our only guide to happiness ... our father, our leader, our light, our food, our redemption, our way, our truth, our life' ... Let them, above all, propagate the faith, through which the Christian is permitted year by year to warm his frozen mind before the crib. Two aspects of Dominici's thought are of special importance for an understanding of the paintings of Angelico. The first is his fear of rhetoric. 'The beautiful form of the poem,' he writes, 'is like clothing. The body is worth more than the clothes which cover it, and the soul worth more than both.' The second is his rejection of personal revelation, that concomitant of mysticism. Whereas

> Savonarola, with his belief in the validity of individual visions, inculcated a personal religious imagery in the artists he inspired, the painting produced under the aegis of Dominici was the expression of collective, and not of individual, mystical experience.
>
> John Pope-Hennessy[8]

The convent of San Marco in Florence was an Observant Dominican house. The visitor can still see the frescoes, with their fresh, glowing colours and simple designs, which Fra Angelico created throughout the convent, now sadly a museum. They are not mere background decoration, but objects for intense contemplation of mind and heart.

And yet equally they are sensuous aesthetic objects, and one can only wonder at the 'artistic certainty' of the artist, knowing before he starts what he wants to 'say' with the picture. All the more so, when we consider how wall frescoes were made at that time. Germaine Greer describes the process, called 'affresco':

> The wall had to be prepared by the application of a granular plaster or *riccio*, which was roughly finished, or, if the walls were already plastered, the old plaster was chipped to provide a rough surface that the painter's fresh *intonaco* [plaster] would adhere to ... The pigment was then applied to the fresh intonaco, which was only laid upon the wall in *giornate*, sufficient, that is, to be painted in a single working day while fresh. The *sinopia*, the underdrawing in red chalk for the whole design, was got in on the riccio, but for the day's work the artist had to proceed by memory, and no *pentimenti* [after painting] were possible, for all colour applied was

instantly amalgamated with the plaster as it
underwent the chemical process of setting.[9]

This, of course, meant that the artist could not see, at the
time of application, what the final colours and colour
relationships would be, because the colours would change
as the plaster dried. Fra Angelico's colours are exquisitely
blended, and there is no doubt that he knew, before he
started, how they would look together.

All the frescoes at San Marco are geared towards the
motivation of the friars as they contemplated the saving
events of Christ, which they would take out to the wider
world in their preaching. So, for example, the entire wall
opposite the entrance to the Chapter Hall is occupied by a
giant fresco showing the crucifixion[10], showing Jesus
between the two thieves, and along the ground in front of
them 17 saints, including the Virgin Mary, John the
Baptist, Mark the Evangelist, Dominic, Francis and
Thomas Aquinas. On the border above the fresco are
hexagonal medallions showing, in the centre, the pelican,
symbol of self-sacrifice, and images of prophets and sybils,
while, below, are 17 circular medallions showing well-
known members of the Dominican order. The whole is,
therefore, a pictorial summary of salvation history, from
the prophets, through the central significance of Christ's
crucifixion, and on to the life and proclamation of the
Church, from the Virgin through to Dominic and his order.
In the cloister of the convent, the visitor soon sees Fra
Angelico's representation of the crucifixion,[11] this time
with Christ alone, and, at the foot of the cross kneeling,
holding the wood of the upright and looking up in
devotion, St Dominic. This image is repeated in all the
novices' cells – a summary of the meaning and purpose of
the convent.

Dominic died in 1221, but we see him as though witnessing the actual moment of the Crucifixion. The scene is bare, with only sky-blue for background, and no other participants but ourselves. And although Christ looks down at the friar, Dominic's eyes do not meet his, but are fixed on some indeterminate distance, like those of a man lost in thought. An eyewitness account of Dominic relates that he used to pray before a sculpted crucifix, weeping for his sins and with love for Christ. But Fra Angelico has not pictured an anecdote from the life of St Dominic any more than he has painted the actual Crucifixion. This is not a carved crucifix but the living Christ – and the two figures inhabit the essence of a landscape rather than a convent interior. What is shown is the object of Dominic's prayerful meditation. We are allowed to see what he sees in his mind's eye, so that his example can be followed by all the members of his Order.

Neil MacGregor[12]

Each of the friars' cells is decorated with an event from one of the great church festivals, including the annunciation, the nativity, the baptism of Christ, the transfiguration, the passion and resurrection, and the coronation of the Virgin. Not all were painted by Angelico, but he was responsible for the designs. Two are particularly striking. *The Mocking of Christ*[13] in Cell 7 represents the Sanhedrin's rough mockery of Jesus at the end of his 'trial', and Christ is certainly blindfolded, but instead of the suffering human figure crouching from his persecutors, we see him seated in a white robe and in calm majesty, the true prince of peace. As for the mockers, they appear in a doubly removed kind of way: they seem to be part of a green picture-within-a-picture behind Christ; and their visibility is limited to their mockery: the head of a man appears out of nowhere, raising his hat in mock salute and spitting at Jesus; three disembodied hands are raised to strike him; and a fourth hand holds a rod for the same purpose. In the front of the picture sit Mary and Dominic, neither looking at Jesus; Mary looks down, deeply pondering; Dominic also looks down, reading a book. It is as though Fra Angelico is representing what Mary is contemplating and Dominic is reading: they both acknowledge Christ as Saviour and King, because of his passion, but they also use the detailed story of his suffering as a way of understanding the meaning of what God has done in him. They focus their thoughts on aspects of the mockery, not on the whole scene. And that is what Fra Angelico shows us, with extraordinary economy and concentration.

The other striking decoration is the *Noli Me Tangere*[14] of Cell 1, a delightful and touching representation of the risen Christ telling Mary Magdalene not to hold on to him, but to go and tell the other disciples that he is going back to the Father.[15] Mary kneels with her back to the blackness of the door of the cave tomb. Flowers spring up all around her. She stretches out her hands to Jesus, but, although he is actually pictured carrying a mattock over his shoulder – Mary thinks he is the gardener – his pierced feet seem to hover an inch or two above the surface of the ground, as he both looks down lovingly upon Mary and also seems to be turning away out of reach of her. The brightness and joy of this image are unforgettable; what a fortunate friar, to get Cell number one!

Dominicans, unlike the members of some other orders, did not sleep in communal dormitories but in individual cells, which they were also expected to use for solitary study and meditation. So the decoration of the novices' cells could be expected to provide the clearest example of how to become a good Dominican: and each of these cells contains an image of Dominic at the foot of the Cross, like the one that greets us in the cloister.

At first sight, all appear to be identical. Only when we look more closely do we notice that in each one the saint is shown in a slightly different pose. In a treatise intended for use by Dominicans, an eyewitness of Dominic's devotions recounts the founder's nine different modes of prayer. Eight were silent, so that only through his gestures was it possible to know what was in his mind. Fra Angelico's frescoes closely follow the painted illustrations in the manuscripts of this treatise – and both illustrations and frescoes are clearly based on a simple theory of imitation. Dominic's states of mind can more easily be evoked and recreated in the viewer if he can replicate the appropriate gestures ...

In these cells built for silent study and prayer, the ultimate purpose of the exemplary images that Fra Angelico and his assistants painted was not private spiritual growth. It was to train the Dominican friar to meditate on and to write about the sufferings of Christ, and to equip him for active apostolic service, preaching to others, in accordance with the Order's motto: 'Things contemplated are to be passed on to others.'

Neil MacGregor[16]

Fra Angelico was called Beato (blessed) during or soon after his life. That, and the very name 'Angelico', bear witness to the regard in which he was held. Two years after his beatification in 1982 Pope John Paul II declared him 'Patron of Catholic artists'.

Here lies the venerable painter Fra Giovanni of the Order of Preachers.

Let me not be praised because I seemed another Apelles, but because I gave my riches, O Christ, to thine.

For some works survive on earth and others in heaven. The city of Florence, flower of Etruria, gave me, Giovanni, birth.

The glory, the mirror, the ornament of painters, Giovanni the Florentine, is contained within this place.

A religious, he was a brother of the holy order of St Dominic, and was himself a true servant of God. His disciples bewail the loss of so great a master, for who will find another brush like his? His fatherland and order lament the death of a consummate painter, who had no equal in his art.

Lorenzo Valla[17]

Creative God,
you gave to Fra Angelico the faith and the
mastery
to depict the story of our salvation in Christ.
Open our eyes to the meaning and beauty of
the Bible,
and give us the power in our way
to help others to see you
in Jesus Christ your Son.

৪০ ៣

Albrecht Dürer
1471–1528

Only the powerful artists will be able to understand this strange speech, that I speak the truth: one man may sketch something with his pen on half a sheet of paper in one day, or may cut it into a tiny piece of wood with his little iron, and it turns out to be better and more artistic than another's big work at which its author labours with the utmost diligence for a whole year. And

> this gift is miraculous. For, God often gives the ability
> to learn and the insight to make something good to one
> man the like of whom nobody is found in his own days,
> and nobody has lived before him for a long time, and
> nobody comes after him very soon.
>
> Albrecht Dürer[18]

Everyone knows the 'Praying Hands'.[19] They have been
reproduced and copied millions of times since Albrecht
Dürer drew them in 1508. They were just one of many
preliminary drawings he did for a large painted altar-piece
he painted for a wealthy cloth merchant in Frankfurt. The
painting itself was destroyed by fire just over 200 years
later, but the 'Praying Hands' have survived – to become
an item of religious kitsch for ever.

This is a strange irony for a deeply serious, intellectual
Christian and artist; and yet it is also oddly appropriate,
for Dürer earned a great deal of his fame, and indeed his
living, from the fact that his wonderfully detailed
woodcuts and copper engravings could be reproduced –
printed and sold around Europe in large numbers of
copies – a publishing industry that he helped to pioneer.

And yet, if you look carefully at the 'Study of an
Apostle's Hands', you will see nothing that is cheap or
sentimental. On the contrary, the brush drawing on blue
primed paper is a wonderfully detailed depiction of real
human hands, with light falling on them from the left. The
artist has looked with great attention, and has drawn with
unbelievable sureness and skill. Such was Dürer's skill that
he became famous in his own lifetime, mixed with many of
the great contemporary artists in Germany, the
Netherlands and Italy, was regarded as the intellectual
equal of people of learning and civic leaders in his home
town of Nürnberg, and received commissions from
aristocrats, prelates and the Emperor Maximilian I. Many
compared him with Apelles, the famous Greek painter of

Alexander the Great, and Konrad Celtis said that his creative powers were not inferior to those of a great thirteenth-century theologian like Albertus Magnus. It was said that on one occasion Dürer's dog had tried to greet his master when he saw him in a self-portrait, so lifelike was it.

> I admit that Apelles was the prince of his art, upon whom no reproach could be cast by other painters except that he did not know when to take his hand off the panel – a splendid kind of blame. But Apelles was assisted by colours, even though they were fewer and less ambitious – still by colours. But Dürer, though admirable also in other respects, what does he not express in monochromes, that is, in black lines? Light, shade, splendour, eminences, depressions; and, though derived from the position of one single thing, more than one aspect offers itself to the eye of the beholder. He observes accurately proportions and harmonies. Nay, he even depicts that which cannot be depicted: fire, rays of light, thunder, sheet lightning, lightning, or, as they say, the 'clouds on a wall'; all the sensations and emotions; in fine, the whole of man as it reflects itself in the behaviour of the body, and almost the voice itself.
>
> Desiderius Erasmus[20]

Albrecht Dürer was born in 1471 in Nürnberg, Germany, which in his lifetime was a flourishing centre of trade. Parchment manufacture, metalworking and book publishing were well established, and the town was known for producing clocks, maps and scientific instruments. Nürnberg also housed the emperor's insignia and holy relics (the Heiltum), and in its busy streets rich merchants rubbed shoulders with manufacturers and humanist scholars. Nürnberg was a Catholic town, but in 1525 it joined Luther's Reformation.

Albrecht was the son of a goldsmith and was initially apprenticed in that craft. But he soon decided that he wanted to be an artist and began an apprenticeship with the painter Michael Wolgemut. Between 1490 and 1494 he travelled in Europe, getting to know other workshops, styles and techniques, and on his return he married Agnes Frey. An arranged marriage, it was apparently not a happy one, and there were no children. Thereafter Dürer left Nürnberg only three times for any substantial period: a journey to Venice straight after his marriage in 1494 (without his wife), to learn from the Italian masters there; another Italian journey in 1505–06, initially to put a stop to the plagiarism of his woodcuts; and a time at Antwerp in the Netherlands in 1520–21, where he went to sort out a pension promised by the Emperor Maximilian I. During this last trip he went out to Zeeland to view a beached whale – it had gone by the time he got there – but he caught a fever there from which, it appears, in due course he died, in 1528, at the age of 57.

Dürer represents in his career the development of the artist from lowly craftsman, working for rich patrons, religious or secular, to the creator who makes his own choices of subject matter and style. He was able to achieve this partly because of his astonishing ability, but also because he could produce and sell many copies of his engravings and woodcuts, and make a living independent of anyone's patronage. Of course he produced many commissioned paintings and drawings, and perhaps he exaggerated the honour he received as a great creative artist in Italy and elsewhere in comparison with the way he was regarded in Nürnberg ('Here [in Italy] I am a gentleman, at home only a parasite'[21]), but there is no doubt of the economic and intellectual autonomy he achieved.

Dürer's development as an artist mirrors the progress of the Renaissance and the Reformation in the fifteenth and sixteenth centuries. The human individual no longer merely accepts and follows the ecclesiastical and political order of the day, but, equipped with new learning, derived from the old classical world, but also new science, geography, mathematics or theology, begins to explore more fully the reality of the world, and above all the meaning of humanity's role within it. Dürer studied the Greek and Roman artists of antiquity and also the contemporary masters, and worked according to strict theories of proportion and correct perspective. He wrote four treatises on human proportions. But he made his own, often quite obscure, choices about motifs and symbols to give deeper meaning to his pictures.

On Friday (17th May) before Whitsunday in the year 1521, came tidings to me at Antwerp, that Martin Luther had been so treacherously taken prisoner; for he trusted the Emperor Karl, who had granted him his herald and imperial safe-conduct. But as soon as the herald had conveyed him to an unfriendly place near Eisenach he rode away, saying that he no longer needed him. Straightway there appeared ten knights and they treacherously carried off the pious man, betrayed into their hands, a man enlightened by the Holy Ghost, a follower of the true Christian faith. And whether he yet lives, I know not, or whether they have put him to death; if so, he has suffered for the truth of Christ and because he rebuked the unchristian Papacy, which strives with its heavy burden of human laws against the redemption of Christ ... Oh God, if Luther be dead, who will henceforth expound to us the holy Gospel with such clearness? What, Oh God, might he not still have written for us in ten or twenty years! Oh all ye pious Christian men, help me deeply to bewail this man, inspired of God, and to pray Him yet again to send us an enlightened man.

Albrecht Dürer[22]

Although he never formally abandoned the Catholic Church, Dürer developed a strong support for Martin Luther and the ideas of the Reformation. Dürer admired Luther because he showed the way through the turmoil of the time in simple and powerful language. 'God helping me, if I ever meet Dr Luther, I intend to draw his portrait carefully from life and to engrave it on copper, to be a lasting remembrance of a Christian man, who helped me out of great distress,' he wrote in 1520 to Georg Spalatin, chaplain to Duke Friedrich, Elector of Saxony.[23] The outburst of anxiety recorded in his diary in the Netherlands in 1521, when he believed Luther to have been captured (in fact Luther had been taken into custody to protect him), shows the strength of his feelings here. He and Luther never met.

Although Dürer must have been glad to live in a Protestant town for the last three years of his life, he also had real anxieties about the chaos which might be unleashed in Europe. In 1526 he painted his 'Four Apostles' for the Nürnberg town council:[24] a pair of paintings showing the life-size standing figures of St Peter and St John on the left and St Paul and St Mark on the right. Underneath these four dignified, powerful figures – heroes of the Christian Reformation – are inscriptions with biblical words of warning from Luther's 1522 translation, chosen by Dürer himself: for Peter there is 2 Peter 2.1–3, warning against false prophets; for John there is 1 John 4.1–3 against those who deny the incarnation; for Paul there is 2 Timothy 3.1–7 against all arrogant and unholy behaviour; and for Mark there is Mark 12.38–40 with Jesus' warning against the scribes. These quotations are introduced with the words:

> Let all worldly rulers in these dangerous times take care not to give heed to human temptation as if it were the word of God. For it is God's will that nothing should be added to his word, or taken from it. These four men, St

Peter, St John, St Paul and St Mark, give warning against this.

Dürer, admirer of Luther and friend of Erasmus, is already warning against the way the Reformation could be spoiled by extreme doctrines, violence and war.

> For the art of painting is employed in the service of the Church and by it the sufferings of Christ and many other profitable examples are set forth. It preserveth also the likeness of men after their death. By aid of delineations the measurements of the earth, the waters and the stars are better to be understood; and many things likewise become known unto men by them. The attainment of true, artistic, and lovely execution in painting is hard to come unto; it needeth long time and a hand practised to almost perfect freedom. Whosoever, therefore, falleth short of this cannot attain a right understanding (in matters of painting) for it cometh alone by inspiration from above.
>
> Albrecht Dürer[25]

Dürer produced two sets of woodcuts illustrating the passion of Christ, and he served the Church by producing countless paintings and drawings. One example of the detailed and symbolic work he produced is the engraving of Adam and Eve, *The Fall of Man,*[26] of 1504. Adam stands on the left next to the Tree of Life and Eve on the right next to the Tree of Knowledge, from which hangs the serpent giving the fruit to Eve. Seven other animals are depicted around them: an elk, a hare, a cat and an ox, and, in the corners of the picture, a mouse, a parrot and a very distant ibex on the edge of a rock. Why has Dürer put in these creatures, other than for 'realistic' effect in the Garden of Eden? The elk, the hare, the cat and the ox represent the four human humours or temperaments in scholastic teaching: the melancholic, the choleric, the phlegmatic and the sanguine. Prior to humanity's fall into sin, it was believed, the soul was in perfect harmony, but now it is all divided and broken up. The cat and the mouse picture the tense conflictual relationship there will now be between the man and the woman, while the distant ibex, teetering on the precipice, is a symbol of their lack of faith. But there is some Christian good news also hidden in the picture: the parrot is a symbol of ideal motherhood and therefore of the Virgin Mary, whose 'Let it be' as the Second Eve will bring about the overcoming of sin.

As for 'preserving the likeness of men after their death', Dürer certainly achieved this in his many portraits, which reveal the appearance and nature of the subject, as Erasmus said, with amazing honesty and uncanny presence. In 1514, two months before his mother died aged 63, he did a charcoal drawing of her.[27] The lined forehead, the stony gaze, the tense unsmiling lips, the hollow bony cheeks and the scraggy neck are unflinchingly recorded: she had borne 18 children, only three of whom had survived. Dürer wrote of her, after her death:

> Her most frequent habit was to go much to the church. She always upbraided me well if I did not do right, and she was ever in great anxiety about my sins and those of my brother. And if she went out or in her saying was always, 'Go in the name of Christ' ... I cannot enough praise her good works and the compassion she showed to all, as well as her high character.[28]

Perhaps the most remarkable of all his portraits was the one he did of himself in 1500 aged 28.[29] Against a completely dark background he is looking straight out of the canvas, in a pose that had usually been reserved for that of Christ (portraits were usually half or three-quarter profile), and with his unblinking stare and the long curly brown hair spread out on either side on his shoulders, he is, to many eyes, the image of Christ. Dürer kept the portrait for the rest of his life, perhaps as a demonstration for his students or customers, but its deepest meaning

seems to be, not a simplistic arrogance, but a sense that
the gift as an artist that he has been given by God (our
gaze is drawn into the picture to the artist's two great
instruments: his hand and his eyes) is not dissimilar to
what God gave in Christ.

> But life in nature manifests the truth of these things.
> Therefore observe it diligently, go by it and do not depart
> from nature arbitrarily, imagining to find the better by
> thyself, for thou wouldst be misled. For, verily, 'art' is
> embedded in nature; he who can extract it, has it; if thou
> acquirest it, it will save thee from much error in thy work
> ... Therefore, never put it in thy head that thou couldst or
> wouldst make something better than God has empowered
> His created nature to produce. For thy might is powerless
> against the creation of God. Hence it follows that no man
> can ever make a beautiful image out of his private
> imagination unless he have replenished his mind by much
> painting from life.
>
> Albrecht Dürer[30]

Dürer studied the human form and human
physiognomy in intense detail. He also filled his pictures
with creatures, real and imaginary, and celebrated
landscape and buildings in many ways. He was fascinated
by strange animals and drew them: a rhinoceros, a walrus,
a lobster, a deformed pig. He did wonderful horses. And
look at the 'Young Hare' of 1502:[31] its huge ears, long black
whiskers, gleaming eyes (the mullion and transom of a
window are reflected in the nearer one), its neat pose –
ready to leap? – and the subtle gradations and shades of
its body fur are miraculously captured. In a way it is more
hare than any live one you might see in a field: as you look
at it, you honour it as a fellow-creature, and you may well
praise God for making you both. Dürer succeeded in
'capturing nature'; there is nothing false about this hare.

In May 1528, after Albrecht Dürer's death, Martin Luther wrote, in reply to Eobanus Hessus, who had written an elegy for Dürer:

> As to Dürer, it is natural and right to weep for so excellent a man; still you should rather think him blessed, as one whom Christ has taken in the fullness of his wisdom and by a happy death from these most troublous times, and perhaps from times even more troublous which are to come, lest one, who was worthy to look upon nothing but excellence, should be forced to behold things most vile. May he rest in peace. Amen.[32]

Creator God,
you gave to Albrecht Dürer
the eye to see and the hand to represent
the truths of life and the gospel.
We too would pay loving attention to all your works.
Help us by, guided by his art,
to keep seeing with new eyes
and to live in love and praise,
for Jesus Christ's sake.

Georges Rouault
1871–1958

At the fall of dusk, after a lovely day, when the first star, shining in the heavenly vault sent a tremor though my heart, an entire world of poetry was born to me. That circus wagon of wandering gipsies halted on the roadside, the old jade browsing the sparse grass, the aging clown seated beside his van patching his glittering, motley-coloured costume, *the contrast* between these scintillating garments of entertainment and this life, of *infinite sadness*, loomed before my eyes. And then ... I suddenly recognized who the 'clown' really was. It was I, you, practically *all of us* ... This richly spangled costume is a gift dealt out by life; we are more or less all of us, *somewhat clowns*, wearing 'a spangled costume'. But if we are suddenly caught unawares the way I caught the old clown, why then, O God! Who'd dare deny that his heart would be rent with infinite compassion? I have the mania, or the failing ... *of stripping everyone of their glamorous or pompous spangled costumes*, be he King or Emperor; with my own eyes must I peer into the soul of the man before me, and the more exalted his position, the more humbly worshipped he be, the greater my misgivings for his soul.

Georges Rouault[33]

So wrote Georges Rouault, the French painter of kings and clowns, of prostitutes and judges. Of course, the sad clown has become a cliché: the symbol of outward jollity and inward loneliness and futility. The cheerful exterior, like the spangled costume of the clown, masks the hollowness of what lies within. Rouault often painted tragic clowns, and often they had his own likeness. It was both a personal and a universal statement: the clown was himself, but also 'all of us'. More than just a cliché, in Rouault's hands it was a powerful symbol.

For Rouault, the conflict between outward ambition and success and inward loneliness and sense of sin was always present, both personally and in the social world as he saw it, and his art turns an intense spotlight on humanity in its arrogance and its suffering, on the evils of a godless society and its victims. A friend of Rouault's was a deputy public prosecutor, and through him Rouault began to frequent the Paris lawcourts. He depicted pitiless judges and fallen women in harsh, unflinching paintings over and over again: a world without the grace of God.

One of Rouault's paintings took 20 years to complete: it's called *The Old King*,[34] and it shows a powerful figure in profile, with black beard and grim visage. He is richly attired in red, gold and blue and has a tight crown upon his head. His eyes appear closed, his jaw set. Perhaps he has weighty decisions to make, decisions of life and death. He is powerful, harsh and very lonely.

Rouault's dark view of human life seems to have had its origin at the very moment of his birth in 1871: his mother was sheltering in a cellar in a slum district during the bombardment of Paris by the cannons of those opposed to the Commune. But he was a convinced Christian, brought up in a Roman Catholic family, though he did not find real faith and conviction until his mid-twenties. How was he, with his unblinking tragic view of humanity, to offer hope and faith and beauty? He became close to Léon Bloy, the Catholic intellectual, who promoted a strongly ascetical and evangelical Catholicism, and who said that modern art needed to 'go on its knees'. In spite of (or perhaps because of) their friendship, Bloy strongly criticized some of Rouault's work:

> This artist that I thought was capable of painting seraphim seems only able to imagine the most atrocious and avenging caricatures ... You are attracted exclusively by the ugly; you seem to be enthralled by the hideous ... If you were a man of prayer, you would not be able to paint such terrible canvases. [35]

It was at the time I lived in Versailles. One day I caught sight of a woman in the doorway of a brothel. She looked divinely beautiful, wrapped in the bright colours cast by the sun. I made straight for home and set to painting her, *just as she was*. In applying my brushstrokes, I rediscovered the woman I had admired,

> for herself and for the sundry reasons that had stirred
> my admiration. Bloy used to say: 'A saint or a trollop.' I
> refuse to judge and pass sentence.
>
> Georges Rouault[36]

Remarkably, in view of the attacks from someone like Bloy who was close to him, Rouault was able to hold on to the integrity of his vision and to fashion an art which looks unwaveringly at the ugliness and isolation of humanity and yet has pity on it, which sees it as lost and yet also as shared and saved in Christ. Between the two world wars he devoted much of his time to engravings for the Paris art dealer, Ambroise Vollard, with whom he had an extended contract. Perhaps the highest point of his achievement as a printmaker was the *Miserere et Guerre*[37] series of a hundred prints, which appeared with texts by the poet André Suarès. The black and white prints were created using nearly every known process of etching and engraving. First the preliminary drawings were photographically transferred on to copper plates using a process known as heliogravure. This then almost disappeared under extensive handwork, Rouault using aquatint, roulette, drypoint line, direct biting with acid, and scraping away parts of the original photo-engraved work. In some instances Rouault made as many as 15 successive impressions of an image before he was satisfied. In the first part of the series, the sufferings of Christ are interwoven with those of humanity, but in the second part, entitled *Guerre* (War), there are many images of death, yet ending with the idea of resurrection and of our salvation through the sacrifice of Christ. In 1929 Rouault designed the sets and costumes for Diaghilev's production of the ballet *The Prodigal Son* with music by Prokofiev.

No doubt, in my youth I was under Rembrandt's spell, then, at the age of thirty, I was suddenly seized with a sort of madness, or maybe favoured with a state of grace, according to one's viewpoint. Anyhow, 'the image of the world changed entirely for me', if I might make so presumptuous a statement. I perceived everything I had seen before, in a different light and harmony. Is it the eye that deceives us at times? And in this solitary world of mine I beheld a procession of clowns, tottering along weary and haggard, of Christs mocked and abused by the mob, Orpheus stripped to rags by Bacchantes. As I transferred these images to canvas, I poured into them, without any deliberate design, my own inner joy or more often my even deeper anguish. On reviewing these canvases today, canvases that are no longer mine, I begin to realize how bitterly I must have disappointed my contemporaries, in particular those who has fostered the hope that one day I would be 'a worthy winner of a Prix de Rome'.

Georges Rouault[38]

It is in the image of Christ, the face of Christ or Christ on the cross, that Rouault 'saves' the harshness of the human condition that he so graphically pictured. Of course, it is not Rouault who 'saves', but Christ, and yet the sense of the identification of Christ with suffering humanity, his pity and compassion, are Rouault's real achievement. He once said, 'My ambition is to be able one day to paint a Christ so moving that those who see him will be converted.'[39]

To claim that he ever achieved this may well go beyond what we can know, but anyone who has seen one of his many portraits of Christ will know of their overwhelming humanity and power. How did he achieve this? It is the bringing together of two elements from his earliest training and development as an artist and adding them to his sense of the pity and misery of human life shared and saved in Jesus Christ.

His training began when he was 14 and an apprentice in a factory producing stained glass. He worked there for five years, and was trained in the restoration of medieval stained glass, such as at Chartres Cathedral. He was deeply influenced by the tight formality and the brilliant colours of the leaded lights, quite apart from the religious subject matter of the windows. The second element emerges from his whole development as an artist. In 1891, aged 20, he entered the École des Beaux-Arts in Paris, where he soon became one of the favourite pupils of the Symbolist painter, Gustave Moreau. After Moreau's death in 1898 Rouault became the curator of a small museum in Paris dedicated to his teacher's work. Henri Matisse had been a fellow-pupil of Moreau's, and for a time Rouault and Matisse were linked together in their painting style. They both exhibited at the Paris Salon d'Automne in 1905, and they and other painters like them were known as *Les Fauves* (the Wild Beasts) because of the primitive savagery of their paintings, their arbitrary use of strong colours and the deliberate flouting of the rules of drawing and perspective. Colour was used as a direct means of *expressing* something rather than as descriptive representation. Until the beginning of the First World War Rouault's most effective medium was watercolour or oil on paper, with dominant blues, dramatic lighting, emphatic forms and an expressive scribble.

The one word always used to describe Rouault's style is *expressionist*. There had been considerable personal turmoil in his life in this period; for a while he was estranged from his family; and he was coming to the commitment of faith that would see him through the rest of his life. It was his Christian commitment that was to separate him from all the great artists who were his contemporaries, but he had a real independence of mind, as he showed also with Léon Bloy. He once wrote:

Just about anybody can be a rebel: it is a much more difficult undertaking to obey silently the dictates of one's soul and to spend one's life looking for the finest means to express one's temperament and talents.[40]

It is clear that Rouault did not think of painting as 'an end in itself and for itself ...' For him the work of art was, as Jacques Maritain said, 'good in relation to something beyond itself'. The beautiful – that word which, fortunately, we no longer spell with a capital letter – was not limited for Rouault to the pleasing, the graceful, the pretty, the hedonistic; it encompassed all the feelings, including the terrible and the terrifying, that affect the human soul. In mid-February 1946 Rouault wrote to me, 'I belong to a much older generation – to a vanished time when those who pretended to uphold the established concept of beauty would excommunicate you from the Grand Salon.' For Rouault, however, art was not a game, a distraction, a luxury intended only to provide relaxation for some wealthy Croesus. It offered the painter the possibility of communicating with other men through drawing and colour, through pigment that the artist has kneaded and worked; it was an outpouring of the heart, the unfolding of a secret launched into space and time, a form of prayer.

Pierre Courthion[41]

If you look at one of Rouault's moving portraits of Christ[42] or one of his Crucifixions, you will at once see how the former stained-glass apprentice and wild expressionist *Fauve* come together in these images. Rouault built up thick layers of intense colour, to give a glowing, almost transparent quality, like the sun shining through a stained-glass window. He also surrounded and divided the main image with heavy black lines, which not only make the colours shine even brighter by contrast, but remind the viewer of the dividing lines of lead in a stained-glass window. The stark and simplified rendering of the face of Christ with the long nose, the dark surround of hair and beard and the huge, black-centred eyes conveys enormous strength and compassion and suffering. If words could do justice to it, we wouldn't need to look at the pictures; but we do need the pictures, for in them we see someone who inhabits the same rough and grief-filled world as the judges, the prostitutes and the clowns and yet one who is able to bear and sustain it – to save it.

Rouault lived until 1958, always continuing to work at his art. Ambroise Vollard, the art dealer who had commissioned so many of his engravings, died in 1939, with many of Rouault's works, often unfinished, still in his possession. Eight years later Rouault successfully sued Vollard's heirs for his right of ownership of these works. He then publicly burned 315 of them, because he felt they did not represent his best work. It is possible that a million euros in today's art values went up in smoke that day.

One day I asked Rouault the question I had already asked Matisse: 'If you were cut off from your fellowmen forever, condemned to live on a desert island until you breathed your last breath, and you knew that your art would never again be seen by anyone, would you go on painting?' Matisse's answer had been no. Rouault's was this: 'Of course I would go on; I would have need of that spiritual dialogue'.

Pierre Courthion[43]

Lord Christ,
our Saviour and our Friend,
who shared the world of kings and
prostitutes, of clowns and judges,

give us time and deep attention for the
images of Georges Rouault,
so that we may know, beyond all words,
that you have borne and transfigured our
corruption and our grief.
We ask this of your eternal compassion.

৵ ৫

Many people were drawn to the National Gallery in 2000 and were profoundly moved by the exhibition *Seeing Salvation,* and this showed that if people were gently and subtly led into the right context for interpreting the works of artists in the Christian tradition, they would experience them as powerfully meaningful, as evoking a spiritual response. Increasingly preachers and retreat leaders are realizing that making works of art a focus for meditation does half the work for them, because many of the greatest artists are also theologians, posing new questions and suggesting new meanings in the familiar Christian story. Such use of theology and spirituality may even succeed in reclaiming some Christian art of the past from the museums and galleries, those secular temples of aestheticism.

৵ ৫

Christ,
image of the invisible God,
artist of wisdom at God's side,
give us the grace to contemplate your beauty
and the glory of all you have made
in the works of those who have served you
faithfully
in pigment, metal, wood and stone.

Chapter 6

Those to whom 'God gave skill that he might be glorified in his works'
Scientists who were Christians

In the letters column of my local newspaper a representative of the British Humanist Association recently suggested that people should honour the 197th birthday in 2006 of Charles Darwin. The purpose of such a secular 'saint's day' was to celebrate the light of truth that had shone in Darwin's theory of the evolution of species and to combat the growing menace of religious groups with their biblical creationist fantasies. My reaction to letters like that is one of discomfort. I accept the evidence for evolution over millions of years, and yet I am certainly not a humanist. I am perfectly happy to interpret the biblical story of 'creation' as an inspired intuition, in story form, of the relationship of God to the cosmos, and specifically to humanity; and so I do not wish, either, to stand with my creationist Christian brothers and sisters in their obsessive attachment to the kind of information I believe the Bible simply cannot give.

What is very clear is that there are still people on both sides willing to continue fighting the 'science versus religion' battle. Seeing Professor Richard Dawkins confronting the leader of an American evangelical mega-church on television increases the discomfort a hundredfold. This is a clash of Darwinian and biblical fundamentalisms, a pointless locking of horns. There has to be another way. Part of that other way must be the celebration of great scientists who were also Christians, people who wanted to investigate the wonders of God's creation and who certainly did not believe they were the Church's 'enemy within'.

Of course, Christianity's difficulties with science as it has developed in the last four centuries must not be minimized. Many of the Bible's myths and miracles have seemed to be undermined by the discovery of scientific 'laws' which exclude the possibility of their occurrence. The more that naturalistic and materialistic explanations for all the phenomena of the cosmos are provided, the less it seems necessary to posit a God as creator and sustainer. And why bother with theological speculation when there is so much fascinating scientific knowledge to be discovered? The thesis of the Church's obstinate and obscurantist opposition to all scientific progress was very strongly proclaimed in Victorian England, and the recent revival of simplistic creationist ideas among many Christians has given that thesis new legs.

But the matter is definitely not as simple as one of age-old ideological conflict. A number of significant things need to be borne in mind:

- From almost the beginning of Christian biblical interpretation, for example, with Origen or Augustine, there was the realization that many texts simply could not be interpreted literally. Christians have never been bound to a one-level literalist (scientific!) interpretation.

- Discovering in detail the 'how' of creation does not in itself lead inevitably to atheism. Quantum mechanics and the many uncertainties about the development of the universe and the progress of evolution leave huge scope for thought and theology about the role of God in all this. Scientists and theologians may well be able to collaborate in attempting to probe the mysteries of the universe – provided both sides are willing to forswear arrogant, overconfident conclusions, recognizing the limits of their knowledge.

- The story of the Church's opposition to scientific enquiry, when investigated in detail, turns out to be by no means so clear-cut as many would have it.

In his book on the history of science and religion John Hedley Brooke wrote:

> Serious scholarship in the history of science has revealed so extraordinarily rich and complex a relationship between science and religion in the past that general theses are difficult to sustain. The real lesson turns out to be the complexity. Members of the Christian churches have not all been obscurantists; many scientists of stature have professed a religious faith, even if their theology was sometimes suspect. Conflicts allegedly between science and religion may turn out to be between rival scientific interests, or conversely between rival theological factions. Issues of political power, social prestige, and intellectual authority have repeatedly been at stake.[1]

Even in the famous case of Galileo, whose evidence that the earth moved round the sun was published in 1632 and who was then forced to recant by the Church, one can adduce factors modifying the apparent intransigence and blindness of the Church leadership and bureaucracy, such as: the fact of considerable sympathy and agreement with Galileo's view in many parts of the Church hierarchy; the political pressures on Rome created by the Reformation churches; Galileo's own arrogance and tactlessness in the way he put forward and published his research.

These factors do not, of course, wipe out the Church's abusive behaviour towards Galileo, but what remains very striking is that Galileo himself remained a committed and convinced Christian. Rodney Stark has recently sought to substantiate the view that it was uniquely western Christianity that provided the world-view and energy for the emergence of modern science. He reviews the rival claims of the ancient Greek world, of China and of Islam, but concludes that Christianity alone depicted God as a rational, responsive, dependable and omnipotent being and the universe as God's personal creation with a rational, lawful, stable structure awaiting human comprehension; and therefore:

> The rise of science was not an extension of classical learning. It was the natural outgrowth of Christian doctrine: Nature exists because it was created by God. To love and honour God, one must fully appreciate the wonders of his handiwork. Moreover, because God is perfect, his handiwork functions in accord with *immutable principles*. By the full use of our God-given powers of reason and observation, we ought to be able to discover those principles.[2]

Laurel C. Schneider maintains a stronger Christian link with classical learning, but sees the same outcome:

> [Thomas Aquinas] argued prodigiously for 'natural theology': a study of the natural world in the style of 'the philosopher' (his shorthand for Aristotle) that would expose God's purposes and meaning in creation. The academic world of the twelfth century West was lodged entirely in ecclesial bodies and monasteries where the emphasis on study had been mystical on the one hand and focused on abstract principles of divinity on the other. Following Thomas meant that Christian scholars could read the pre-Christian, pagan Aristotle, open the doors of the church, and begin again to take account of empirical data without risking theological censure. This deceptively simple change in focus ushered in a new era of scholarship, one that would eventually explode into the heavens and begin what the West calls the scientific revolution.[3]

What is certain is that most of the pioneers of modern science were committed Christians, and while the extra freedom of mind that the Reformation contributed was an additional positive factor, we actually find the great names of the scientific revolution in the sixteenth and seventeenth centuries to be pretty equally spread between Protestant and Catholic adherence. Many of these scientists experienced a joyful wonder as they contemplated the beauty and order of what they uncovered in the working of God's world.

> In late eighteenth- and early nineteenth-century Europe, it was not unusual to hear naturalists speaking of their scientific awakening in terms that might be used of a religious conversion. One could experience a sense of ecstasy at the disclosure of nature's secrets and a sense of the sublime in contemplating its works.[4]

This 'conversion' could of course lead to a wholly secular stance in which science completely replaced religion; and that brings us into the modern world, in which scientific enquiry is completely autonomous and does not have to relate itself to the requirements and theology of any religious institution, and in which many scientists are either indifferent or positively antagonistic towards religion.

But many scientists are still religious and see no conflict between their research and their faith. John Polkinghorne has expressed the relationship of science and theology like this:

> [They] are concerned with the exploration of different aspects of human experience: in the one case, our impersonal encounter with a physical world that we transcend; in the other, our personal encounter with the One who transcends us. They use different methods: in

the one case, the experimental procedure of putting matters to the test; in the other, the commitment of trust which must underlie all personal encounter, whether between ourselves or with the reality of God. They ask different questions: in the one case, how things happen, by what process; in the other, why things happen, to what purpose. Though these are two different questions, yet, the ways we answer them must bear some consonant relationship to each other.[5]

And yet the old narrative in which religion opposes science still holds sway over many minds. Richard Harries recently wrote:

I wonder whether we Christians actually celebrate science enough? I don't just mean its achievements but the very fact that it has given us a way into understanding the world in which we live and the daily miracles about us that sustain us in being. It could be that the popular myth that religion is opposed to science would be dissipated somewhat if it was clearly seen that Christians are not just on the side of science but celebrating it and caring about the vocations of those who work in scientific fields.[6]

One way of demonstrating that science can be grounded in a religious understanding of existence is by celebrating and studying the lives and careers of some of the great scientific pioneers who were also Christians, like Roger Bacon, Robert Boyle, Gregor Mendel, and many others.

Roger Bacon
c. 1214–c. 1292

Roger Bacon was born about 1214, possibly at Ilchester in Somerset, and he died in 1292, probably at Oxford. He studied and possibly lectured on arts in Oxford, and later lectured at Paris, where he was a pioneer in teaching Aristotle's natural philosophy. After some time, and influenced by Robert Grosseteste (later to be Bishop of Lincoln) and the Franciscan school at Oxford, he had a significant change of interest, and began to study scientific and technological subjects. He was also influenced by a work attributed to (but in fact not written by) Aristotle, the *Secretum Secretorum* (The Secret of Secrets), which is in the form of a long letter on kingship to Alexander the Great and strongly recommends the usefulness of philosophy, science and medicine. At some point, perhaps about 1257, Bacon joined the Franciscan order, which was certainly not a natural step for someone of his intellectual and curious nature. He also returned to live in Paris for about 10 years.

> For twenty years in which I specifically worked on the study of wisdom, turning away from the opinion of the common herd, I expended more than two thousand pounds on this, because of secret books and different experiments and languages and instruments and tables etc; also for seeking out friendships with wise people, and for assistants in languages, in designs, in mathematics, in tables, in instruments and many other things.
>
> Roger Bacon[7]

The first of his major writings emerged from a friendship with Guy Foulquois, who, formerly a lawyer and soldier, became a cardinal in 1261 and three years later Pope Clement IV. The new pope commanded Bacon to send him an account of his theories and wisdom in writing, and so Bacon quickly got down to work, eventually sending off the *Opus Maius* (the bigger work) which was in seven parts covering the causes of human ignorance, the relation of the other sciences to theology, grammar and the power of languages, mathematics (which included astronomy and astrology), optics, experimental science and moral philosophy. As soon as he had sent the book, a writer's natural anxieties started gnawing at Bacon: Would the work get lost on the way? What if it were too bulky for a busy pope to wade through? What about the subjects he'd been forced to leave even out of so huge a tome? So he started on the *Opus Minus* (the smaller work), which summarized and supplemented the larger work, and eventually entrusted it to his favourite pupil John to take to Pope Clement. He then wrote an *Opus Tertium* (the third work); we don't know if it was ever sent; and we don't even know whether the pope received and read any of Bacon's work – he died only four years after his election.

A thorough consideration of knowledge consists of two things, perception of what is necessary to obtain it and then of the method of applying it to all matters, that they may be directed by its means in the proper way. For by the light of knowledge the Church of God is governed, the commonwealth of the faithful is regulated, the conversion of unbelievers is secured, and those who persist in their malice can be held in check, by the excellence of knowledge, so that they may be driven off from the borders of the Church in a better way than by shedding of Christian blood.

Roger Bacon[8]

Bacon continued to write, aiming to produce a compendium or systematic treatise of all his knowledge. By about 1270 he was back in Oxford, but then found himself in trouble from his order. In 1278 the master-general of the Franciscans, Girolamo da Ascoli, 'condemned and disapproved of the teaching of Brother Roger Bacon, Englishman, Doctor of Sacred Theology, as containing certain suspect novelties on account of which the said Roger was condemned to be imprisoned' (Chronica XXIV Generalium). He may well have remained a prisoner until 1290, when the new master-general, Raimondo Gaufredi, had him released – at the age of almost 80, and not long before his death. We do not know precisely what the charges were that were brought against Bacon, but he could well have made himself unpopular by the contempt with which he wrote about other contemporary intellectuals, and for his keenness to study astrology.

In what sense was Bacon a pioneer of modern science?

We can glimpse the scientific spirit in a number of areas of his work.

- He felt that the ancients had the key to much wisdom, and therefore good, accurate translations of their work were vital.

- He drew on the recently translated work of the Arabic scientist, Ibn al-Haytham (Alhazen), on optics, agreeing with him that vision was effected by light and colour coming into the eye rather than by visual rays being projected out of it, although he still thought there must be some action proceeding outwards from the eye. Bacon had several parabolic burning mirrors, as described by al-Haytham, made for his own use. It is clear from his writing that he made numerous observations in the field of optics which could properly be described as experiments.

If a man looks at letters or other small objects through the medium of a crystal or a glass or of some other transparent body placed above the letters, and it is the smaller part of a sphere whose convexity is towards the eye, and the eye is in the air, he will see the letters much better and they will appear larger to him. For in accordance with the truth ... all conditions are favourable for magnification ... Therefore this instrument is useful to the aged and to those with weak eyes. For they can see the letter, no matter how small, sufficiently enlarged.

Roger Bacon[9]

- Bacon wrote much about astrology and believed in the influence of the celestial bodies in human events on earth, but towards the latter part of his life he modified his view about the absolute reliability of astrology alone; now he said that a good practitioner would need other skills as well, such as knowledge of physiognomy, alchemy, agriculture and so on – and it might help if the expert himself had been born under the right celestial configuration! This, we might say, is a rational application of medieval knowledge.

- Bacon believed that an important way to restore human knowledge, which had been corrupted since the time of the wise figures of long ago, was through what he called *scientia experimentalis*. This 'experimental science' was something very new for the thirteenth century, but a long way from what we would understand by that term. By it Bacon meant everything from the accumulated experience of human beings in both ordinary and even quasi-mystic mode through to the testing of something in repeated practice, but he himself did not carry out experiments in any *systematic* way. He was more like a modern science writer than a practising

183

scientist. Nevertheless, when he writes about the formation of rainbows or of haloes round the sun and moon, he seems quite close to modern science.

As he writes about the knowledge of one Petrus Peregrinus, who was possibly a contemporary military engineer and who was famous for his work on magnetism, we get an idea of what Bacon meant by 'experimental science'.

> He investigated all works of founding metals, and all things that are worked with gold, silver, other metals and all minerals; and he knew all that pertained to warfare and arms and hunting; and he examined all that were for agriculture and the measurement of fields and rural works; also he considered the experiments, divinations and charms of old women and all magicians, and similarly the illusions and devices of all jugglers, so that nothing that should be known would be hidden from him, and he would know how far to reject them as false and magical.
>
> Roger Bacon[10]

Bacon was certainly concerned to reject what was false and magical, and to find a rational or naturalistic theory to explain things. He thought that substances radiated likenesses, or 'species', of themselves in all directions, and that this could include everything from heat emanating from the sun to the astrological influence of the stars, and even to a set of words uttered with a certain psychic power and intention. He thought that heavenly influences could explain why people differed from each other in custom and culture; and – another flash of rational or 'scientific' thinking in the midst of irrational and unproved assumptions – he believed that if you used a big mirror to beam back again whatever influence was heading your way from the sky, you could nullify its action.

Roger Bacon cannot be counted the happiest of men. He evidently 'thought too much' for his contemporaries and sailed too close to the wind, so that he failed to reach the eminence he believed he deserved and instead found imprisonment and obloquy in his old age. Even after his death his fame was as an alchemist and as a magician, and he was caricatured as a sort of Franciscan mad professor. Today he is beginning to earn some just praise, as the one who took some of the first steps in thinking 'outside the church box' and beginning that empirical enquiry which is science's mainspring.

> To neglect knowledge is to neglect virtue; the intellect lightened by the flame of goodness cannot help but love it. Love is only born of knowledge. Reason is the guide of a right will. It is reason which leads us to salvation. The true and the good are one; in order to do good one must know it; in order to avoid evil one must discern it; ignorance is the mother of sin; the man surrounded by darkness throws himself into evil as a blind man into a ditch; the enlightened man, on the contrary, may neglect his duty but his conscience returns to repentance and to right ideas.
>
> Roger Bacon[11]

Now, O God, we see reality as in a mirror, darkly,
but you speak truth to us in revelation and reason.
Open our eyes wide through the spirit of Roger Bacon to all we can know of your beauty,
and so prepare us for the full majesty of your glory,
when we shall see you face to face.

৪০ ୧୫

Robert Boyle
1627–91

> The *virtuosi* I speak of ... those, that understand and cultivate experimental philosophy, make a much greater and better use of experience in their philosophical researches. For they consult experience both frequently and heedfully; and, not content with the phenomena, that nature spontaneously affords them, they are solicitous, when they find it needful, to enlarge their experience by trials purposely devised; and ever and anon reflecting upon it, they are careful to conform their opinions to it; or, if there be just cause, reform their opinions by it. So that our *virtuosi* have a peculiar right to the distinguishing title that is often given to them, of experimental philosophers.
>
> Robert Boyle[12]

The Christian Virtuoso which Robert Boyle published in 1690, near the end of his life, is an apologia for the role of the scientist who is a Christian. In contrast to those who base their theories on speculation, popular tradition or abstract reason, the good virtuoso constantly and systematically conducts experiments and reflects on the results, providing solid ground on which to understand the workings of the world and therefore refining our sense of the intricate wonders of God's creation. It is no exaggeration to say that Boyle's own life was a rich exemplification of the Christian virtuoso. He was both a committed Christian and a committed scientist (or, in the language of his day, a natural philosopher).

Robert Boyle was born in 1627 into one of the wealthiest families in Britain. His father was the First Earl of Cork and, following his mother's death in 1630, his father was responsible for his education, until at the age of eight he went to Eton College. Following a short period with a tutor, then travels in Europe, including a time of study in Geneva, Robert returned to England in 1644. After some months in London staying with his sister, Lady Ranelagh, he moved to Stalbridge in Dorset, where his father had bequeathed him the manor house and estate. Here he began his career as a writer, with ethical and devotional tracts, although he published nothing until 1655.

In his autobiographical writing, Boyle described a strong religious experience during his time in Europe, caused by an awe-inspiring thunderstorm. This, he said, had had a formative influence on the rest of his life. But an equally powerful change happened to him in 1649 when he set up a laboratory in the house at Stalbridge and began to carry out experiments, with chemical and alchemical trials involving mercury and other substances, and the use of microscopes to view the minute structure of living things. About the same time he also became very interested in the original languages of the Bible, in which his later expertise impressed his contemporaries. So the stage was set for his role as the Christian virtuoso, the experimental scientist and Christian apologist, to which he devoted the rest of his life.

And indeed, the experimental philosophy giving us a more clear discovery, than strangers to it have, of the divine excellencies displayed in the fabrick and conduct of the universe, and of the creatures it consists of, very much indisposeth the mind, to ascribe such admirable effects to so incompetent and pitiful a cause as blind chance, or the tumultuous justlings of atomical portions of senseless matter; and leads it directly to the acknowledgement and adoration of a most intelligent, powerful, and benign author of things, to whom alone such excellent productions may, with the greatest congruity, be ascribed.

Robert Boyle[13]

At the end of 1655 Boyle moved to Oxford and joined the lively group of natural philosophers based at Wadham College under the auspices of John Wilkins. After the latter left for Cambridge in 1659, the group met at Robert's lodgings on the High Street. In 1655 Boyle was created doctor of physick, the only academic degree he acquired. Here Robert Hooke became his associate, assisting in some of his crucial experiments, including the ones with the air pump, which Hooke himself had constructed. With the pump they were able to investigate air pressure and the vacuum, and their discoveries were published in Boyle's first scientific publication, *Experiments Physico-Mechanicall, Touching the Spring of the Air and its Effects* (1660). They were able to reject the notion that 'nature abhors a vacuum', showing how it was perfectly possible to produce one. They illustrated the characteristics and functions of air by studying the effects of its withdrawal on flame, light, sound and living creatures. One of their findings (published in 1662) later became known as Boyle's Law: this expresses the inverse relationship which exists between the pressure and volume of a gas. It was determined by measuring the volume occupied by a constant quantity of air when compressed by differing weights of mercury.

In such works as *The Sceptical Chymist* (1661) and *The Origine of Forms and Qualities* (1666) Boyle advocated a 'mechanical philosophy', seeing the universe as like a huge machine or clock. All his experiments were geared to discovering the precise workings of the 'mechanism' of creation, and he regarded this approach as revealing the order and beauty and purpose which the mind of God had built into and maintained in the world. He stood out against the atheistic materialism of Thomas Hobbes, against Descartes' view that God was not involved in the detailed running of the world, and against the older Aristotelian idea that everything was based on the interplay of four elements (earth, air, fire, water) or the alchemists' scheme of the three prime elements (sulphur, salt, mercury). Instead he built on the ideas of Francis Bacon, followed by Gassendi and Descartes, and said that natural changes and sensory effects were caused by interactions between minute bodies, which he called 'corpuscles'. Boyle refrained from using the term 'atoms' for them, because that term was part of the old Epicurean view which saw the world as the accidental result of chance movements and combinations of 'atoms', and he was quite clear, the more he discovered about the processes and designs of nature, that there was a divine mind fully and directly responsible for them.

> He, that sees the admirable fabric of the coats, humours, and muscles of the eye, and how excellently all the parts are adapted to the making up of an organ of vision, can scarce forbear to believe, that the author of nature intended it should serve the animal, to which it belongs, to see with ... When, upon the anatomical dissection, and the optical consideration, of a human eye, we see it as exquisitely fitted to be an organ of sight, as the best artificer in the world could have framed a little engine, purposely and mainly designed for the use of seeing; it is very harsh and incongruous, to say, that an artificer, who is too intelligent either to do things by chance, or to make a curious piece of workmanship, without knowing what uses it is fit for, should not design it for an use, to which it is most fit.
>
> Robert Boyle[14]

From the late 1650s, after the move to Oxford, Robert Boyle was intensely involved in scientific research, and books outlining his own findings and those of others, together with his own reflections on natural philosophy and theology, poured from him. He published over 40 books in his lifetime, comprising more than three million words, not counting the many unpublished papers that exist. After a serious illness in 1654 his eyesight was badly affected, forcing him to depend upon assistants to write down his prose. This undoubtedly gave his style a certain expansive digressiveness, reflecting his actual manner of speaking.

In comparison with his research and writing, politics and national and ecclesiastical affairs took second place in his life. On the Calvinist wing of the Church of England in the tempestuous times of the Civil War and the Commonwealth, he nevertheless always had a concern for religious tolerance and co-existence. After the Restoration he had personal contact with royalty. He became governor of the Company for the Propagation of the Gospel in New England and used considerable sums of his own money to support evangelical activities. For example, he helped pay for a Turkish New Testament and Catechism, supported a Lithuanian exile in his efforts to get a Lithuanian Bible published, and supported rural ministers in Ireland. Attempts were made by the Earls of Clarendon and Southampton to persuade Boyle to become a bishop – he was, of course, a layman, throughout his life – but he declined on the ground that he had 'never felt the Inward Vocation'. One of the codicils to his will provided for the setting up of lectures for the defence of the Christian religion against atheists and others, the Boyle Lectures.

> That the consideration of the vastness, beauty, and regular motions, of the heavenly bodies; the excellent structure of animals and plants; besides a multitude of other phaenomena of nature, and the subserviency of most of these to man; may justly induce him, as a rational creature, to conclude, that this vast, beautiful, orderly, and (in a word) many ways admirable system of things, that we call the world, was framed by an author supremely powerful, wise, and good, can scarce

> be denied by an intelligent and unprejudiced considerer.
>
> Robert Boyle[15]

From the time of the Restoration Boyle continued to live in Oxford, but was frequently in London. He was present at the inauguration of the Royal Society on 28 November 1660 and was very involved in its activities and publications on experimental philosophy in its early years. In 1668 he moved permanently to London and lived for the rest of his life on Pall Mall with his beloved sister, Lady Ranelagh. Here he had his own quarters and also a laboratory, located in a 'back house'. The laboratory became a place of pilgrimage for admirers near and far, and John Evelyn could claim that 'one who had not seene Mr Boyle, was look'd-on as missing one of the most valuable Objects of our Nation'. In 1670 Boyle suffered a stroke, which curtailed some of his outside activities, but his experiments and publications continued. He died on 31 December 1691, just eight days after his sister. A vast crowd attended his funeral at St Martin-in-the-Fields.

Robert Boyle was a fervent scientist and a fervent Christian. He had himself taken a vow of lifelong chastity, and he was a man of scrupulous, possibly over-scrupulous, probity and piety. 'The very Name of God was never mentioned by him without a Pause and a visible stop in his Discourse.' He was also totally committed to the experimental method of science and he was convinced that such rigorous experimentation could only reveal more of the exquisite intricacies of God's creative power. And yet he was always ready to acknowledge that there were things in God's omniscience and power which were beyond human knowing and which might sometimes transcend the regulating laws of the cosmos. But that should never inhibit the reverent investigator of God's world, of whom he was such a supreme example.

And, for my part, I am apt to think, there is more of admirable contrivance in a man's muscles, than in (what we yet know of) the coelestial orbs; and that the eye of a fly is, (at least as far as appears to us,) a more curious piece of workmanship, than the body of the sun ... And there is incomparably more art expressed in the structure of a dog's foot, than in that of the famous clock of Strasburg.

Robert Boyle[16]

The heavens are telling your glory, Lord,
and your artful design is revealed in the eye
of a fly.
May we study you in the book of nature,
like Robert Boyle, with rigour and precision,
humility and trust,
refusing sentimental speculation,
not fearing questions,
and begin to find you,
a God not too small.

ଚ୦ ଓଃ

Gregor Mendel
1822–84

Yes, his laurels shall never fade,
Though time shall suck down by its vortex
Whole generations into the abyss,
Though naught but moss-grown fragments
Shall remain of the epoch
In which the genius appeared.
May the might of destiny grant me
The supreme ecstasy of earthly joy,
The highest goal of earthly ecstasy,

That of seeing, when I arise from the tomb,
My art thriving peacefully
Amongst those who are to come after me.

Gregor Mendel[17]

That adolescent hope, written by one Johann Mendel about Johann Gutenberg, the inventor of movable type, while Mendel was at school in the Gymnasium at Troppau in Moravia, was to be in a striking fashion fulfilled. The obscure monk of the nineteenth century was to be feted and admired only after his death by the scientists of the following century. But this is a story not only of an individual's determination and genius but also of a Roman Catholic monastery's institutional commitment to science.

Johann Mendel was born of peasant stock in Heizendorf (Hyneice today, in the Czech Republic) in 1822. He was a gifted child, and after leaving the Gymnasium at the age of 16, he took a two-year course at the Philosophy Institute at Olomouc University, but poverty was a constant threat and drain upon him. In a brief curriculum vitae which he wrote, in the third person, in 1850, about his earlier life, he said, about the period at Olomouc: 'The anxious, dreary outlook which the future offered him affected him so powerfully at that time that he fell sick and was compelled to spend a year with his parents to recover.'[18] His sister then gave up part of her dowry, and this enabled him to finish his course.

Then came the critical decision of Mendel's life. He had already developed a deep interest in natural science, but his lack of resources made it impossible for him to think of going on to higher education. What was to be done? One of his professors at Olomouc suggested that he should join the Augustinian monastery of St Thomas at Brünn (Brno). Mendel entered the novitiate at St Thomas in September 1843 and took the name Gregor. He began his theological studies, and five years later he was ordained priest. He remained a monk of St Thomas for the rest of his life.

This was no ordinary monastery. It was already playing an important part in the practical and intellectual life of Moravia, thanks to its abbot, Cyrill Napp. The beginning of the nineteenth century saw a huge growth of interest in the agricultural and scientific challenges of breeding, whether of sheep or fruit trees or vines. Such improvements were vital to agriculture and scientific development. After The Agricultural Society of Moravia and Silesia was formed in 1806, agriculture and natural history became part of the university curriculum at Olomouc and Abbot Napp established an experimental nursery in his monastery. In 1825 he wrote a manual on how to grow improved varieties of fruit. When Mendel arrived at St Thomas, he found not only the experimental garden and fellow monks who were botanists, but also a fine library and colleagues who were philosophers, mathematicians and mineralogists.

Mendel soon discovered that teaching, not pastoral ministry, was his forte. Exposure to the sick and dying in a local hospital brought him close to a nervous breakdown. But he taught maths and classics for one year in the Gymnasium at Znojmo, and later began regular employment at the Realschule in Brno, teaching natural history. In spite of twice failing his teacher's qualification examination in Vienna, he was considered an excellent teacher and science demonstrator and was well loved by his pupils. Abbot Napp believed Gregor to be clever enough to be sent to Vienna University for two years (1851–53), where he studied physics, maths and chemistry, as well as entomology, palaeontology, botany and plant physiology. It was after this that he began, in the large new greenhouse built by the abbot in St Thomas, his research on the heredity of peas.

During the fifties and sixties of the nineteenth century, anyone passing [through the garden of the Augustinian monastery] might have seen, on fine spring days, a vigorous, short, rather sturdily built and somewhat corpulent man engaged in a laborious occupation which would have been puzzling to any uninstructed observer. Here there were to be seen, clinging to staves, the branches of trees, and stretched strings, hundreds of pea-plants of the most various kinds, with white and with violet blossoms, both tall and dwarf, some destined to bear smooth and others wrinkled peas. The gardener would move from one flower to another, opening with fine forceps the blossoms that had not opened spontaneously, removing the keel, and carefully detaching the anthers. Then with a camel-hair brush he would dust the pollen upon the stigma of another plant and would subsequently enwrap the flower thus treated in a little bag of paper or calico, to prevent any industrious bee or enterprising pea-weevil from transferring pollen from some other flower to the stigma thus treated, and in this way invalidating the result of the hybridization experiment.

Hugo Iltis[19]

For seven years (1856–63) Mendel grew generations of peas (*Pisum sativum*) in the monastery garden. He began by letting them self-pollinate, to isolate those that bred 'true', then he systematically cross-bred them, watching what happened to a specific and limited number of characteristics – for example: seed shape (round or wrinkled), colour of unripe pod (green or yellow) or height (tall or dwarf) – as the plants were crossed with each other and produced a whole series of new generations. A vital and pioneering aspect of his experiments was that he used very large numbers, counting the peas and pea-plants that were produced in each generation, and so arriving at statistically reliable proportions of each characteristic.

One wonders whether counting peas, for Mendel, almost took the place of counting rosary beads; perhaps the effect was equally hypnotic and in a strange way prayerful.

Two fundamental facts of genetics emerged from Mendel's research in the cross-fertilization of peas. They are now known as the Law of Independent Assortment and the Law of Segregation.

The first of these tells us that offspring are not just a simple blend or mixture of their parents' characteristics. What happens is that, for each separate characteristic (for example, its pod colour for a pea), the offspring receives – quite independently from other factors – one factor (now called a 'gene') from each parent. If both parental genes received are for green, the new pea pod will be green; if both parental genes are for yellow, the new pea will be yellow; *but* if one parental gene is for green and the other for yellow, the new pea will be ... yellow. Why? Because the gene for yellow is 'dominant', while the gene for green is 'recessive'. But the yellow offspring (with its recessive green gene) may become parent of a green child if the child receives another gene for green in fertilization. The green pea pod colour may disappear for generations, only to reappear much later. The gene for green, though recessive and not affecting the outward appearance of the succession of yellow pods, had never gone away. Mendel was able to calculate the predictable proportions of green to yellow peas down the generations, and how many would actually have a recessive gene for green even though the pod looked yellow.

The other law is the Law of Segregation. Each parent has, of course, two genes, inherited from *its* parents, for any one characteristic (for example two genes for green pod, or two for yellow, or one of each), but this parent only contributes *one* of these to its child, the other parent providing the other gene. Mendel realized that the process of 'selecting' which of its two genes to pass on to its child was in fact not a selection at all, but an absolutely random process, like tossing a coin. So a hundred parents that had a green and a yellow gene for pod colour were likely, on average, to contribute 50 green and 50 yellow genes to their offspring, but entirely at random.

The investigator's patience was indefatigable. At the end of [Mendel's] second letter to Nägeli [Professor of Botany at Munich], we read, 'The experiments progress slowly. At first a certain amount of patience was needed, but I soon found that matters went better when I was conducting several experiments simultaneously. Thus from spring right on into autumn I was able, day after day, to approach my work with reawakened interest, and the labour I devoted to my protégés was richly rewarded. My happiness will be redoubled if, by my experiments, I can only succeed in finding the solution of the problem.' His fondness for his plants was shown by a little joke he often made ... When visitors came, and he had taken them for a turn in the garden, he would say apropos of nothing in particular, but quite seriously: 'Now I am going to show you my children!' Having noted with a smile the astonishment that would naturally be aroused by such a remark from a priest, he would lead the visitors to see the peas in his experimental plot.

Hugo Iltis[20]

Mendel reported on his research with peas in two lectures given to the Brno Natural Science Society early in 1865. The lectures, entitled *Experiments on Plant Hybrids*, were published in the Society's *Proceedings*, and Mendel sent reprints to respected scientists throughout Europe. The result was not overwhelming. No one recognized the great scientific breakthrough that Mendel had achieved, and even Professor Nägeli at Munich, with whom he corresponded for six years, did not 'get it'. In 1862 Mendel had visited London with a group from Brno to see the first London Annual Exhibition. He had not yet read Charles Darwin's *On the Origin of Species*, although he was soon to do so, and it is highly unlikely that he ever met its author. Had he done so, or if his pea experiments had been taken up and understood by the scientific community, he would have been able to throw considerable light on the precise way species may change and adapt through the generations.

In 1868 Gregor Mendel was elected abbot of St Thomas following the death of Cyrill Napp. This inevitably severely curtailed his opportunities for further research, as he took responsibility for the leadership and administration of the monastery. He became vice-president of the Brno Agricultural Society, and this involved him in much work offering expert advice and sitting on committees. He spent a lot of time and energy cultivating new strains of fruit trees in the monastery. For some years after the pea experiments, he tried to set up similar programmes with other plants such as beans and hawkweed (Hieracium). Hawkweed had been suggested by Professor Nägeli, but its pollination needed a magnifying glass, and Mendel's eyesight was failing; nor did they realize that hawkweed uses asexual reproduction, which made clear results impossible to achieve. One other factor curtailed Mendel's botanical researches: as he wrote to Professor Nägeli,

> My plan of studying Hieracium in situ during the present summer was only fulfilled to a very moderate extent. Of course lack of time was the main trouble; but, besides this, I am no longer well fitted for botanical expeditions, seeing that Heaven has blessed me with an excess of avoirdupois, and this makes long walks and especially hill climbing very difficult for me in a world where universal gravitation prevails.[21]

Mendel's last years were clouded by failing health and by an endlessly protracted struggle over new taxation which he refused to pay from the monastery to the government. One consolation was a happy relationship with his sister's sons; he was able to support them financially in their medical education, and so repay his sister's sacrifice for his own education. He died on 6 January 1884.

Exploiting fully the opportunities offered by the monastic life, the late abbot had devoted himself to the study of natural science and the pursuit of truth. Mendel's path was not a straightforward one; yet shortly before his death a future abbot of the monastery, Fr F Barina, heard him recall: 'Though I have suffered some bitter moments in my life, I must thankfully admit that most of it has been pleasant and good. My scientific work has brought me a great deal of satisfaction, and I am convinced that it will not be long before the whole world acknowledges it.'

Vitezslav Orel[22]

It was in fact another 16 years after Mendel's death before, in 1900, three botanists, Hugo de Vries, Carl Correns and Erich Tschermak, independently realized the true significance of Mendel's research. The new science of genetics was on its way.

Mendel is a curious wraith in history. His associates, his followers, are all in the next century. That is when his influence began. Yet if we are to understand him and the way he rescued Darwinism itself from oblivion we must go the long way back to Brünn in Moravia and stand among the green peas in a quiet garden. Gregor Mendel had a strange fate: he was destined to live one life painfully in the flesh at Brünn and another, the intellectual life of which he dreamed, in the following

century. His words, his calculations were to take a
sudden belated flight out of the dark tomblike volumes
and be written on hundreds of university blackboards,
and go spinning through innumerable heads.

Loren Eisley[23]

God of unfolding time,
in the evolution of living beings
and in the energies of Christendom
you brought forth Gregor Mendel,
to grasp the complex patterns of generation.
May we also hear your invitation
to investigate all the mysteries
of what we are.

℘ ℆

Albert Einstein once said, 'The most beautiful thing we
can experience is the mysterious. It is the source of all true
art and science.' It is perhaps striking that when
contemporary preachers seek for illustrations of their
theme most head towards the arts rather than the
sciences, but if religion concerns itself with that ever-
shifting point at which the known begins to shade into the
unknown, evoking a sense of power and mystery, then the
models and narratives of science ought to be used too. The
lives of those who first created those models and revealed
those narratives could then play an important role. The
current lists of those lives the Church recommends to its
members show little awareness of this possibility, wrongly
confirming the long-held suspicion that Christianity is
inimical to science.

℘ ℆

God, source and sustainer of the universe,
your Spirit drove the curiosity of human
beings to test ideas and intuitions in
experiments,
and to add reason to revelation.
As we thank you for the faith of so many
scientists,
we pray that their work will improve our
common life
and enlarge our wonder for the world you
have given us.
We ask this in Jesus' name.

Chapter 7

Those who 'were wise in their words of instruction'
Heroes of other faiths

It might well be objected that, for Christians to honour and celebrate people of other faiths is rather like the golf club giving trophies to cricketers, because they simply have no relevant authority to do so. Some Christians might well say that it is worse than that: more like a rugby team giving away 10 free points to the opposing team before the game even starts. Our task, it might be said, is to promote and celebrate the uniqueness of Jesus Christ and also the unique faith and actions of those who have followed him most closely; don't do the work of other faith communities for them.

Such views are of a very myopic religious character. For one thing, they are contradicted by that gospel tradition which tells us that, when a Roman centurion asked for Jesus' help for his slave who was ill and was willing to trust him implicitly, Jesus said, 'Truly I tell you, in no one in Israel have I found such faith.'[1] For the centurion's response of faith was not about desiring to become a Jew, let alone a Christian, at this moment in time, but, we may say, a pagan's awareness of the presence of God and his trust in it, in the hands of Jesus. Now that we have reached the twenty-first century, when the globe has become such a small place and people of other faiths are our neighbours, Christianity and all the world faiths must finally learn to live together, and be tolerant and respectful towards each other. Such respect and tolerance need not imply a desire to minimize or hide the unique qualities and tenets of each belief system, or involve the attempt to sweep them into one all-purpose theology, spirituality and ethic.

It may not, of course, be so easy. John Hick's famous parable suggests why that is so:

> We have been like a company of people marching down a long valley, singing our own songs, developing over the centuries our own stories and slogans, unaware that over the hill there is another valley, with another great company of people marching in the same direction, but with their own language and songs and stories and ideas; and over another hill yet another marching group – each ignorant of the existence of the others. But then one day they all come out onto the same plain, the plain created by modern global communications, and see each other and wonder what to make of one other. You might think that the different groups would then simply greet one another as fellow companies of pilgrims. But in fact that is made difficult by part of the content of our respective songs and stories. For if we are Christians, we have been singing for centuries that there is no other name given among men, whereby we may be saved, than the name of Jesus. And if we are Jews, we have been singing that we are God's only chosen people, a light to lighten the world. And if we are Muslims, we have been singing that Muhammad (peace be upon him) is the seal of the prophets, bringing God's latest and final revelation. And if we are Buddhists or Hindus, we have been singing yet other songs which imply that we have the highest truth while others have only lesser and partial truths.[2]

If we are to learn how to 'greet one another as fellow companies of pilgrims', then staying tightly within our communities is not an option. I am suggesting here that, from the Christian side, one aspect of our 'moving out' could be our remembering and honouring figures from the history of other religious groups. But if we did begin such remembering and honouring, would there be any dangers? It looks as though there could be two equal and opposite dangers: the danger of turning Christianity into a syncretistic soup in a rush to 'blend in' people of a very different religious world-view; and the danger of pouring a distinctive but patronizing Christian sauce all over the sharply differing features of people of radically other faiths.

We live, however, in a pluralist world, a world in which, in spite of the secularization theorists, the different religions with their unique characters are not suddenly going to fade away, and a world which now knows its need of respectful dialogue and deeper understanding across the boundaries of the faith communities. This is a world, moreover, in which we are just beginning to find out how it is possible to maintain our striking differences and intense commitments of faith and culture and politics, and yet still honour and understand (and engage in dialogue with and occasionally be influenced by) people of very different character and confession. Of course, there are many counter-examples to this claim – people who live in mutual ignorance, hatred and incomprehension; people who live in indifference, sweeping all religious ideas and differences into one (largely ignored) pot – but I repeat that the world knows quite clearly that the only way forward for people in different religious groups is education, equality of respect, dialogue and freedom of response. We should, therefore, know how to avoid the two dangers, of Christianity becoming subsumed under a generalization of all faiths, or of Christianity trying to colonize and tame the other faiths.

A number of factors, therefore, have motivated me in this section. The first is to open eyes to the distinctive riches which exist outside our Christian world, and to do it not in terms of systematic faith explanation, but rather through individual lives of brilliance and courage. Secondly, I wanted to counteract what can only be described as the tribal character of most Christian canonization until now, that is, the way in which the Spirit of God has only been recognized at work in people of orthodox faith (and sometimes indeed only in the more cautiously conservative, or only in priests and religious). For most of the 2,000 years of Christianity one would not have expected anything very different, of course, but now we live in a much changed world, and a sign of Christian strength and magnanimity would be for us to have some way of signalling our belief that the Spirit of God had been at work in people outside our tradition. We would not be denying the uniqueness of our faith, but enlarging our sense of God's power and possibilities.

Thirdly, it seemed good to me to choose some figures from other faiths who had had some relationship with or influence upon Christianity. There is a paradox here: a faith becomes distinctive and unique not only through its key foundational individuals and events but also through the outside influences that the world brings to bear on it. The more we as individual human beings derive from strong influences around us, the more we become ourselves; the greater the variety of influences, the stronger and more rounded our self becomes. So with the Church: having to accept the world of Greek philosophy immensely extended its intellectual range; the work of the scholastic theologians, above all Thomas Aquinas, would scarcely have been possible without the work of Islamic and Jewish theologians like al-Ghazali and Maimonides, passing on much ancient philosophy to them. Al-Ghazali shows us not just the giving up of wealth and possessions, like St Francis, but also the willingness to surrender intellectual power. And twentieth-century Christians received great inspiration from Mahatma Gandhi, who, although he could not bring himself to accept the Christian doctrine of the cross and resurrection of Christ, nevertheless lived in a more Christ-like way than even outstanding Christians and helps us to see what Jesus was really getting at in the unique combination of the personal and the political. These influences and relationships have helped the Church to be itself, only more so. They can still help Christians to be better Christians.

Finally, it is of immense spiritual benefit to 'read' the lives of great souls of other faiths, as David Tracy recommends we read the religious classics:

> Religious questions deliberately ask the question of the meaning and truth of Ultimate Reality not only as it is in itself but as it is existentially related to us. The religious classics are testimonies to the response of the religions to those questions. They are testimonies by human beings, who, like ourselves, have asked these questions and believe that they have received a response from Ultimate Reality itself. They believe, therefore, that some revelation has occurred giving them a new possibility of enlightenment or even some new way to formulate the question. They believe in following some way of religious liberation by which they may become related to all reality through a trusting relationship to that Ultimate Reality that as ultimate is the origin and end of all ... Any interpreter who is willing to ask the fundamental questions to which the religious classics respond can and should converse with them.[3]

It is – in contrast to some of the other Christian figures in this book – not at all surprising that the heroes and heroines of other faith systems were never honoured by the Church in past times. Perhaps even now it seems like a step too far. And yet in view of the desperate need for global and local harmony, perhaps the conversation with them could be an important statement that institutional definition and defensiveness are not the be-all and end-all – for the Christian Church, or for anybody.

Mohammad Al-Ghazali
1058–1111

> From my early youth, since I attained the age of puberty before I was twenty, until the present time when I am over fifty, I have ever recklessly launched out into the midst of these ocean depths, I have ever bravely embarked on this open sea, throwing aside all craven caution; I have poked into every dark recess, I have made an assault on every problem, I have plunged into every abyss, I have scrutinized the creed of every sect, I have tried to lay bare the inmost doctrines of every community. All this have I done that I might distinguish between true and false, between sound tradition and heretical innovation.
>
> Mohammad Al-Ghazali[4]

Just over a century before St Francis abandoned wealth and worldly glory for a life of poverty, prayer and compassion, an Islamic scholar who had achieved intellectual position and fame in Iraq also reached a point of no return and gave everything up for a life without his accustomed physical and rational support systems.

Abu Hamid Muhammad Al-Ghazali was a brilliant, indefatigable searcher for God. He was born in Tus in Persia in 1058 and, after his father's early death, he was brought up and taught by teachers in the Sufi tradition, the mystical tradition of Islam. His education would have started with the Qu'ran and the *ahadith* (the traditions about the example of the Prophet Muhammad) and included the teachings of the Sufi saints, inculcating asceticism, frequent prayer and works of compassion, but Al-Ghazali also studied theology, philosophy, natural science and jurisprudence. Even at an early age, he showed his brilliance of mind in writings and lectures and in a certain relentless scepticism of enquiry. His teacher, Al-Juwayni, described him as 'a sea to drown in', so large was the scope of his speculation.

Returning to Tus [after study in Jurjan], he met with an adventure which is recorded by most of his biographers, on the word of Al-Ghazali himself. The party was attacked by highway robbers, who carried off all that the travellers had with them. Al-Ghazali went after them, though warned by the chief of the brigands that he imperilled his life by so doing. He persisted, however, and begged only for the return of his precious note-books, which could be of no value to them. 'What are your note-books?' asked the robber chief, and Al-Ghazali explained that they contained notes of the lectures he had recently heard and represented his knowledge of them. The robber laughed and said, 'How can you lay claim to this knowledge when we have taken it from you? Being separated from your knowledge, you remain without it.' Then he ordered one of his men to restore the note-books to their owner. Al-Ghazali felt that the words of the robber were to be taken as divine guidance to him, and when he had reached Tus, he betook himself to study for three years, during which time he committed to memory all the contents of his note-books, so that if he were robbed again, he could not be deprived of his learning.

Margaret Smith[5]

Al-Ghazali's reputation as a scholar in all fields led Nizamulmulk, the powerful vizier of the Turkish sultan, to appoint him to the chair of theology at the Nizamiyya *madrasah* (college) at Baghdad in 1091. At the age of 33

Al-Ghazali had attained one of the most distinguished positions in the academic world of his day. He astonished the Baghdadis by the excellence of his lectures, his fluent delivery, the extent of his learning, the subtlety of his allusions and the lucidity of his explanations. His lectures attracted large numbers, including all the leading scholars. He was asked for rulings on matters of law from across the Mediterranean. He, his wife and young family lived with all the comforts of wealth that his position brought him.

And yet in 1096 he gave it all up. Why? He did so because, in spite of his exhaustive searches, he could not find an absolutely irrefutable, completely certain way to God. In the apologia written towards the end of his life, *al-Munqidh min ad-Dalal* (Deliverance from Error), he describes his investigations in the field of *kalam* (Islamic theology), *falsafah* (philosophy), the Ismaili tradition of the authority of the Imam, and in the teachings of the Sufi mystics (Al-Ghazali's writings are much occupied with all these), but how he came to the realization that there is a huge difference between knowing *about* God and knowing God. He had come as far as he could on the rational route and felt as far away as ever.

> It had already become clear to me that I had no hope of the bliss of the world to come save through a God-fearing life and the withdrawal of myself from vain desire. It was clear to me too that the key to all this was to sever the attachment of the heart to worldly things by leaving the mansion of deception and returning to that of eternity, and to advance towards God most high with all earnestness. It was also clear that this was only to be achieved by turning away from wealth and position and fleeing from all time-consuming entanglements. Next I considered the circumstances of my life, and realised that I was caught in a veritable thicket of attachments. I also considered my activities, of which the best was my teaching and lecturing, and

realised that in them I was dealing with sciences that were unimportant and contributed nothing to the attainment of eternal life. After that I examined my motive in my work of teaching, and realised that it was not a pure desire for the things of God, but that the impulse moving me was the desire for an influential position and public recognition. I saw for certain that I was on the brink of a crumbling bank of sand and in imminent danger of hell-fire unless I set out to mend my ways.

For nearly six months beginning with July 1095, I was continuously tossed about between the attractions of worldly desires and the impulses towards eternal life. In that month the matter ceased to be one of choice and became one of compulsion. God caused my tongue to dry up so that I was prevented from lecturing. One particular day I would make an effort to lecture in order to gratify the hearts of my following, but my tongue would not utter a single word nor could I accomplish anything at all. The impediment in my speech produced grief in my heart, and at the same time my power to digest and assimilate food and drink was impaired; I could hardly swallow soup or digest a single mouthful of food. My powers became so weakened that the doctors gave up all hope of successful treatment. 'The trouble arises from the heart,' they said, 'and from there it has spread through the constitution; the only method of treatment is that the anxiety which has come over the heart should be allayed.'

Mohammad Al-Ghazali[6]

The doctors' diagnosis was correct: it was a deep depression, caused by profound inner conflict without resolution. Finally, however, Al-Ghazali did resolve the conflict. He told everyone that he was making the pilgrimage to Mecca, but in fact, having left money to provide for his wife and children, he 'dropped out' and lived the life of a wandering ascetic for something like 10 years. He spent his time 'simply in retreat and solitude, self-discipline and self-mortification, being preoccupied with the cleansing of the soul, the amendment of character, and the purification of the heart for the recollection of God most high'. He followed the way of the Sufi, no longer merely as a theoretical study. He wore coarse clothing, carried a bag for his scanty provisions and a staff, ate dry bread and wandered from place to place. He spent time as a servant in a monastery at Damascus, praying often shut up in the minaret of the mosque there. For a time he was in Jerusalem, praying in the great mosque of Omar. Later he did make the pilgrimage to Mecca, and spent time in Egypt. After a time he attracted companions and followers. Eventually he resumed teaching and preaching and writing, and spent time in both Baghdad and Tus. In 1106 a new vizier invited Al-Ghazali to return to teach at the Nizamiyya college, and this he did for a while, before finally retiring to Tus, where he established a college for students of theology and a monastery for Sufis.

For Al-Ghazali's retreat was not ultimately a purely self-centred, escapist episode; he remained profoundly concerned to communicate what he had experienced and discovered. Karen Armstrong writes:

> [He] returned to Iraq ten years later to write his masterpiece, *Ihyah ulum al-Din* (The Revival of the Religious Sciences). It became the most quoted Muslim text after the Quran and the *ahadith*. It was based on the important insight that only ritual and prayer could give human beings a direct knowledge of God; the arguments of theology (*kalam*) and Falsafah, however, could give us no certainty about the divine. The *Ihyah* provides Muslims with a daily spiritual and

practical regimen, designed to prepare them for this religious experience. All the Shariah rules about eating, sleeping, washing, hygiene and prayer were given a devotional and ethical interpretation, so that they were no longer simply external directives, but enabled Muslims to cultivate that perpetual consciousness of the divine that is advocated by the Quran. The Shariah had thus become more than a means of social conformity, and a slavish exterior imitation of the Prophet and his *sunnah* (custom): it became a way of achieving interior *islam* (surrender to the will of God). Al-Ghazali was not writing for the religious experts, but for devout individuals.[7]

In waking from sleep endeavour to be awake before daybreak. Let the first activity of heart and tongue be the mention of God most high. Say here: 'Praise be to God who has made us alive after making us dead; to him are we raised up again. It is for God that we and all creation have come to this day. His is the greatness and the authority, his is the might and the power, Lord of the worlds. In the disposition of surrender to God have we come to this day, and in the word of sincerity, in the religion of our prophet Muhammad (God bless and preserve him) and in the community of our father Abraham, surrendered to God, not one of the idolaters. O God, we beseech thee that thou wouldest direct us this day to all good. I take refuge with thee from committing evil this day and from bringing evil upon a Muslim. O God, through thee have we come to this day, and through thee have we come to the night; through thee do we live, through thee do we die, and to thee are we raised up. We beseech thee for the good of this day

and of what is in it; we take refuge with thee from the
evil of this day and of what is in it.'

Muhammad Al-Ghazali[8]

Abu Hamid Mohammad Al-Ghazali died on 18
December 1111. His brother, Ahmad, wrote that at dawn
on the day of his death Al-Ghazali performed his ablutions
and prayed, and then said, 'Bring me my shroud,' and
taking it he kissed it and laid it over his eyes and said,
'Most gladly do I enter into the presence of the King,' and
he stretched out his feet and went forth to meet him, and
so passed into the paradise of God, 'worthy of all honour,
of loftier station than the stars, giving more guidance to
men than the full moon when darkness has fallen'.[9]

Once I had been a slave: lust was my master.
Lust then became my servant: I was free.
Leaving the haunts of men, I sought thy presence;
Lonely, I found in thee my company.

Not in the market-place is found the treasure
Nor by the ignorant, who know not thee,
Who taunt me, thinking that my search is folly,
But at the end, thou wilt be found with me.

Attributed to Mohammad Al-Ghazali[10]

O God,
you are the only God
and beside you there is no god;
in your hand is our living and our dying.
In your compassion and mercy
move us from attachment to intellectual and
social success
and, with Mohammad Al-Ghazali, towards
the inner vision of your glory,

to lives of simplicity, praise and service,
where we may dwell with you for ever.

ଊ ଓ

Moses Maimonides
1135–1204

As the tourists wander around the old town in Cordoba in the southern province of Andalucia in Spain, they will inevitably come to the old synagogue, and, not far away, a bronze statue of a seated figure. He wears a long robe and a turban; with pursed lips and pointed beard he looks solemnly and meditatively into the distance. The guide will tell the visitors that if they touch the figure's toe which protrudes from his robe, they will gain some of his wisdom. The toe is already shiny and worn from a thousand hopeful rubbings. The statue is of Rabbi Moses Ben Maimon, known to Jews as the RaM BaM, from the initials of his name, and in the West as Maimonides. He was born in this town of Cordoba in 1135.

Maimonides' father was Rabbi Maimon, the *dayan* or judge of Cordoba, a learned man from an ancient and illustrious Jewish family. It is presumed that he taught his son from the Torah and the Talmud but Moses also learned mathematics, astronomy and philosophy. Ever since the ninth century, Spain had been part of the Muslim world, which stretched from there around the north of Africa and into the Middle East. The rulers of the time were tolerant towards Jews and Christians, and the country's achievements in culture, science, medicine and philosophy outstripped anything in the contemporary Christian world. Maimonides inherited the advantages of this world but, unfortunately when he was thirteen a less tolerant, dynasty, the Almoravids, came to power, and this led, after some years, to a necessity for the family to leave Cordoba.

I have now finished this work (Commentary on the Mishnah) in accordance with my promise, and I fervently beseech the Almighty to save us from error. If there be one who shall discover an inaccuracy in this Commentary or shall have a better explanation to offer, let my attention be directed unto it; and let me be exonerated by the fact that I have worked with far greater application than anyone who writes for the sake of pay and profit, and that I have worked under the most trying circumstances. For Heaven had ordained that we be exiled, and we were therefore driven about from place to place; I was thus compelled to work at the Commentary while travelling by land, or crossing the sea ... I, Moses, the son of Maimon, commenced it when I was twenty-three years old, and finished it in Egypt, at the age of thirty-three years.

Maimonides[11]

So the family wandered in exile, and, after short stays in Morocco and the Holy Land, settled in Fostat, the old city of Cairo, discovering a more tolerant Muslim rule. Moses passed most of his life there, supported at first by his brother David, who carried on a trade in precious stones, and then, after his brother's death, serving as physician to the royal court of Saladin, Regent of Egypt, and as leader of the Jewish community there, until his death in 1204.

My duties to the sultan are very heavy. I am obliged to visit him every day, early in the morning, and when he or any of his children or any of the inmates of his harem are indisposed, I dare not quit Cairo, but stay during the greater part of the day in the palace ... Hence, as a rule, I leave for Cairo very early in the day, and even if nothing unusual happens, I do not return to Fostat until the afternoon. Then I am almost dying with hunger ... I find the antechamber filled with people, both Jews and gentiles, nobles and common people, judges and bailiffs, friends and foes, a mixed multitude who await the time of my return. I dismount from my animal, wash my hands, go forth to my patients and entreat them to bear with me while I partake of some slight refreshment, the only meal I take in the twenty four hours. Then I go forth to attend to my patients, and write prescriptions and directions for their various ailments. Patients go in and out until nightfall, and sometimes even, I solemnly assure you, until two hours or more in the night. I converse with and prescribe for them while lying down from sheer fatigue; and when night falls, I am so exhausted that I can scarcely speak.

Maimonides[12]

Maimonides wrote 10 books on medicine, and he is still celebrated as a medical authority who pioneered a holistic approach to health. On one occasion one of Saladin's sons sought Maimonides' opinion when he was suffering from depression, anorexia, vomiting, constipation and indigestion, and the resulting 'consultant's report', which he published as the *Regimen Sanitatis* (or *The Preservation of Youth*), includes therapeutic, preventative and health promotional ideas. In spite of that he saw his medical work as a distraction from the theological works he was constantly engaged upon, as this remark from a letter reveals:

> Although from my birth the Torah was betrothed to me, and continues to be loved by me as the wife of my youth, in whose love I find a constant delight, strange women whom I at first took into my house as her handmaids have become her rivals and absorb a portion of my time.[13]

In the letter to Shmuel ibn Tibbon Maimonides says that he only has the Sabbath for instructing the faithful.

Nevertheless, Maimonides's reputation is based above all on his voluminous writings in theology and philosophy. Among many other works, we should note three: the commentary on the Mishnah (1168), the *Mishneh Torah* (c. 1180) and the *Moreh Nevuchim* (*Guide for the Perplexed*) (1190).

The first of these includes a short enumeration of the thirteen fundamental beliefs of Judaism. These thirteen principles are the nearest Judaism has come to having a creed, and they can usually be found in Jewish prayer books, to be said every day at the end of morning prayers. Hans Küng has written:

> Maimonides' confession of faith ... expresses the elements of faith which Judaism shares with Christianity and Islam (belief in the existence, unity, incorporeality and omniscience of God, and in retribution and resurrection) as clearly as what divides the three religions: over against Christianity, the absolute simplicity of God and belief in a messiah who is still to come, and over against Islam and its Qur'an, the eternal validity of the Torah of Moses.[14]

1. I believe and affirm that the Creator created and guides all creatures, and that he alone has accomplished, accomplishes and will accomplish all works.

2. I believe and affirm that the Creator is one, with a oneness which is absolutely unique, and that he alone was, is and will be our God.

3. I believe and affirm that the Creator is not a body, that there is nothing bodily about him and that none is like him.

4. I believe and affirm that the Creator is the first and will be the last.

5. I believe and affirm that the Creator alone is worthy of worship and that we should not worship anything other than him.

6. I believe and affirm that all the words of the prophets are true.

7. I believe and affirm that the prophecy of our teacher Moses is true and that he is the father of all the prophets, both of those who came before him and those who followed him.

8. I believe and affirm that the Torah which is in our possession today is the same Torah as was handed down to our teacher Moses.

9. I believe and affirm that this Torah will not be abrogated, nor shall another Torah come from God.

10. I believe and affirm that the Creator has knowledge of all the deeds and thoughts of men, for scripture says, 'He who has formed all their hearts also understands their doings'.

11. I believe and affirm that the Creator rewards those who obey his commandments and punishes those who transgress his prohibitions.

12. I believe and affirm that the messiah will come. Even should he tarry, I still long for his advent.

13. I believe and affirm that a resurrection of the dead will take place at a time which will be well pleasing to the Creator.

Praised be his name and praised be his memory for ever and ever.

Maimonides[15]

The *Mishneh Torah* took Maimonides 10 years to write; it is a systematic codification of the Jewish law. It is the only book he wrote in Hebrew; all his other works were written in Arabic. As for the *Guide for the Perplexed*, it is a work of some 400 close-printed pages in the English translation, and in its three parts it seeks to reconcile the teaching of the Old Testament about God with Aristotelian philosophy. Many have doubted whether it really achieves this reconciliation, and Keith Ward, in his own book *God: A Guide for the Perplexed*, comments humorously: 'The title of the book is rather ironic, because if you were perplexed when you began to read it, you certainly would be by the time you finished it.'[16]

There are two reasons for this. One is that Maimonides indulges in a great amount of speculative philosophical argumentation and exegesis of Old Testament texts. The other, more fundamental, reason is that there is real conflict between a scriptural and an Aristotelian view of God and creation. Aristotle sees God not as creator, but simply as the ultimate unchanging Being who produces change in the world just by drawing things by attraction; God himself does not change or move; he is the unmoved mover. The Bible, by contrast, sees God as the one who creates everything by his sovereign word out of nothing. For Aristotle, matter is eternal; it never began, and it will never finish; for the Bible, there was a beginning, and there will be an end. Maimonides presents both sides of the argument very fully indeed, and in the end admits that reason alone cannot decide between them. His conclusion is to trust those great prophets, such as Moses or Abraham, who intuited the truth of creation through mystical revelation.

Perhaps Maimonides' greatest insight is into the utter otherness and unknowableness of God. In this he was following great Muslim thinkers, such as Ibn Sina (Avicenna), Al-Ghazali and Ibn Rushd (Averroes). The knowledge of God's ways can certainly be approached, both through the prophetic revelation of the Bible and through the rational thinking of the philosophers, but it will always fall short of the full reality of God.

> For in the same way as all people must be informed, and even children must be trained in the belief that God is One, and that none beside Him is to be worshipped, so must all be taught by simple authority that God is incorporeal; that there is no similarity in any way whatsoever between Him and his creatures; that his existence is not like the existence of his creatures, his life not like that of any living being, his wisdom not like the wisdom of the wisest of men; and that the difference between Him and his creatures is not merely quantitative, but absolute.
>
> Maimonides[17]

Therefore the only absolutely true things that you can say about God are negative: God is not wise as human beings are wise, God is not good as we know goodness, and so on – God is infinitely more so! And that also means that when we read in the Bible that God is angry, likes the smell of a good sacrifice, argues with Abraham, or has fingers, these things are not literally true: they are parables, images, analogies, pointing to a reality far beyond their absolute grasp.

Maimonides lived in a world in which there was real interchange and intercourse between faiths. As a Jew he lived in a Muslim world and derived much from the freedoms and the intellectual culture of that world. He was part of a movement of both Arabic and Jewish theologians who searched for truth in the rationality of philosophy as well as the revelations of scripture, and that movement powerfully influenced the Christian theologians of the thirteenth century, Albert the Great and Thomas Aquinas. Perhaps we may hope that the twenty-first century will see a real rapprochement among the three Abrahamic faiths, and that, as the Swiss theologian Hans Küng so profoundly hopes, the reconciliation of these may be a source of peace for the world. Perhaps it will need a third Moses to achieve this.

Certainly, after Moses ben Maimon died, it was often said among the Jews: 'From Moses (of the Torah) to Moses (Maimonides), there was none like Moses.'

> *God of Abraham, God of Moses, eternal*
> *source of all being,*
> *save us from the arrogance of certainty;*
> *teach us at the feet of Rabbi Maimonides*
> *to search for you with all our mind;*
> *and reassure us that, though we may not find*
> *you, you will find us,*
> *in the deepest meditations of our faith.*
> *We ask this, seeking understanding, in faith*
> *and love.*

ഇ ഌ

Mohandas Gandhi
1869–1948

What I want to achieve – what I have been striving and pining to achieve these thirty years – is self-realization, to see God face to face, to attain moksha [salvation]. I live and move and have my being in pursuit of this goal. All that I do by way of speaking and writing, and all my ventures in the political field, are directed to this same end. But as I have all along believed that what is possible for one is possible for all, my experiments have not been conducted in the closet, but in the open; and I do not think that this fact detracts from their spiritual value ... But for me, truth is the sovereign principle, which includes numerous other principles. This truth is not only truthfulness in word, but truthfulness in thought also, and not only the relative truth of our conception, but the Absolute Truth, the Eternal Principle, that is God. There are innumerable definitions of God, because His manifestations are innumerable. They overwhelm me with wonder and awe and for a moment stun me. But I worship God as Truth, only I have not yet found Him, but I am seeking after Him. I am prepared to sacrifice the things dearest to me in pursuit of this quest. Even if the sacrifice demanded be my very life, I hope I may be prepared to give it.

Mohandas Gandhi[18]

Gandhi was shot dead by a Hindu on 30 January 1948 as he was on his way to an evening prayer meeting in Delhi. He was 78 years old. His 'sin' in the young Hindu's eyes was that he was at that time striving to bring healing and reconciliation between Hindus and Muslims in the riot-torn areas of Bengal and Bihar following the partition of British India into separate states along religious lines. Gandhi had spent most of his adult life in the forefront of the Indian struggle for rights of freedom and for independence from British rule, and this culminated in the Mountbatten Plan of 1947, which created the two new dominions of India and Pakistan, but it was entirely against his whole vision that the division separated a Muslim state from a Hindu one.

If we ask where Gandhi's campaign against imperialism began, we might point to his refusal to remove his turban when ordered to do so in a Durban law court soon after he arrived as a barrister in South Africa in 1893, and to an incident on a train at Pietermaritzburg.

The train reach Maritzburg, the capital of Natal, at about 9pm. Beddings used to be provided at this station. A railway servant came and asked me if I wanted one. 'No,' said I, 'I have one with me.' He went away, but a passenger came next, and looked me up and down. He saw that I was a 'coloured' man. This disturbed him. Out he went and came in again with one or two officials. They all kept quiet, when another official came to me and said, 'Come along, you must go to the van compartment.'

'But I have a first class ticket,' said I.

'That doesn't matter,' rejoined the other. 'I tell you, you must go to the van compartment.'

'I tell you, I was permitted to travel in this compartment at Durban, and I insist on going on in it.'

'No, you won't,' said the official. 'You must leave this compartment, or else I shall have to call a police constable to push you out.'

'Yes, you may. I refuse to get out voluntarily.'

The constable came. He took me by the hand and pushed me out. My luggage was also taken away. I refused to go to the other compartment and the train steamed away.

Mohandas Gandhi[19]

Gandhi spent a freezing night in the station, but already he had made up his mind to do what he could to root out the disease of colour prejudice, and to defend his and other people's dignity as Indians and as human beings. A remarkable transformation now took place. During his education in India and at the Inner Temple in London, where he trained as a lawyer, he had never appeared strong or intellectually outstanding, and indeed had been overcome with shyness in situations where he had to speak. And yet there was in him an inner passion for righteousness and truth, and a steely determination to achieve personal standards, which blossomed, in the time he worked as a barrister in South Africa, into his becoming the leader of a struggle for the rights of Indians in South Africa, and a very effective political campaigner. He organized petitions, kept up a steady stream of reasoned statements to the press and the government about Indian grievances, founded the Natal Indian Congress, and finally, in 1906, persuaded a mass meeting of Indians to commit themselves to disobey a proposed law for the registration of the Indian population and gladly to bear all the penalties of their defiance. Thus was born *satyagraha*.

Satyagraha literally means insistence on truth. This insistence arms the votary with matchless power ... Such a universal force necessarily makes no distinction between kinsmen and strangers, young and old, man and woman, friend and foe. The force to be so applied can never be physical. There is in it no room for violence. The only force of universal application can, therefore, be that of *ahimsa* or love. In other words, it is soul-force.

Love does not burn others, it burns itself. Therefore a *satyagrahi*, i.e. a civil resister, whilst he will strain every nerve to compass the end of the existing rule, will do no intentional injury in thought, word or deed to the person of a single Englishman.

As an individual, a *satyagrahi*, will harbour no anger.

He will suffer the anger of the opponent.

In so doing he will put up with assaults from the opponent, never retaliate; but he will not submit, out of fear of punishment or the like, to any order given in anger.

When any person in authority seeks to arrest a civil resister, he will voluntarily submit to the arrest, and he will not resist the attachment or removal of his own property, if any, when it is sought to be confiscated by authorities.

If a civil resister has any property in his possession as a trustee, he will refuse to surrender it, even though in defending it he might lose his life. He will, however, never retaliate.

Non-retaliation excludes swearing and cursing.

Mohandas Gandhi[20]

Gandhi left South Africa in 1914, having achieved some real concessions from the South African government; thousands of Indians, including Gandhi himself, had endured jail, and many had suffered violence, in the process; but *satyagraha* had proved its effectiveness. It was to do so again in the years that followed, as Gandhi became the leader of the Indian struggle against British imperial rule, refashioned the Indian National Congress into an effective force, organized countrywide demonstrations of non-violent resistance and added fasting in prison to the peaceful strategies of non-co-operation. He resigned from the Congress Party in 1934, feeling that his leading colleagues were adopting non-violence merely as a political expedient rather than from deeper spiritual motive and integrity, and the final ending of British rule came without his direct involvement, and with a partition of Indian from Pakistani which was against his vision.

Gandhi retired to the ashram (community) at Sevagram. He had set up farm colonies in South Africa, and Sevagram was the second ashram in which he lived in India. Although married by arrangement at the age of 13 and the father of several children, he early on took a vow of chastity, although continuing to live with his wife,

Kasturbai, usually in open, communal settings. He felt an irresistible attraction to a life of simplicity, manual labour and austerity: when someone gave him a copy of John Ruskin's book *Unto This Last* in 1904, it was a revelation for him. The teachings of the book he understood to be:

1 That the good of the individual is contained in the good of all.

2 That a lawyer's work has the same value as the barber's, inasmuch as all have the same right of earning their livelihood from their work.

3 That a life of labour, i.e. the life of the tiller of the soil and the handicraftsman, is the life worth living[21].

The result of this was the first farm settlement, and a lifetime of living usually in community, in extreme austerity and simplicity, happily doing the most menial domestic tasks and travelling third class, and in using the considerable sums that he earned mostly in his public activities. Gandhi radically eschewed all the trappings of power and wealth. After his retirement from the Congress Party, he focused his energies in attempting to build the nation, India, 'from the bottom up'. This included the promotion of handspinning, weaving and other cottage industries to supplement the earnings of underemployed peasants, seeking to evolve a system of education suited to the needs of the people, and striving to bring the Untouchable caste into mainstream life.

Gandhi's religious quest, his relentless succession of 'experiments with truth', was the driving force of his whole life. It began in his childhood homes at Porbandar and Rajkot, in Vaishnavism (worship of the Hindu god Vishnu), with a strong influence of Jainism, and he always took for granted the principles of *ahimsa* (non-injury to all living beings), vegetarianism, fasting for self-purification and mutual tolerance between adherents of different creeds. He became convinced of the 'subtlety and profundity' of Hinduism and treated the *Bhagavadgita* as his 'spiritual dictionary'. His interest in other faiths, especially Christianity, was stimulated by Christian friends and acquaintances in London and South Africa. He could never accept the exclusive claims of Christianity, but he was intensely attracted by the figure of Jesus and by his teaching. In his early days in London he met a Christian from Manchester in a vegetarian boarding house; the latter gave him a Bible, and Gandhi ploughed through the Old Testament. The chapters after Genesis invariably sent him to sleep.

> But the New Testament produced a different impression, especially the Sermon on the Mount which went straight to my heart. I compared it with the *Gita*. The verses, 'But I say unto ye, that ye resist not evil; but whosoever shall smite thee on thy right cheek, turn to him the other also. And if any man take away thy coat let him have thy cloak too,' delighted me beyond measure.[22]

Gandhi attends a Christian Convention in South Africa:

> The Convention lasted three days. I could understand and appreciate the devoutness of those who attended it. But I saw no reason for changing my belief – my religion. It was impossible for me to believe that I could go to heaven or attain salvation only by becoming a Christian ... It was more than I could believe that Jesus was the only incarnate son of God, and that only he who believed in him would have everlasting life. If God could have sons, all of us were His sons. If Jesus was like God, or God Himself, then all men were like God and could be God Himself. My reason was not ready to believe literally that Jesus by his death and by his blood

redeemed the sins of the world. Metaphorically there might be some truth in it ... I could accept Jesus as a martyr, an embodiment of sacrifice, and a divine teacher, but not as the most perfect man ever born. His death on the Cross was a great example to the world, but that there was anything like a mysterious or miraculous virtue in it my heart could not accept.

Mohandas Gandhi[23]

For he [Jesus] was, certainly, the highest example of one who wished to give everything asking nothing in return, and not caring what creed might happen to be professed by the recipient. I am sure that if he were living here now among men, He would bless the lives of many who perhaps have never heard His name, if only their lives embodied the virtues of which He was a living example on earth; the virtues of loving one's neighbour as oneself and of doing good and charitable works among one's fellow-men.

What then does Jesus mean to me? He was one of the greatest teachers humanity has ever had. To His believers He was God's only begotten Son. Could the fact that I do not accept this belief make Jesus have any more or less influence in my life? Is all the grandeur of His teaching and of His doctrine to be forbidden to me? I cannot believe so.

Mohandas Gandhi[24]

Gandhi was loved and admired by very many different people, people of every religious and political persuasion. In the eyes of millions of his compatriots he was the Mahatma – the great soul. He came perhaps as near as any Christian saint to fulfilling that 'available love' which Christ embodied and taught. He initiated and was a major catalyst of three shining lights in a dark century – the struggle against colonialism, against racism and against violence.

Gilbert Murray wrote of Gandhi:

> Persons in power should be very careful how they deal with a man who cares nothing for sensual pleasure, nothing for riches, nothing for comfort or praise, or promotion, but is simply determined to do what he believes to be right. He is a dangerous and uncomfortable enemy, because his body which you can always conquer gives you so little purchase upon his soul.[25]

ℬ ℭ

God of truth,
you reveal yourself to those who seek you
in purity of heart and integrity of will.
Show us in the life and mission of Mahatma Gandhi
how to defeat evil with love alone,
in ourselves and in our world,
and so prove ourselves your true sons and daughters.
We ask it in the name of Jesus your Son.

ℬ ℭ

Many other figures of insight, holiness and compassion could have been chosen from the great faiths of the world. No one can understand and experience from the inside the genius and power of the whole range of faith systems and cultures; what *is* possible, however, is for us to learn of the life and witness of a key figure in a faith other than our own, and when we do that with just one extraordinary life, the experience is salutary and humbling, for we then face the ignorant prejudice in which we so casually belittle faiths we know almost nothing about. If the churches were really serious about inter-faith understanding, they could ask the leaders of other faith groups to recommend a number of their greatest figures who could become 'honorary heroes of faith' to Christians too.

ଓ ଓଃ

Holy God,
you are beyond all human conceiving,
pictured, approached, celebrated and obeyed
in myriad ways across the earth and down
the centuries.
Give us the grace to see the reflection of your
face in lives and customs different from our
own,
and so to find the unity of holiness
for peace in a world of infinite variety.

Chapter 8

Those who 'led the people by their counsels'
Forgotten Pioneers

I want to reflect, in this chapter, on some of the reasons why great Christians get forgotten, even though they do not fall into the categories of those, like the heroes of the previous chapters, who are regarded as being 'beyond the pale' or among those to whom the churches have turned a blind eye.

First of all, they may come to be thought of as the 'B-team'. Great composers living in Vienna at the time of Mozart or Beethoven ran the risk, whether or not they knew it, of being relegated to second-rate-ness or oblivion, just because they weren't those towering geniuses. Fortunately Haydn is now being restored to his true glory, but there may not be any hope for Salieri or Spohr. George Whitefield was at least as famous a preacher as John Wesley in his day, and he actually led the way in open-air preaching, but he has disappeared from view in comparison with the Wesleys. Of course, Whitefield failed to set up the educational/ecclesial structures that were the great Wesleyan legacy, but is that sufficient reason to forget the undoubted power of his gifts?

Another reason for the greater likelihood of oblivion is that one was a lay person, not a priest or religious. It has been noted that the religious orders in Catholicism have the time and energy and resources to put forward the causes of their outstanding members for canonization; and the intense clericalism of many church denominations has inevitably meant that priests and ministers have been 'noticed', but lay people much less often. Consider Dwight Moody: a great American evangelist with an enormous influence on world Christianity, but a layman; he is largely forgotten within many mainstream denominations.

Dwight Moody reminds us of another reason for neglect, and that is a kind of snobbishness among some Christians, especially those of a more Catholic habit of mind or of intellectual bent. Popular evangelists have often been regarded with suspicion and contempt by established Christian elites, and both Whitefield and Moody came under that kind of negative scrutiny. A tough Calvinist theology also put such preachers further beyond mainstream acceptability. It is hard to imagine – to put it mildly – anyone within the Church of England or the Roman Catholic Church pressing for the inclusion, after their deaths, of Pat Robertson or Cliff Richard! But I believe there is a profoundly ecumenical imperative about such a consideration. Outstanding Christians in the low church tradition are, of course, very much less likely to be remembered and celebrated after their deaths within their *own* traditions, but it could well be recommended to such traditions that they would be immensely enriched by such deliberate remembrance; and this would also act as ecumenical convergence.

I wrote in the introduction of this book about the Church of England's current rule of thumb, that no one except a martyr is included in the calendar until they have been dead for 50 years, for fear of bowing to the cult of the moment. This may be wise, but it may also have the effect of casting into permanent oblivion those who deserved better. It's often the case that great writers or composers become deeply unfashionable immediately after their deaths, as culture and sensibilities move on, and it may take many decades or even centuries before they are rediscovered and freshly celebrated. There were many early twentieth-century pioneers of social care, of political engagement, of ecumenism, of health and healing, of popular apologetic, but we have allowed such names as Leslie Weatherhead, Dick Sheppard, George Bell and Paul Couturier to sink without much trace. Florence Allshorn was a remarkable Christian, a woman of great wisdom and vision, a pioneer in 'earthed spirituality', but she died in 1950 – just the right moment for her currently to be forgotten.

Finally, I need to return to the question of the representation of women in the roll of great Christians remembered. They have always figured less prominently among the named saints, and this book has been, I admit, no exception to that rule. The future will be very different, as women find their place at all levels of the Church and in much greater equality of visibility, but I believe that there is certainly much more work to be done, to restore many hidden women from the centuries of the Church – and from outside the Church – to knowledge and celebration.

I offer here the lives of George Whitefield, Dwight Moody and Florence Allshorn as a small act of restitution for so many Christian lives of total dedication consigned to the margins of ecclesiastical memory.

George Whitefield
1714–1770

In his classic work, *The Varieties of Religious Experience*, the American philosopher and psychologist, William James, gave copious examples of those who had undergone sudden religious conversion.

> These [examples] will show you how real, definite, and memorable an event a sudden conversion may be to him who has the experience. Throughout the height of it he undoubtedly seems to himself a passive spectator or undergoer of an astounding process performed upon him from above. There is too much evidence of this for any doubt of it to be possible. Theology, combining this fact with the doctrines of election and grace, has concluded that the spirit of God is with us at these dramatic moments in a peculiarly miraculous way, unlike what happens at any other juncture of our lives. At that moment, it

> believes, an absolutely new nature is breathed into us, and
> we become partakers of the very substance of the Deity.
>
> William James[1]

Two hundred years ago, revivalist Christian preaching
was producing thousands upon thousands of conversions,
often to the disapproval of the established churches: on
the European continent in the Pietist and Quietist
movements, in Britain with Evangelicalism, and in
America in the Great Awakening. In Britain and America
the Methodist movement played a great part, and in that
movement two figures played a predominant role, one still
well known and honoured, the other to a considerable
extent forgotten. Their names were John Wesley and
George Whitefield (pronounced Whitfield). Why has
Whitefield been neglected? Perhaps because, although
younger than Wesley, he died 21 years before him, and did
not, like Wesley, follow up his preaching with the
organizational infrastructure – the local preachers, the
class meetings, the annual conference and the rest – which
was the foundation of the Methodist Church. And perhaps,
too, because, although he was undoubtedly a more
charismatic preacher than Wesley, he chose a tougher
(Calvinist) theology than Wesley, a theology that proved
less attractive to a Methodist future so profoundly
influenced by Wesley. That theology, and the reason why
Whitefield and Wesley ceased their collaborations in 1741,
was around the question of Christian conversion.

And the question was this. Both Wesley and Whitefield,
as children of the Reformation, believed that the human
sinner was saved and justified by God's grace in Christ
through their faith alone; no good works or church rituals
could achieve this. But still there remained a question:
could absolutely anyone be saved, or had God already
chosen those whom he would save? For Wesley, who
followed the teaching of Jacobus Arminius, the sixteenth-
century Dutch theologian, what God had done in the death

and resurrection of Christ (his prevenient grace) was always available to anyone, enabling them to respond to the preaching of Christ, and so be converted, and everyone was free to accept or reject it. It followed logically from this that those who had accepted Christ were still free, either to advance towards a greater perfection in the Christian life, or indeed to lose their salvation, by turning away from what they had once received.

This Arminian doctrine, which had been rejected by mainstream Calvinists, following John Calvin himself, was repugnant, too, to George Whitefield. For them, it allowed far too much to human freedom and human self-will, and far too little to the sovereignty of God. They believed that God knew and had decided from all eternity which people would receive his grace and mercy, and which would not. The purpose of preaching, then, was to awaken the awareness of their salvation in those who had been saved; and once that awareness had been made, God's choice and grace were absolutely unchangeable and unloseable – the recipients could live in a state of certitude and grace, knowing indeed that they remained miserable sinners, but completely certain that they were the unmerited beneficiaries of salvation by God's gracious gift. This was the theology of George Whitefield. To put it very simply: Wesley defended the freedom of the individual human being, Whitefield the sovereign decision of God; but both believed passionately in taking God's grace in Christ to those who did not know it. Both realized the need to preach to people outside church walls, but Whitefield realized it first.

Before we can ever have peace with God, we must be justified by faith through our Lord Jesus Christ, we must be enabled to apply Christ to our hearts, we must have Christ brought home to our souls, so that his righteousness may be made our righteousness and his merits imputed to our souls ... You must not build upon

---

> a work within you, but always come out of yourselves to the righteousness of Jesus Christ without you. Come away, my dear brethren – fly, fly, fly for your lives to Jesus Christ, fly to a bleeding God, fly to a throne of grace; and beg of God to break your hearts, beg of God to convince you of your actual sins, beg of God to convince you of your self-righteousness, beg of God to give you faith, and enable you to close with Jesus Christ.
>
> George Whitefield[2]

Whitefield and Wesley first met at Oxford University. John Wesley was already a fellow at Lincoln College in 1732 when George Whitefield arrived at the age of 18 as a servitor (an undergraduate not charged fees by the college) at Pembroke College. George had grown up in Gloucester, where his widowed mother ran the Bell Inn. He became acquainted with John and Charles Wesley and the other members of the 'Holy Club' or 'Methodists' (so called because of their methodical approach to leading a holy life), and his Christian faith, until now relatively unformed, became the central reality of his life. He lived a life of self-denial, fasting twice a week, eating the poorest food and wearing very scruffy clothes. He read the Bible voraciously and Reformation and Puritan classics of the Christian life, but for many weeks the reassurance of faith did not come to him.

> Whenever I knelt down, I felt great pressure both on body and soul, and have often prayed under the weight of my sorrows, till the sweat came through me. God only knows how many nights I have lain upon my bed, groaning under what I felt. Whole days and weeks have I spent in lying prostrate on the ground in silent or vocal prayer.[3]

Then, upon recovery from a prolonged period of (probably self-induced) sickness, came the moment of conversion.

After having undergone innumerable buffetings of Satan and many months in expressible trials by night and day under the spirit of bondage, God was pleased at length to remove the heavy load, to enable me to lay hold on His dear Son by a living faith, and by giving me the spirit of adoption, to seal me, as I humbly hope, even to the day of everlasting redemption. But O! with what joy – joy unspeakable – even joy that was full of, even big with glory, was my soul filled, when the weight of sin went off, and an abiding sense of the pardoning love of God, and a full assurance of faith broke in upon my disobedient soul! Surely it was the day of my espousal – a day to be had in everlasting remembrance. At first my joys were like a spring tide, and, as it were, overflowed the banks. Go where I would, I could not avoid singing of psalms almost aloud; afterwards they became more settled, and, blessed be God, saving a few casual intervals, have abode and increased in my soul ever since.

George Whitefield[4]

Whitefield was ordained deacon in the Church of England in 1736 by Bishop Benson of Gloucester. He had not sought this out, but the bishop had heard of his character and sent for him. His first sermon – at St Mary-le-Crypt in Gloucester – was the first of some 18,000 sermons that he was to preach in the next 34 years, and it already established the brilliant, passionate style that was to make him a household name. He wrote afterwards that 'I have since heard that a complaint was made to the bishop that I drove fifteen mad ... The worthy prelate wished that the madness might not be forgotten before next Sunday.' In little more than a year, at the request of the Wesley brothers who were already there, Whitefield had set sail for the American colony of Georgia. Already by then he had established himself as the preacher to be heard in London churches; already the established clergy were growing suspicious of him, scandalized by his preaching of new birth as something still needed by the baptized. This first voyage to America was to be followed by six others, on each of which he conducted preaching tours and took funds for an orphanage near Savannah in Georgia. The orphanage was to be a care and burden for the rest of his life. On his return from the first tour, he was ordained priest in early 1739 by Bishop Benson. Soon he began his open-air preaching.

The next day he came to London again; and on Sunday, the 21st, preached twice. But though the churches were large, and crowded exceedingly, yet many hundreds stood in the churchyard, and hundreds more returned home. This put him upon the first thought of preaching in the open air. But when he mentioned it to some of his friends, they judged it to be mere madness: so he did not carry it into execution till after he had left London. It was on Wednesday, February 21, that, finding all the church doors to be shut in Bristol (beside, that no church was able to contain one half of the congregation), at three in the afternoon he went to Kingswood, and preached abroad to near two thousand people. On Friday he preached there to four or five thousand; and on Sunday to, it was supposed, ten thousand! The number continually increased all the time he stayed at Bristol; and a flame of holy love was kindled, which will not easily be put out. The same was afterwards kindled in various parts of Wales, of Gloucestershire, and Worcestershire. Indeed, wherever he went, God abundantly confirmed the word of his messenger.

John Wesley[5]

Those who at first thought it 'mere madness' to preach out of doors included John and Charles Wesley. Whitefield began his preaching to the miners of Bristol with words on the Beatitudes (Matthew 5). By the time he was preaching to thousands, it was a major advantage that he had, as Benjamin Franklin said, 'a voice like an organ'. Two months later Whitefield began open-air preaching in London. Thousands flocked to hear him. John Wesley soon changed his mind on this subject. Whitefield now began a life which consisted of little else but travelling the length of Britain and across to America, and preaching, outdoors and indoors.

> Having no righteousness of their own to renounce, [the colliers] were glad to hear of a Jesus who was a friend to publicans, and came not to call the righteous but sinners to repentance. The first discovery of their being affected was the sight of the white gutters made by their tears, which plentifully fell down their black cheeks, as they came out of their coal-pits. Hundreds of them were soon brought under deep conviction, which, as the event proved, happily ended in a sound and thorough conversion. The change was visible to all, though numbers chose to impute it to anything rather than the finger of God. As the scene was quite new, it often occasioned many inward conflicts. Sometimes, when twenty thousand people were before me, I had not in my own apprehension a word to say either to God or them. But I was never totally deserted, and frequently ... was so assisted that I knew by happy experience what our Lord meant by saying, 'Out of his belly shall flow rivers of living water'. The open firmament above me, the prospect of the adjacent fields, with the sight of thousands, some in coaches, some on horseback, and some in the trees, and at times all affected and in tears, was almost too much for, and quite overcame, me.
>
> George Whitefield[6]

In 1739 John Wesley preached a sermon on 'free grace' at Bristol. While Whitefield was away on his second visit to America, Wesley published this sermon, which was a clear attack on Whitefield's Calvinist view of God's predestining some to salvation and some to damnation. In 1741, after he had returned, Whitefield ended many attempts to persuade Wesley to retract his views, and the two men went their separate ways, building separate chapels and forming separate societies. (Later Whitefield became a chaplain in the Countess of Huntingdon's Calvinist Methodist society.) But the two men's personal friendship was not broken for long, there remained a strong mutual affection and respect, and, after Whitefield's death at the age of 56 in America in 1770, Wesley preached a memorial sermon at Whitefield's chapel on Tottenham Court Road and at the Tabernacle at Greenwich. Among many other things he said on those occasions, Wesley paid tribute to Whitefield's personal openness and friendship, in spite of differences of opinion.

Mention has already been made of his unparalleled zeal, his indefatigable activity, his tender-heartedness to the afflicted, and charitableness towards the poor. But should we not likewise mention his deep gratitude to all whom God had used as instruments of good to him? – of whom he did not cease to speak in the most respectful manner, even to his dying day. Should we not mention that he had a heart susceptible of the most generous and the most tender friendship? I have frequently thought that this, of all others, was the distinguishing part of his character. How few have we known of so kind a temper, of such large and flowing affections! Was it not principally by this that the hearts of others were so strangely drawn and knit to him? Can anything but love beget love? This shone in his very countenance, and continually breathed in all his words, whether in public or private. Was it not this, which, quick and penetrating as lightning, flew from heart to

> heart? Which gave that life to his sermons, his conversation, his letters? Ye are witnesses!
>
> John Wesley[7]

Wesley ended his sermon with a passionate plea to Christians not to let differences of theology lead to conflict and party strife, and to have that 'catholic love – that sincere and tender affection which is due to all those who, we have reason to believe, are children of God by faith', that catholic love which he now ascribed to his departed friend and brother, George Whitefield.

William James believed that 'the real witness of the spirit of the second birth is to be found only in the disposition of the genuine child of God, the permanently patient heart, the love of self eradicated. And this, it has to be admitted, is also found in those who pass no crisis, and may even be found outside of Christianity altogether.'[8] Without for one moment impugning the value and reality of the conversion George Whitefield underwent and spent his life persuading others to give themselves up to, are we not also allowed to wonder whether the tender love and compassion he gave and inspired in others – which must have contributed so much to his effectiveness as a preacher and which allowed him to stay in fellowship with those he disagreed with – were not also in part natural, in-born gifts which he exercised as one of God's free children?

> He made another tour through Pennsylvania, the Jerseys, and New York. Incredible multitudes flocked to hear, among whom were abundance of Negroes. In all places the greater part of the hearers were affected to an amazing degree. Many were deeply convinced of their lost state, many truly converted to God. In some places, thousands cried out aloud; many as in the agonies of death; most were drowned in tears; some

turned pale as death; others were wringing their hands; others lying on the ground; others sinking into the arms of their friends; almost all lifting up their eyes, and calling for mercy ... Toward the close of his journey he made this reflection: 'It is the seventy-fifth day since I arrived at Rhode Island, exceeding weak in body; yet God has enabled me to preach an hundred and seventy-five times in public, besides exhorting frequently in private! Never did God vouchsafe me greater comforts: never did I perform my journeys with less fatigue, or see such a continuance of the divine presence in the congregations to whom I preached.'

John Wesley[9]

It is easy, Lord, for those who are intelligent
and successful to feel that they do not need to
change their lives.
But let us hear again the powerful word of
George Whitefield
and learn that our very best works
are as nothing in the light of your fierce love.
Thankful for the freedom you have given us,
help us still always to be ready to come to
you with nothing in our hands,
ready only to receive your justifying grace
in Jesus Christ our Saviour.

℘ ℘

Dwight Moody
1837–99

It seems strange to us that a single American evangelist, who died a few days before the year 1900 began and who was never ordained, could be influential both in twentieth-century fundamentalism *and* the ecumenical movement. But that is the case with Dwight Lyman Moody, who began life in 1837 on an impoverished farm in Northfield, Massachusetts, whose father died when he was four and whose education was minimal. The man who wrote – honestly – about his own spelling, 'I am always sure of the first letter and the last, and anywhere between may be upstairs or downstairs,' was later to make a very big impression on Cambridge University.

How did this come about? Moody was a man of enormous energy who, especially in his early days, lived life in a constant whirlwind of activity. He read the Bible voraciously, never doubting for one second its ability to provide divine guidance and power for himself and others, and was completely untouched by questions raised by its critical study. He made many strong friendships with Christian leaders of all denominations, believing that a focus on mission could overcome church sectarianism and division. He had the ability to interpret the Bible in attractive, natural, humorous and urgently emotional ways. His passion and driving energy could make him brusque and impatient at times, but there was a self-discipline and determined Christian spirit in him that would always quickly seek forgiveness and harmony if he had overstepped the mark. The two major human supports of his life were his wife Emma, who gently smoothed away some of the rough edges of his youth, and Ira Sankey, whose beautiful singing was indispensable to the effectiveness of his preaching on many evangelistic campaigns. He was, in later life, a very stocky substantial figure with a bull neck and a big brown beard. He loved physical exercise and being out of doors; he was a great one for practical jokes of a simple character; and he enjoyed playing with his children and grandchildren. There was in him a natural force and intelligence together with a single-minded evangelical conviction that overcame most obstacles that he faced.

In an age of ponderous English sermons when Spurgeon, most popular of all preachers, mouthed rolling periods, piled metaphor upon metaphor, Moody merely chatted 'to thirteen thousand as to thirteen', on what the Bible showed him. He made it alive in the context of every day. Daniel in the lions' den takes out his watch to check if it is the hour of prayer. Scoffers before the Flood 'talk it over in the corner groceries, evenings: "Not much sign of old Noah's rain-storm yet!"' Bartimaeus, suddenly seeing ('the first object that met his gaze was the Son of God himself'), rushes into Jericho 'and he says, "I will go and see my wife and tell her about it" – a young convert always wants to talk to his friends about salvation – Away he goes down the street 'n he meets a man who passes him 'n goes on a few yards 'n then turns round 'n says, "Bartimaeus, is that you?" "Yes." "Well, I thought it was, but I couldn't believe my eyes! How've you gotten your sight?" "Oh, I just met Jesus of Nazareth outside the city and asked him to have mercy on me." "Jesus of Nazareth! What! Is he in this part of the country?" "Sure. Right here in Jericho." "I should like to see him!" and away he runs down the street ...'

J.C. Pollock[10]

Moody's fame – as part of the partnership of Moody and Sankey – was launched on the British tour of 1873–75. Up to that time, and after a few years as a shoe salesman, his life had been principally based in Chicago, where he had launched a non-denominational Sunday School which developed into the Illinois Street Church, and where he worked for the Young Men's Christian

Association as a tireless city missionary, rising to become its President and a popular speaker at YMCA conventions. The Chicago fire of 1871 destroyed the Illinois Street Church, the YMCA hall and the Moody's home among much else in the city, and this, together with a powerful spiritual experience a few weeks later in New York, had the effect of launching Moody on to wider preaching missions. Of the overpowering sense of the presence of God he experienced, he wrote, 'I can only say that God revealed Himself to me, and I had such an experience of His love that I had to ask Him to stay His hand.' Prior to this moment 'I was all the time tugging and carrying water. But now I have a river that carries me.'[11]

The British evangelistic campaign of Moody and Sankey began fairly inconspicuously in York, continuing in Sunderland and Newcastle.

> There was a great crowd at Mr Leitch's church. At the meeting, which was opened by Mr Leitch and myself, the chief peculiarity was the singing of a Mr Sankey with harmonium accompaniment, under the direction of a Mr Moody, an American gentleman who has been labouring in Newcastle for five weeks. The singing was very impressive, the congregation striking in at the choruses with thrilling effect. The address by Mr Moody though thoroughly Yankee was deeply earnest and produced a great impression. It was on the grace of God, and had many happy strokes though here and there grotesque. The audience was fairly carried away at times by this mingled impulse of singing and appeal, and at the close a good many persons, impressed for the first time, waited to be spoken with.
>
> John Cairns, United Presbyterian minister[12]

The campaign burst into flames in Edinburgh, crowds flocking nightly to the Corn Exchange, which held almost

600 people, to hear Moody and Sankey. Key elements in its success were energetic and thorough publicity beforehand – using mass media, door-to-door canvassing, collaboration with local churches and financial support from business leaders – and, afterwards, the enquiry room or after-meeting where those who had stood up to give their lives to Christ could be counselled and brought to a greater resolution. Moody emphasized to his Scottish fellow-workers that they should, in these after-meetings, give 'patient and thorough dealing with each case, no hurrying from one to another'. They should 'wait patiently, and ply them with God's word, and think, oh! think, what it is to win a soul for Christ, and don't grudge the time spent on one person'. After missions in Glasgow and other parts of Scotland, then Belfast, Dublin, Manchester, Sheffield, Birmingham and Liverpool, the tour came to a huge climax in London, where Moody addressed some 2,500,000 people in four venues over more than four months. There were inevitably criticisms – from High Churchmen, of the 'vulgarity' of it all, from Calvinists, of the indiscriminateness of the preaching; but Moody's missions made an impact on all classes of society, including the poorest classes, and brought many people into the regular life of the Church. They even received a cautious welcome from the Archbishop of Canterbury, A.C. Tait.

At Islington Hall those Revivalists Yankee
Pious pair D L Moody and Ira D Sankey,
Are drawing, they tell us, immense congregations
By eccentric devotions and droll ministrations.
Their manner seems strangely at odds with their
    matter,
The former grotesque and most serious the latter.
They proclaim Gospel truths, in spite of grave
    prepossessions,
In colloquial slang, and commercial expressions,

State Scriptural facts in American phrases,
And interpolate jokes 'twixt their prayers and their
praises.

Satirical poem from *Punch*[13]

While the two men were in Edinburgh, Moody read a copy of the *Christian Age* and came across an anonymous poem entitled 'The Lost Sheep'. He told Sankey it would make a brilliant evangelistic hymn if it had a tune, and then forgot about it. Meanwhile Sankey began thinking of musical phrases, but on the very next day the theme of the noonday meeting was 'The Good Shepherd', and after the addresses Moody turned to Sankey and said, 'Have you a solo appropriate for the subject, to close the service with?' Sankey thought he had not, but then he thought of the 'The Lost Sheep' poem.

> Placing the little newspaper slip on the organ in front of me, I lifted my heart in prayer, asking God to help me so to sing that the people might hear and understand. Laying my hands upon the organ I struck the key of A flat and began to sing:
>
> > There were ninety and nine that safely lay
> > in the shelter of the fold;
> > But one was out on the hills away,
> > far off from the gates of gold –
> > away on the mountains wild and bare,
> > away from the tender Shepherd's care,
> > away from the tender Shepherd's care.
>
> After the first verse I was very glad I had got through, but overwhelmed with fear that the tune for the next verse would be greatly different from the first. But again looking up to the Lord for help in this most trying moment, He gave me again the same tune for all the remaining verses, note for note.[14]

The song had a huge emotional impact, with Moody and half the audience in tears. It swept Scotland. Sankey's *Sacred Songs and Solos*, which included his own and many other songs in his repertoire, was first published 1873, there were many subsequent editions, and the profits funded many of Moody's later ventures.

Moody returned to Britain several more times and organized similar evangelistic campaigns throughout America for the rest of his life. He also turned his attention to education and training for evangelism throughout the world. In 1879 he established the Northfield Seminary for Young Women, and in 1881, nearby, the Mount Hermon School for Young Men. In 1887 he established the Bible-Work Institute of the Chicago Evangelization Society, which became the Moody Bible Institute after his death. Annual summer conferences were held at Northfield, nurturing personal networks among conservative Protestants of various denominations. These institutions became important sources and centres of interdenominational fundament-alism in the twentieth century.

Moody and Sankey came to Cambridge in 1882, and on 5 November the Corn Exchange began to fill with around 1,700 rowdy undergraduates. Some dons and clergy led the two evangelists on to the platform to hoots and cheers. When Sankey sang 'The Ninety and Nine' the students beat the floor with canes and umbrellas and shouted, 'Hear, hear!' at the end of the first verse, and each verse produced cries of 'Encore!' When Moody got up to preach, the mockery continued: the audience mimicked his American accent and expressions and the way he said 'Dan'l' instead of Daniel; there was loud laughter and shouts of 'Well done'. Moody was visibly affected by all this, but kept his countenance and continued to the end of his words. At the end a further prayer meeting was held, and 400 students stayed behind, including some of those who had mocked. Next day Gerald Lander of Trinity

College came to see Moody. 'I want to apologize, sir. And I've brought a letter of apology from the men.' By the end of the week the Corn Exchange was full and no one could doubt Moody's significant impact in the university.

He had not spoken half a dozen words before I felt as though he and I were alone in the world ... After a scathing and indignant invective on sin, he turned to draw a picture of the hollow, drifting life with feeble, mundane ambitions – utterly selfish, giving no service, making no sacrifice, tasting the moment, gliding feebly down the stream of time to the roaring cataract of death. Every word he said burned into my soul. He seemed to me to probe the secrets of my innermost heart; to be analyzing, as it were, before the Judge of the world, the arid and pitiful constituents of my most secret thought. I did not think I could have heard him out – his words fell on me like the stabs of a knife. Then he made a sudden pause, and in a peroration of incredible dignity and pathos he drew us to the feet of a crucified Saviour, showed us the bleeding hand and the dimmed eye, and the infinite heart behind. 'Just accept Him,' he cried; 'in a moment, in the twinkling of an eye you may be His – nestling in His arms – with the burden of sin and selfishness at His feet.'

Arthur C. Benson, after hearing Moody at Cambridge[15]

The Cambridge mission played a vital role in the world mission enthusiasm of many students. Three years later, in 1885, the 'Cambridge Seven' sailed for China amidst much publicity, and that same year, at the sixth of Moody's Northfield Conferences, it was agreed to issue an 'Appeal to Disciples Everywhere', urging that if all the churches took the missionary call seriously, the entire earth could be evangelized by 1900. (Evangelization did not mean conversion; the aim was for every human being to have had the chance to hear the claims of Christ.) In his later years Moody spoke a great deal in American universities, and in 1886 he held the first of his student conferences at Northfield. At that conference, with the enthusiasm of Robert Wilder and John R. Mott, 100 students signed a declaration of willingness to serve overseas, and so began the Student Volunteer Movement, which played a major role in recruiting students for mission in the following years and which was a vital forerunner of the International Missionary Council set up at the Edinburgh World Missionary Conference of 1910. John R. Mott was the chair of the IMC, and the Edinburgh Conference effectively marked the beginning of the twentieth-century ecumenical movement, as the churches sought to work together in mission.

D.L. Moody died on 22 December 1899. His influence, both during and after his lifetime, is hard to overestimate. John R. Mott said, 'Next to the words of the Bible, and possibly those of Bunyan, Moody's words have been translated into more tongues than those of any other man.'

Lord Jesus Christ,
in whom God's love and mercy are made
known to us in the challenge of words and
deeds and in death undergone,
free us from prejudice and intellectualism
to hear again,
from the mouth of Dwight Moody,
the simple consolations and requirements of
your gospel.
We ask this for your precious name's sake.

৪০ ৫৪

Florence Allshorn
1887–1950

Today many Christians go 'on retreat'. Many retreat houses around the country offer thematic programmes, spiritual guidance, silence and tranquillity, and, above all, physical comfort and TLC. Many are run by monks and nuns, but many also by lay people; they offer people the chance to spend a few days perhaps mainly in silence, in order to get some perspective on life, freed from all immediate demands, and freed to listen a little harder for what God may be saying. This need not be a form of escapism; retreatants inevitably take with them their lives, their relationships, all their strengths and weaknesses. In the quiet setting many people feel the working of God's Spirit in them, changing their outlook, and continuing in their lives long after the retreat has ended.

People who go on retreat can be thankful for the life of Florence Allshorn, a significant pioneer in the first half of the twentieth century of the role of the modern retreat house as we know it. She was also someone who made a profound spiritual impression on all who knew her.

> I only met Florence Allshorn a few times – over a supper table, at a bazaar, in church. Each time I had an unforgettable and almost incommunicable impression of something I had never encountered before, a feeling that she was living in two worlds simultaneously, mine and one she brought with her. This seemed to show itself in a strange and delightful contradiction in her personality. She was at once gay and yet profoundly serious around her gaiety. She appreciated and offered the best of material pleasures and comforts and beauties and yet one suspected that they really meant nothing to her. She looked ready to share one's most trivial or sordid experience and one knew she would be untouched by it at the same time as bearing it. She gave

> me the impression of toughness and delicacy, like silver
> wire. I believe, of course, that I am trying to describe
> saintliness.
>
> Athene Seyler[16]

Born in 1887, Florence was brought up in Sheffield
from the age of three by a Miss Jackson, governess to her
mother's family. Both Florence's parents had died by then,
and her two brothers both died while still young men.
Florence studied art, then domestic science after leaving
school, but a turning-point in her life came when she met
Dr Gresford Jones, who was appointed Vicar and
Archdeacon of Sheffield in 1913. She became closely
involved in the work of Sheffield Cathedral, starting a club
for factory girls which soon reached a membership of
more than 80. 'My first memory of her', wrote Bishop
Gresford Jones, 'is at the centre of a group of rough factory
girls. No one had been really able to reach them before,
when lo! the miracle had happened, and there was this gay
company in the parish hall, as happy as could be, and
Florence the soul of it all.'[17] From 1918 she was a full-time
member of the Cathedral staff, running Bible classes and
doing pastoral work. She read novels, biography and
theology at this time, and covered half Derbyshire in long
walks over the heather.

Florence's Sheffield life came to an end in 1920, when
she was accepted, without further training, by the Church
Missionary Society, and sailed out to Uganda. At the
Iganga station in Busoga she was faced with an unenviable
challenge: to take over a girls' school singlehanded, and to
live with a single missionary colleague worn out by her
years there. We get a vivid impression of Florence's spirit
in the words of her first letter home:

> Busoga at last, and it is a job! It's the girls'
> boarding school for the whole of Busoga. No
> one can speak English, and the other
> European lady is the worker among the

women and in the dispensary. She's nervy, and the lady whose place I am taking has gone dicky with her nerves. So I am in the soup. But it's a great job, because it's the place on which the raising of the status of the women of Busoga depends. Isn't that a gorgeous bit of work to tackle? I'm jolly glad of it. Thank God for something absolutely impossible.[18]

It was the experience of the way 'something absolutely impossible' became possible in the four years Florence spent in Uganda that set the parameters for the rest of her life. This was not in the school responsibilities she had, which she seems to have managed with great energy and command, nor in the rats in her bedroom, the hyenas, leopards and jackals in the garden, the seven-foot snake outside her bedroom door or the hundreds of ant bites, but rather in the relationship she had with her older colleague. Florence's two guiding principles were the two great commands to love God and neighbour, but she became acutely aware that the apparently 'good work' that she and her colleague were doing was fatally undermined by the sourness of her colleague, into which she had allowed herself to be drawn. 'My colleague has stuck it,' she wrote in a letter. 'It just happens not to have affected her health, but it has absolutely rotted her nerves, and she has the most dreadful fits of temper. Sometimes she doesn't speak at all for two days. Just now we've finished up three weeks of never a decent word or smile.'[19] This was the crisis of Florence's life, and from what now happened flowed the rest of her life's strength and vision.

One day the old African matron came to me when I was sitting on the verandah crying my eyes out. She sat at my feet and after a time she said, 'I have been on this station for fifteen years and I have seen you come out, all of you saying you have brought to us a Saviour, but I have never seen this situation saved yet.' It brought me to my senses with a bang. I was the problem for myself. I knew enough of Jesus Christ to know that the enemy was the one to be loved before you could call yourself a follower of Jesus Christ, and I prayed, in great ignorance as to what it was, that this same love might be in me, and I prayed as I have never prayed in my life for that one thing. Slowly things rightened. Whereas before [my colleague] had been going about upsetting everybody with long deep dreadful moods, and I had been going into my school depressed and lifeless, both of us found our way to lighten each other. She had a great generosity and I must have been a cruel burden to her, worn out as she was. But I did see that as we two drew together in a new relation the whole character of the work on the station altered. We had some little real love to show to the people on it; they were freer with us, and less uneasy of what sort of attitude they would meet in us when they came. It is a long story and I could not put in half here, and it reads as though I had been the great reconciler. But that is certainly not true. She had been beaten in that place, and I was only in the process of being beaten, and the old matron saved me.

Florence Allshorn[20]

Florence read 1 Corinthians 13 every day for a whole year. 'Before we can hope to move things out here, I believe we have just got to be *living* 1 Corinthians 13. I am certain of it, I feel nothing else matters in comparison at all, organizations, gifts of speech – *nothing*.'[21] She knew she had discovered the power of God to make love victorious. Years later she wrote: 'To love a human being means to accept him, to love him as he is. If you wait to love him till he has got rid of his faults, till he is different, you are only loving an idea. He is as he is now, and he is to be loved now, as he is.'[22] But she had discovered a lot of other things too:

I have done a lot since I came here – been an influence for good, learned to whack girls over the head with a plate or anything you have in your hand, lead in extempore prayer, cook beautifully, entertain, help at confinements, keep my head when I wanted to lose it, keep calm with an obnoxious insect the size of my hand down my back, to use my tongue, to think a theatre is the height of earthly bliss, to think men are poor worms and that the only hope is in women, to bear with a lofty patience the fact that people don't realize that I've given my young life up to them, to suffer fools gladly (perhaps), and oh a lot more.[23]

Florence could be very earnest, but honesty and irony and gaiety kept breaking out.

By the time she got home on furlough, Florence looked thin and emaciated. She was diagnosed with a cavity in her lung, and spent time in England and Switzerland recuperating. In 1928 she was invited by the Church Missionary Society to become warden of one of their two training colleges for women missionaries, and six years later she became principal when the two colleges were combined into one. Her great aim and achievement in this time was to offer and provide her students with the solid spiritual and relational resources which they would need, in addition to the technical or professional expertise they would take to the mission field. Without being grounded in the love of God and in some understanding of human relationships, she believed, they would be little better than 'sounding brass or clanging cymbal'.

However many complacent excuses we may make about 'not being perfect', we are called to be 'saints', and a saint is a person who has learned to be possessed by God with whose love she confronts enemy as well as friend. If this definite learning of the love of God in reality and truth does not in practice and act take first place in our training at home or abroad, what strength and clarity of direction have we in our training? St Catharine of Sienna ... after seeing God became one of the most famous and one of the most powerful women of her century, endlessly active, travelling, shaping the life of Christendom. Why do we not set our pattern towards her experience? ... That every recruit has a true and effective spiritual life is taken too much for granted, and we have a queer belief that the Holy Spirit will do the job for us if we ask, occasionally in some little ardent way, and hundreds of times coldly ... Therefore we do not want secular colleges with a religious bias, pushing in knowledge of theology, anthropology, Bible etc., as if they were matters to be learned like maths. For the second stage of training at all events we want a religious house (with its connotation) for the training – not a religious house divorced from the world of sinners and worldly men, but a community of people struggling to become God-possessed, where they will find the world too as well as the deeper commitments of God.

Florence Allshorn[24]

But spirituality without emotional self-awareness and maturity would not be enough.

It is in the emotional life – this queer hinterland which is in all of us – that there huddle the anxieties, timidities, antagonisms, self-deceptions, inferiorities, revenge attacks, superiorities and withdrawals which somehow our spiritual life does not go deep enough to touch, where all the fighting and friction and the wreckage begin and end. If a woman fails to adjust her emotional life and goes on unconsciously working with a sense of failure there, then the one spot where she can find success is in 'the job'; but the almost inevitable result of a sense of failure in the inner life of a woman is an urgent desire for power. I believe that to be the chief reason why women missionaries ... so often lose that integral quality of Christ-likeness, humility, and become so hard and dominating and so rabid about their work.

Florence Allshorn[25]

It was during the Second World War that Florence's thoughts turned increasingly towards the idea of establishing a small community house of women, to provide a place of beauty and comfort for missionaries on furlough or for anyone else who, battered or drained by life and work, needed a place of rest and refreshment, both physical and spiritual.

I want to do something, where I can still go on serving you with what I have of experience and real caring for you. I have a dream of a house in some lovely quiet place where you could come and be quiet and rest and read and talk ... I believe that as the need for spiritual leadership becomes more and more urgent, as it is doing, we shall have to keep times of quiet and re-creation and being still to know God, not only on first furlough but on every furlough. Also for church people at home who go on and on and on in the same rut.[26]

A first house was found in 1941, then came a move in 1943 to St Julian's Barns Green, and finally in 1950 to charming and extensive premises at St Julian's Coolham near Horsham in Sussex. Florence died within months of the move to Coolham, but the community of St Julian's continued, from her founding inspiration, until the end of the century, offering quietness and regular prayer, a good library, beautiful surroundings and physical comfort for those who sought it. Breakfast in bed was de rigueur! Florence turned her back decisively on the prevailing tradition of austerity in Christian community life and retreat provision; beauty and quality of surroundings were vital to the apprehension of God's glorious love. She hated shoddiness and the attitude of 'it will do'; she loved the story of the woman who came to Jesus with the alabaster jar of ointment. St Julian's, now renamed St Cuthman's, is still a retreat house and is currently run by the Roman Catholic Diocese of Arundel and Brighton.

Florence Allshorn made a huge impact on all who knew her. She had a clear vocation to singleness and was felt by many to be 'way ahead' of them, but she also had a great gift of friendship, and the inevitable tensions and clashes of personality among the St Julian's community members were always worked through with determination, practicality and unsentimental love. Florence set herself the highest possible standards of openness to God, of closeness to Christ and of selflessness in love, and that meant she expected them in others, and indeed drew them out of others, often by sheer inspiration and example, and sometimes by an almost frightening sternness. The great enemy was half-hearted shallowness – going through the motions of religion without having plumbed the depths (of human sinfulness) or scaled the heights (of God's love). She loved a saying of Charles Péguy: 'A word is not the same with one writer as with another. One tears it from the guts, the other pulls it out of his overcoat pocket.' She experienced God with great intensity and great joy in the beauties of the created order, in the words of scripture, in other people, in art and literature – and sometimes, too, she struggled in loneliness and doubt. But the joy and inspiration of her faith were never far away.

> If I have any advice to give at all, I would beg you to study Jesus Christ in his dealings with men, until the stand he takes every time glows and burns within your hearts, so that you yourselves can do no other when the

same things happen to you, and I would beg you to pray that you may learn to love as Jesus Christ loved, with more passion and with more insistency than anything you have ever prayed for in your life, and then refuse defeat. Perhaps you will be able to do no more, but refuse defeat!

Florence Allshorn[27]

'When I first met her,' wrote one of Florence's former students, 'she impressed me – startled me – with a quality I can best call life, that vivid flame-like quality, so much more than mere moral goodness, which crackles through all the greatest saints.'[28]

You and I, before we pass away from here, have one little track to make in this life away from self to God. The trouble is that we are creatures of two dimensions – and we do not take the one as seriously as we take the other. An eternal you and a temporal you, and the first matters most, the eternal in you matters most. If only we could look and think a little bigger. If we could see, beyond our ordinary seeing, our place in the incredible destiny of human life, and see that we really take our stand somewhere in the millions and millions who age beyond age, year after year, have struggled and fallen, risen and triumphed. If we could for once hear the great universal cry of unhappiness, the horror before God of untruth, the bitter little self-defending defiances, the dreary litanies of self-pity, the great surging tides of self-will rearing themselves against all that is perfect love – happening all the time below the frozen gloss of what we are pleased to call being normal; and against that, the steadying wise cry of those who against every odd have kept life fresh and sweet and smiling and true – the undefeated ones with their grand earthly secret, 'He showed Himself alive in me'; if we could hear, see it as it is – reality as it is –

how we should choose, once for all choose which way
we should go, once for all determine to have no truck
with the surly self-wills, resentments, sour things, self-
defensiveness, untruths. How we should surrender
once for all. We must look and keep the edges of our
single-mindedness clear.

Florence Allshorn[29]

Florence Allshorn always refused defeat.

> *God of love,*
> *we pray that we may see the true beauty of*
> *your creation,*
> *taught by the intense vision of Florence*
> *Allshorn,*
> *and learn how to love you and to love all*
> *others with clearsighted determination and*
> *unsentimental faith,*
> *refusing defeat, today and tomorrow,*
> *in the presence and strength of Jesus Christ.*

℘ ℆

I want to end this chapter with two modest proposals,
approaching the problem of neglected saints from
opposite ends.

The first is that we should perhaps return to the
practice in the early centuries of the Church, when saints
were honoured just in particular localities and by popular
acclaim. Any church could add an extra layer of
celebration to the funeral eulogies and the books of
remembrance for their most outstanding members, by
remembering them each year on the day of their deaths –
not just the mention of a name on All Saints' or All Souls'
Day, but the deliberate recalling of a particular life and the
details of its holiness and achievements. This would be

inspiring and moving, especially for those who had known the person in question. Anglican dioceses actually have the power to create official celebrations in the calendar for local saints. Truro Diocese has a good number of local Cornish saints. If not everyone wants to celebrate Florence Allshorn, why not just the Diocese of Sheffield, where she spent her formative years?

My second proposal is based on the assertion that it is a powerfully healthy and ecumenical act to remember and celebrate *a saint that you would have disagreed with.* In fact, this is already built into the system of saints' days, because many of them lived in cultures or had positions which encouraged actions, such as crusades or physical self-mortifications, that contemporary people would find deeply unacceptable. In the Church of England both Protestant and Catholic martyrs of the sixteenth century are included in the calendar. Yet Anglicans may celebrate Thomas More as well as Thomas Cranmer, but we don't celebrate Edmund Campion, and the Roman Catholics don't celebrate Nicholas Ridley – yet. We need to be brave and forgiving and magnanimous enough to celebrate the lives of our old opponents.

ଚ୦ ଔ

God of our fathers and mothers,
you have brought into being a great
communion of saints,
people of the Spirit, both great and small,
prominent and hidden.
In the body of your Son you draw together
the celebrated and the neglected,
in a wholeness embracing all our quarrels
and differences.
Open our eyes to other kinds of life,
and expand our conception of discipleship
within the love of Jesus Christ.

Epilogue: Judas Iscariot

'Judas! traitor!' I ejaculated. 'You are a hypocrite, too, are you? a deliberate deceiver?'[1] So says Nellie Dean as she catches Heathcliff embracing Isabella Linton in Emily Brontë's *Wuthering Heights*. 'Judas' and 'traitor' have become synonyms, through 2,000 years of Christian history. And that reflects the way Judas makes his appearances in the New Testament: in the lists of the 12 disciples he always appears last and as the one who betrayed Jesus; in all four gospels he leads the Jewish authorities to Jesus at night, betraying Jesus with a kiss in all the gospels except John; and Matthew and Luke describe the bitter end to which he came (Matthew – he hanged himself; Luke – he fell headlong and his bowels gushed out). John's Gospel adds to the villainous portrait of Judas by having him help himself from the common purse and by having Jesus call him 'a devil'.

So Judas is the ultimate villain: disloyal, greedy, envious, he brings about the death of the innocent Son of God. And as if that were not enough, he commits suicide in some kind of remorse and despair (according to Matthew), thus adding another major sin – in the eyes of later Christian thought – to his tally. John Calvin concluded that Judas' repentance was merely the 'legal' kind, and that he together with Cain or King Saul

> perceived the heinousness of their sins, and dreaded the divine anger; but, thinking only of God as a judge and avenger were overwhelmed by the thought. Their repentance, therefore, was nothing better than a kind of threshold to hell, into which having entered even in the present life, they began to endure the punishment inflicted by the presence of an offended God.[2]

So Judas is, if you like, the ultimate test case for the rescue or rehabilitation of those whom later tradition has vilified, ignored or merely failed to celebrate. If Judas can be 'rescued', then anyone at all can be rescued, but if he can't be, this may place a question mark against some fashionable attempts to rehabilitate despised or ignored historical figures and show them to be mere special pleading.

Certainly Judas has been the object, in the last couple of centuries, of more attempts to restore his name than almost any other figure of religious or historical significance. Richard III can't compete!

In poems and novels and plays Judas has been accorded a measure of sympathy or even seen as a flawed hero. In George Russell's poem *Germinal* Judas' behaviour is given a psychological explanation: 'In the lost boyhood of Judas Christ was betrayed'; while in representations of the gospel by Robert Graves, Nikos Kazantzakis, Anthony Burgess, right up to *Jesus Christ Superstar*, Judas emerges as a bit of a star himself. Two 'good' ways of construing Judas' behaviour emerge. He can be seen as desperate for the kingdom of God to break in, and therefore willing, as it were, to 'force God's hand' by betraying Jesus and bringing the great conflict between good and evil to a head. On this reading, everything seems to go wrong when Jesus is actually executed, and Judas hangs himself in shame and chagrin. Or else the whole thing can be seen as part of the good intention of God, to lead to the saving death on the cross, and so Judas can be seen to have an honourable part in bringing that about. The twentieth-century Argentine writer Jorge Luis Borges wrote a story, *Three Versions of Judas,* in which a theologian came to regard Judas as the true Messiah, because he bore not just death but eternal damnation and everlasting vilification, for his part in the passion drama!

Why do modern people want to rehabilitate Judas? Well, we are much more aware of our mixed personalities and of moral ambiguities; we tend to love anti-heroes and underdogs; and I suppose we're arrogant enough to think that, with our superior understanding, we can overturn thousands of years of uncritical assumptions imposed by arrogant hierarchies. On the other hand, perhaps it's not arrogant to say that it is unfair that a human life should be eternally blackened on the basis of a few lines in the New Testament. Surely Judas did lots of good things along with the rest of the disciples? And actually some of the later legends about him do imagine him getting a few hours out of hell on the basis of some small acts of charity he had done.

A better reason for deflecting odium from Judas is as part of the modern attack on Christian-inspired anti-Semitism. St Jerome in the fourth century said, 'The Jews take their name, not from that Judah who was a holy man, but from the betrayer. From the former we [Christians] are spiritual Jews; from the traitor come the carnal Jews.'[3] Dante in his *Inferno* placed Judas, together with Brutus and Cassius (who betrayed Julius Caesar), in the ninth circle of hell; his head and upper torso are chewed eternally by the front mouth of Lucifer's three faces. Dante calls this part of hell 'la Guidecca', a name which was used later for the Jewish ghettoes of Europe. Judas is frequently portrayed in medieval art as the typical nasty caricature of the Jew: the red hair and beard, the ruddy skin, the large hooked nose, big lips and bleary eyes, the yellow robe and money bag. Both Jewish and Christian modern writers have called attention to the way in which Judas had become the archetypal Jew – envious, greedy, untrustworthy. Of course, a much more powerful attack on Christian anti-Semitism is provided by rediscovering the Jewishness of Jesus himself; but a subordinate element in that campaign should be the rescuing of Judas from his role as the 'essential Jew'.

A third reason for revisioning Judas in the modern period lies in our anxieties about eternal damnation. In the third century, Origen thought that even the devil would finally turn and be saved, but theologians from

Augustine to Calvin and beyond have thought that very many were predestined to be lost for ever, and, if so, Judas was a prime candidate – both for his betrayal of Jesus and for his suicide. Many liberal western people now feel anxious about this view and would want to side with Origen. Are we to say that God judges them as harshly as they clearly judge themselves?

Finally even the Roman Catholic Church has shown signs of wishing to pass a more merciful judgement on Judas. In January 2006 it was announced that Monsignor Walter Brandmuller, head of the Pontifical Committee for Historical Science, was to lead a new examination of the acts of Judas from the point of view that his betrayal had actually been divinely inspired, in order to 'resolve the problem of an apparent lack of mercy by Jesus towards one of his closest collaborators', and perhaps also to rebuild more bridges with the Jewish community. The headlines said, 'Catholic Church Sends Judas to Rehab', and 'Vatican Makeover for Judas Iscariot'. At more or less the same moment in time there was publicity about a *Gospel of Judas*, originating from a Gnostic sect, the Cainites in Egypt in the second century AD, which, having been discovered in the 1970s, was about to be published. In it Jesus apparently encourages Judas to betray him and Judas is called 'Jesus' true disciple'. In my view, this apparently ancient document fits with the late twentieth-century desire to exonerate Judas just a little *too* well. I would not be in the slightest surprised if it turned out to be a forgery.

There are, then, strong motivations for the modern desire to reinstate Judas, but the resulting pictures of Jesus' betrayer undoubtedly say more about the modern authorities than about Judas. In this book I, too, have been strongly motivated to reinstate for Christian consideration lives and careers of genius and faith which have been despised or ignored or simply overlooked, as flesh-and-blood sources of inspiration for us, and there can be no doubt that, as a person of modern conditioning, my motivation has been strongly based on twentieth- and twenty-first-century factors of a liberal kind. Nevertheless I have striven here to be faithful to the best historical sources and view of the lives I have presented, and to avoid the cruder kind of hagiography or special pleading.

So if we look at Judas in a ruthlessly historical assessment, what do we find? That most puritanical of New Testament critics, John Dominic Crossan, in his book *Who Killed Jesus?*[4] believes that Mark created the earliest account we have of the events after Gethsemane on the basis of the story of King David leaving Jerusalem during the revolt of his son Absalom: the role of Judas is then portrayed as like that of Ahithophel, who was disloyal to David and finally committed suicide. Crossan believes that some of the events described by Mark may be historical, but that the whole story line is Mark's creation. His final *guess* is that Judas may have betrayed to the authorities who precisely had carried out the disruption of the Temple sacrifices and then told them where they could find Jesus; and that he died soon afterwards. So the likelihood is that Judas's was very much a 'bit part' in the complex series of events and the multiple personalities and motivations of all the people who brought Jesus to his death.

My considered opinion, then, whether on that basis or on the basis of the New Testament reports themselves, is that we do not have enough material to rehabilitate Judas. A *Times* editorial on 12 January 2006 in response to the Vatican initiative said,

> To see him as a victim is surely too generous – even by modern standards. To contend that he did not know what he was doing does not square with the biblical evidence. To conclude that he was only obeying orders is not satisfactory either ... The Vatican may decide to be very kindly towards him. Yet, Judas is surely a bad chap.[5]

Well, who knows? As Jean Rhys wrote in *Wide Sargasso Sea,* 'What does anyone know about traitors or why Judas did what he did?'[6] One thing I do know is that all the heroes of faith presented in this book were certainly 'good chaps', focusing their faith *in skills and disciplines and searchings which have been too little celebrated as true vehicles of holiness and charity.* Their charity was often of a different kind from what was institutionally approved, a charity of genius and communication, a charity recognized by the seventeenth-century sage, Sir Thomas Browne, when he wrote:

> I hold not so narrow a conceit of this virtue, as to conceive that to give Alms is only to be Charitable, or think a piece of Liberality can comprehend the Total of Charity. Divinity hath wisely divided the act thereof into many branches and hath taught us in this narrow way many paths unto goodness; as many ways as we may do good, so many ways we may be charitable. There are infirmities not only of Body, but of Soul, and Fortunes, which do require the merciful hand of our abilities. I cannot contemn a man for ignorance, but behold him with as much pity as I do Lazarus. It is no greater Charity to cloth his body, than apparel the nakedness of his soul.[7]

The dispensers of charity celebrated in this book, wisdom's children, have left the Church and the world deeply in their debt.

As for the eternal fate of Judas, even if he were a double-dyed villain, what can we say? When we know of the possibility of forgiveness and reconciliation after horrific offences here on earth, are we going to say that such things are impossible *post mortem*? How can a faith which sees the providential good emerging from the evil doings of Joseph and his brothers, out of the early deaths of Naomi's sons-in-law, and supremely in the whole history of Israel leading to the unjust trial and execution of Jesus, say that there could be no providential goodness available for Judas? Of course, these can only be questions, but if Christ died for all, how could Judas be outside the scope of God's love?

&) (og

Dear God,
how can we look into the lives of other human
beings
and know what love and faith burn in their hearts?
Judas, too, had a part to play as a friend of Jesus,
but we pray that neither he nor anyone
may put themselves beyond your reach.
As we thank you for all who put their genius at
your service,
save us from betraying, in a false trail of holiness,
the actual skills and gifts you have given us;
help us to use them in the realization of your
kingdom here and hereafter.

Notes

Inspire gratefully acknowledges the use of copyright items. Every effort has been made to trace copyright owners, but where we have been unsuccessful we would welcome information which would enable us to make appropriate acknowledgement in any reprint.

Introduction

1. Tom Stoppard, *The Real Inspector Hound and Other Plays,* Faber & Faber, 1993, p. 7.
2. Robert Atwell (ed.), *Celebrating the Saints: Daily Spiritual Readings for the Calendar of the Church of England*, Canterbury Press, 1998, p. ii.
3. Karl Rahner, quoted in Robert Ellsberg, *All Saints*, Crossroad, 1997, p. 2.
4. Robert Ellsberg, *All Saints*, pp. 4–5.
5. Mark 9.40.
6. Mark Santer, quoted in Robert Atwell, *Celebrating the Saints*, p. vii.
7. Kathleen Jones, *Who are the Celtic Saints*, Canterbury Press, 2002, p. xvii.
8. Jonathan Swift, *A Tale of a Tub*, 1704, Dedication.

Chapter 1

1. Matthew 11.11, 13–14.
2. Hebrews 11.39–40.

3. Hebrews 9.15.

4. Justin Martyr, *First Apology 46,* quoted in L.W. Barnard, *Justin Martyr: His Life and Thought,* Cambridge, 1967, p.89.

5. Mark van Doren, 'The People of the Word', from *Spring Birth and Other Poems,* 1953.

6. Robert Carroll, *Jeremiah,* SCM Press, 1986, pp. 63–64.

7. N.T. Wright, *The Resurrection of the Son of God,* SPCK, 2003, p. 152.

8. Wilfred Owen, 'Futility', in *Selected Poems,* Bloomsbury, 1995, p. 51.

Chapter 2

1. Maurice Wiles, *Archetypal Heresy: Arianism Through the Centuries,* OUP, 1996, p. 2.

2. *Theology,* Vol. CVIII, No. 845, September–October, 2005, p. 353.

3. G.R. Evans, *A Brief History of Heresy,* Blackwell, 2003, p. 164.

4. Homily 34 [PG13. 1886] on the parable of the Good Samaritan (Latin version by St Jerome), quoted in David Lyle Jeffrey (ed.), *A Dictionary of Biblical Tradition in English Literature,* Eerdmans, 1992, p. 315.

5. Henri Crouzel, 'Origen', in *The Oxford Companion to Christian Thought,* OUP, 2000, p. 503.

6. Origen, *de Principiis* IV.2.4, in G.W. Butterworth, *Origen on First Principles,* SPCK, 1936.

7. Origen, commentary on Matthew's Gospel in R.B. Tollinton (ed.), *Selections from the Commentaries and Homilies of Origen,* SPCK, 1929.

8. Origen, *de Principiis* IV.4.10, quoted in Joseph Wilson Trigg, *Origen,* SCM Press, 1985, p. 129.

9. William Ralph Inge, quoted in Joseph Wilson Trigg, *Origen*, p. 258. Inge was Dean of St Paul's Cathedral (1911–34).

10. Herbert B. Workman and R. Martin Pope (eds.), *The Letters of John Hus*, Hodder & Stoughton, 1904, pp. 275–76 (from Internet Modern History Sourcebook www.fordham.edu/halsall/mod/ 1415janhus.html)

11. Pope John Paul II, *Address to the international congress of historians on Jan Hus*, 17 December 1999. www.vatican.va/holy_father/john_paul_ii/ speeches/1999/documents/hf_jp-ii_spe_17121 (my translation from original German).

12. Jan Hus, *Postilla*, quoted in Matthew Spinka, *John Hus's Concept of the Church*, Princeton University Press, 1966, pp. 296–97.

13. Jan Hus, letter to his university colleagues and students, written 10 days before his death, quoted in Matthew Spinka, *John Hus's Concept of the Church*, pp. 391–92.

14. Jan Hus, *Postilla*, quoted in Matthew Spinka, *John Hus's Concept of the Church*, pp. 304–5.

15. Jan Hus, *Vyklad viry*, quoted in Matthew Spinka, *Joh Hus's Concept of the Church*, p. 320.

16. John William Colenso, *Natal Sermons II*, quoted in Peter Hincliff, *John William Colenso, Bishop of Natal*, Nelson, 1964, p. 175.

17. B.B. Burnett, *Anglicans in Natal*, 1953, quoted in Peter Hincliff, *John William Colenso, Bishop of Natal*, p. 68.

18. John William Colenso, *The Pentateuch and the Book of Joshua Critically Examined*, Longman, Roberts and Green, 1862, Preface, p. vii.

19. John William Colenso, *St Paul's Epistle to the Romans: Newly Translated, and Explained from a*

Missionary Point of View, Pietermaritzburg Ekukanyeni Mission Press, 1861, p. 107.

20. John William Colenso, *The Pentateuch and the Book of Joshua Critically Examined*, Introductory Remarks, p. 13.

21. J.W. Rogerson, *Old Testament Criticism in the Nineteenth Century: England and Germany*, SPCK, 1984, p. 236.

22. Limerick in *The Natal Witness* 1863, quoted in Jeff Guy, *Class, Imperialism and Literary Criticism: William Ngidi, John Colenso and Matthew Arnold*, Journal of South African Studies, Vol. 23 No. 2, June 1997, p. 219.

23. Anthony Trollope, *Clergymen of the Church of England: The Clergyman who subscribes for Colenso*, Chapman and Hall, 1866, pp. 124–28.

24. Alister E. McGrath, *Christian Theology: An Introduction*, Blackwell 1994, p.175.

Chapter 3

1. Ephesians 5.19.

2. *Catechism of the Catholic Church* 1156, Geoffrey Chapman, 1994.

3. Augustine, *Confessions* 9.6, quoted in *Catechism of the Catholic Church* 1157.

4. Augustine, *Confessions*, 10.33.

5. Augustine, *Confessions*, 10.33.

6. David Wyn Jones, *Oxford Composer Companions, Haydn*, OUP, 2002, p. 214.

7. T. S. Eliot, 'Little Gidding' 242, *Four Quartets*, Faber & Faber, 1944.

8. Hans Küng, *Mozart: Traces of Transcendence*, SCM Press, 1992, p. 33.

9. William Byrd, *Preface to the First Book of Madrigals*, 1588.

10. Henry Walpole, 'Why do I use', 1581, quoted in Imogen Holst, *The Great Composers: Byrd*, Faber & Faber, 1972, p. 40.

11. William Byrd, *Dedication of the Second Book of* Gradualia *to Baron Petre of Writtle* 1607, translated from the Latin, quoted in Imogen Holst, *The Great Composers: Byrd*, p. 67.

12. Dr Julius Bayer, *Recorded recollection for BBC2* Workshop *documentary, OAMDG*, 1968, quoted in Stephen Johnson, *Bruckner Remembered*, Faber & Faber, 1998, p. 107.

13. Carl Hruby, *Meine Erinnerungen an Anton Bruckner*, Vienna 1901, quoted in Stephen Johnson, *Bruckner Remembered*, p. 73.

14. Julia Bayer, *Anton Bruckner in Steyr,* reproduced in Grassberger and Partsch (eds.), *Bruckner-skizziert*, Vienna 1991, quoted in Stephen Johnson, *Bruckner Remembered,* pp. 79-80.

15. Stephen Johnson, *Programme note to CD of Bruckner 9th Symphony* LSO Live, The London Symphony Orchestra conducted by Sir Colin Davis.

16. Karl Kobald (ed.), *In Memorian Anton Bruckner*, Zürich, Vienna and Leipzig 1924, quoted in Stephen Johnson, *Bruckner Remembered,* pp. 172–73.

17. 1 Corinthians 13.12.

18. Franz Gräflinger, *Anton Bruckner, Bausteine zu seiner Lebengesichte*, Munich 1911, quoted in Stephen Johnson, *Bruckner Remembered,* pp. 21–22.

19. Revelation 10.5–6 (The New Jerusalem Bible).

20. Claude Samuel, *Conversations with Olivier Messiaen*, English ed. trans. Felix Aprahamian, Stainer & Bell, 1976, p. 11.

21. Claude Samuel, *Conversations with Olivier Messiaen*, p. 6.

22. Claude Samuel, *Conversations with Olivier Messiaen*, p. 2.

23. Oliver Messiaen, *Notes in the score of Visions de l'Amen.*

24. *Guardian*, 17 June 2005.

Chapter 4

1. *A Dictionary of Biblical Tradition in English Literature*, Eerdmans, 1992, p. xi.

2. Quoted in *The Oxford Companion to Christian Thought*, 2000, p. 545.

3. John 16.12–13.

4. John Milton, *Psalm 136*, 1–24 in H.C. Beeching (ed.), *The Poetical Works of John Milton*, Oxford, 1919, p. 9-10.

5. John Milton, *Paradise Lost XII*, 509–519 in H.C. Beeching (ed.), *The Poetical Works of John Milton*, pp. 444f.

6. John Milton, *Sonnet XVI* in H.C. Beeching (ed.), *The Poetical Works of John Milton*, p. 85.

7. John Milton, *Paradise Regain'd* IV, 606–17, in H.C. Beeching, (ed.), *The Poetical Works of John Milton*, p. 501.

8. John Milton, *Paradise Lost* XII, 561–69, in H.C. Beeching, (ed.), *The Poetical Works of John Milton*, p. 446.

9. John Milton, *Paradise Lost* XII, 641–49, in H.C. Beeching, (ed.), *The Poetical Works of John Milton*, p. 448.

10. Fyodor Dostoyevsky, *The Brothers Karamazov*, trans. David Magarshack, Penguin, 1958, p. 287.

11. Nicholas Berdyaev, *Dostoyevsky*, Sheed and Ward, 1936, pp. 30–31.

12. Letter to Mrs Fonvizin, quoted in Matthew Spinka, *Christian Thought from Erasmus to Berdyaev*, Prentice-Hall, 1962, pp. 196–97.

13. Konstantin Mochulsky, *Dostoyevsky* 1973, quoted in *The Oxford Companion to Christian Thought*, 2000, p. 179 (article by Donald Nicholl).

14. Fyodor Dostoyevsky, *Notes from the Underground*, 1864, quoted in *The Oxford Companion to Christian Thought*, p. 180.

15. Fyodor Dostoyevsky, *The Brothers Karamazov*, p. 308.

16. Nicholas Berdyaev, *Dostoyevsky*, pp. 207–8.

17. Dorothy L. Sayers, *Letter to John Wren-Lewis*, 1954, quoted in David Coombes, *Dorothy L. Sayers: A Careless Rage for Life*, Lion, 1992, pp. 205–6.

18. Dorothy L. Sayers, *The Man Born to be King*, 1943, Ignatius Press, San Francisco, 1990, pp. 14–15.

19. Dorothy L. Sayers, 'The Mocking of Christ' in *Catholic Tales and Christian Songs*, The Anglican Library, 2000, www.anglicanlibrary.org/sayers/catholictales/index.htm

20. Dorothy L. Sayers, *Murder Must Advertise*, quoted in Mary Brian Durkin, *Dorothy L. Sayers: A Christian Humanist for Today*, Christian Century, 14 November 1979, p. 1114. www.religion-online.org/cgi-bin/relsearchd.dll/showarticle?item_id=1267

21. *Biographisch-Bibliographisches Kirchenlexicon*, Verlag Traugott Bautz, 1998, p. 1412 (my translation).

22. Dorothy L. Sayers, 'The Zeal of thy House' in *Four Sacred Plays*, Gollancz, 1948, pp. 102–3.

23. Dorothy L. Sayers, *Creed or Chaos?* Quoted in Mary Brian Durkin, *Dorothy L. Sayers: A Christian Humanist for Today*.

24. Dorothy L. Sayers, 'The Greatest Drama Ever Staged' in *Creed or Chaos? and other Essays in Popular Theology*, reproduced in Ann Loades (ed.), *Dorothy L. Sayers: Spiritual Writings*, SPCK, 1993, p. 117.

25. Quoted in Mary Brian Durkin, *Dorothy L. Sayers: A Christian Humanist for Today*.

26. Dorothy L. Sayers, *The Man Born to be King*, p. 256.

27. Dorothy L. Sayers, *The Dogma is in the Drama*, in Ann Loades (ed.), *Dorothy L. Sayers: Spiritual Writings*, p. 54.

Chapter 5

1. Exodus 20.4.

2. Régis Debray, *The New Testament Through 100 Masterpieces of Art*, Merrell, 2004, pp. 7–8.

3. Régis Debray, *The Old Testament Through 100 Masterpieces of Art*, Merrell, 2004, p. 4.

4. John Drury, *Painting the Word: Christian Pictures and their Meanings*, Yale, 1999, pp. 155–75.

5. Book of Common Prayer.

6. Desiderius Erasmus, *Moriae Encomium* 1511, trans. John Wilson, *In Praise of Folly* 1668, Dover Publications, 2003, p. 32.

7. Vasari, *Life of Fra Angelico*, quoted in John Pope-Hennessy, *The Paintings of Fra Angelico*, Phaidon, 1952, p. 1.

8. John Pope-Hennessy, *The Paintings of Fra Angelico*, pp. 2–3.

9. Germaine Greer, *The Obstacle Race*, Martin Secker and Warburg Ltd, 1979, pp. 173–74.

10. Fra Angelico, *Crucifixion with Saints*, Convento di San Marco, Florence. Most of the pictures I refer to

can be accessed through the Bridgeman Art Library (www.bridgeman.co.uk) or as Google images.

11. Fra Angelico, *St Dominic Adoring the Cross*, Convento di San Marco, Florence.

12. Neil Macgregor with Erika Langmuir, *Seeing Salvation*, BBC, 2000, p. 153.

13. Fra Angelico, *The Mocking of Christ*, Convento di San Marco, Florence.

14. Fra Angelico, *Noli Me Tangere*, Convento di San Marco, Florence.

15. John 20. 10–18.

16. Neil Macgregor with Erika Langmuir, *Seeing Salvation*, pp. 153–56.

17. Lorenzo Valla, *Inscription on Fra Angelico's tomb*, quoted in John Pope-Hennessy, *The Paintings of Fra Angelico*, p. 31.

18. Albrecht Dürer, *Treatise on Proportion*, quoted in Erwin Panofsky, *The Life and Art of Albrecht Dürer*, Princeton, 1954, p. 283.

19. Albrecht Dürer, *Praying Hands*.

20. Desiderius Erasmus, Dialogue *De recta Latini Graecique sermonis pronuntiatione*, quoted in Erwin Panofsky, *The Life and Art of Albrecht Dürer*, Princeton, 1954, p. 44.

21. Albrecht Dürer, *Letter from Venice to Willibald Pirckheimer 13 October* 1506, in Richard Friedenthal, *Letters of the Great Artists*, Random House, 1963, p. 58.

22. Albrecht Dürer, *Journal,* quoted in William Martin Conway, *Literary Remains of Albrecht Dürer*, Cambridge, 1889, pp. 158–59.

23. Albrecht Dürer, *Letter to Georg Spalatin*, quoted in Otto Benesch, *The Art of the Renaissance in Northern Europe*, Harvard University Press, 1945, p. 23.

24. Albrecht Dürer, *Four Apostles*.

25. Albrecht Dürer, *Treatise on Painting*, quoted in W.M. Conway, *Literary Remains of Albrecht Dürer*, p. 177.

26. Albrecht Dürer, *The Fall of Man*.

27. Albrecht Dürer, *Portrait of his Mother*.

28. Albrecht Dürer, *Family Chronicle*, quoted in W.M. Conway, *Literary Remains of Albrecht Dürer*, p. 78.

29. Albrecht Dürer, *Self Portrait* 1500.

30. Albrecht Dürer, *Treatise on Proportion*, quoted in Erwin Panofsky, *The Life and Art of Albrecht Dürer*, p. 279.

31. Albrecht Dürer, *Young Hare*.

32. Martin Luther, *Letter to Eobanus Hessus*, quoted in W.M. Conway, *Literary Remains of Albrecht Dürer*, p. 136.

33. Georges Rouault, *Letter to Édouard Schuré* c. 1905, in Irina Fortunescu trans. Richard Hilliard, *Rouault: Anthology of Texts, Selection of Illustrations and Chronology*, Meridiane Publishing House, Bucharest, 1975, p. 8.

34. Georges Rouault, *The Old King*.

35. Quoted in Edward Knippers, Commentary on the Exhibition of Prints from 'Miserere' at Christ Church Cathedral, Montreal, June 1997 www.montreal.anglican.org/cathedral/english/roua ult.htm

36. Georges Rouault, *Thoughts and Recollections* in *Roualt: Anthology of Texts*, p. 8.

37. Georges Rouault, *Miserere et Guerre*.

38. Georges Rouault, *Letter to Georges Chabot* 1927, in *Rouault: Anthology of Texts*, p. 10.

39. Quoted in Knippers, Commentary on the Exhibition of prints from 'Miserere'.

40. Quoted in Jose Maria Faerna, Rouault Cameo (Great Modern Masters Series) Harry N. Abrams, 1997, p.5.

41. Pierre Courthion, *Georges Rouault*, Thames and Hudson, 1978, p. 23.

42. E.g. Georges Rouault, *Christ Mocked by Soldiers* 1932, *Christ* 1937, *The Holy Face* 1956.

43. Pierre Courthion, *Georges Rouault*, pp. 22–23.

Chapter 6

1. John Hedley Brooke, *Science and Religion: Some Historical Perspectives*, CUP, 1991, p. 5.

2. Rodney Stark, *For the Glory of God: How Monotheism led to Reformations, Science, Witch-hunts, and the End of Slavery*, Princeton University Press, 2003, p. 157.

3. Laurel C. Schneider, in Susan Brooks Thistlethwaite (ed.), *Adam, Eve and the Genome*, Fortress Press, Minneapolis, 2003, pp. 28–29.

4. John Hedley Brooke, *Science and Religion: Some Historical Perspectives*, p. 31.

5. Quoted in Peter Barrett, *Science and Theology Since Copernicus*, T. & T. Clark, 2004, p. 10.

6. Richard Harries, 'Religion and Science – Old Enemies or New Friends?', *Modern Believing* 47:1, January 2006, p. 26.

7. Roger Bacon, *Opus Tertium*, quoted in Theodore Crowley, *Roger Bacon: The Problem of the Soul in his Philosophical Commentaries*, Louvain Editions de l'Institut Supérieur de Philosophie 1950, p. 29 (my translation from the Latin).

8. Roger Bacon, *Opus Maius*, quoted in Winthrop Woodruff, *Roger Bacon*, James Clarke and Co., London (no date), p. 78.

9. Roger Bacon, *Opus Maius*, quoted in Winthrop Woodruff, *Roger Bacon*, p. 142.

10. Roger Bacon, *Opus Tertium*, quoted in *Oxford Dictionary of National Biography*, 2004, Vol. 3, p. 179.

11. Roger Bacon, *Opius Tertium,* quoted in E. Westacott, *Roger Bacon in Life and Legend*, Rockliff, 1953, pp. 40–41.

12. Robert Boyle, *The Christian Virtuoso* 1690 1st Part from Robert Boyle, *Works*, 5 vols, London, 1744, in D.C. Goodman (ed.), *Science and Religious Belief 1600-1900*, Open University, 1973, p. 125.

13. Robert Boyle, *The Christian Virtuoso* 1st Part, in D.C. Goodman (ed.), *Science and Religious Belief 1600–1900*, Open University, 1973, p. 125.

14. Robert Boyle, *A Disquisition about the Final Causes of Natural Things* 1688, in D.C. Goodman (ed.), *Science and Religious Belief 1600–1900*, Open University, 1973, p. 107.

15. Robert Boyle, *The Christian Virtuoso* 1st Part in D.C. Goodman (ed.), *Science and Religious Belief 1600–1900*, Open University, 1973, p. 126.

16. Robert Boyle, *A Disquisition about the Final Causes of Natural Things* in D.C. Goodman (ed.), *Science and Religious Belief 1600–1900*, Open University, 1973, p. 111.

17. Gregor Mendel, quoted in Robin Marantz-Henig, *A Monk and Two Peas*, Weidenfeld and Nicholson, 2000, p. 17.

18. Gregor Mendel, quoted in Vitezslav Orel, *Mendel*, OUP, 1984, p. 22.

19. Hugo Iltis, trans. Paul Cedar and Eden Paul, *The Life of Mendel*, W.W.Norton & Co., New York, 1932, pp. 108–9.

20. Hugo Iltis, trans. Paul Cedar and Eden Paul, *The Life of Mendel*, p. 108.

21. Gregor Mendel, quoted in Hugo Iltis, trans. Paul Cedar and Eden Paul, *The Life of Mendel*, p. 110.

22. Vitezslav Orel, *Mendel*, p. 93.

23. Loren Eisley, quoted in Jan Sapp, *Genesis: The Evolution of Biology*, OUP, 2003, p. 119.

Chapter 7

1. Matthew 8.10.

2. John Hick, quoted in Reinhold Bernhardt, *Christianity Without Absolutes*, SCM Press, 1994, p. 159.

3. David Tracy, *Plurality and Ambiguity*, SCM Press, 1988, pp. 88–89.

4. Mohammad Al-Ghazali, *al-Munqidh min ad-Dalal* (Deliverance from Error), trans. W. Montgomery Watt, *The Faith and Practice of Al-Ghazali*, Oneworld, 2000, p. 18.

5. Margaret Smith, *Al-Ghazali the Mystic*, Kazi Publications, Lahore (no date), pp. 13–14.

6. Mohammad Al-Ghazali, *al-Munqidh min ad-Dalal* (Deliverance from Error), trans. W. Montgomery Watt, *The Faith and Practice of Al-Ghazali*, pp. 58–60.

7. Karen Armstrong, *Islam: A Short History*, Weidenfeld and Nicolson, 2000, p. 76.

8. Mohammad Al-Ghazali, *Bidayat al-Hidayah* (The Beginning of Guidance), trans. W. Montgomery Watt, *The Faith and Practice of Al-Ghazali*, pp. 101–2.

9. Quoted in Margaret Smith, *Al-Ghazali the Mystic*, pp. 35–36.

10. Poem attributed to Mohammad Al-Ghazali, quoted in Margaret Smith *Al-Ghazali the Mystic*, p. 84.

11. Maimonides, *Note to the Commentary on the Mishnah*, quoted in M. Friedländer, *The Guide for the Perplexed by Moses Maimonides*, Dover Publications, 1956, p. xviii.

12. Maimonides, *Letter to Rabbi Shmuel ibn Tibbon*, quoted in M. Friedländer, *The Guide for the Perplexed by Moses Maimonides*, p. xiv.

13. Maimonides, *Letter*, quoted in M. Friedländer, *The Guide for the Perplexed by Moses Maimonides*, p. xxiii.

14. Hans Küng, *Judaism*, SCM Press, 1992, pp. 158–59.

15. Maimonides, *Commentary on the Mishnah*, quoted in Hans Küng, *Judaism*, p. 158.

16. Keith Ward, *God: A Guide for the Perplexed*, Oneworld, 2002, p. 45.

17. Maimonides, *The Guide for the Perplexed* I.xxv, trans. M. Friedländer, p. 49.

18. M.K. Gandhi, *An Autobiography, or the Story of My Experiments with Truth*, Penguin Books, 1982, pp. 14–15.

19. M.K. Gandhi, *An Autobiography, or the Story of My Experiments with Truth*, p. 113.

20. M.K. Gandhi, *Some Rules of* Satyagraha, 27 February 1930 in Rudrangshu Mukherjee (ed.), *The Penguin Gandhi Reader* 1993, pp. 157–58.

21. M.K. Gandhi, *An Autobiography*, pp. 274–75.

22. M.K. Gandhi, *An Autobiography*, pp. 77.

23. M.K. Gandhi, *An Autobiography*, p. 135.

24. M.K. Gandhi, *Modern Review* October 1941 in V. Geetha (ed.), *Soul Force, Gandhi's Writings on Peace*, Tara Publishing, 2004, pp. 387–88.

25. Gilbert Murray, *Hibbert Journal* 1918, quoted in 'Gandhi, Mohandas Karamchand', *Encyclopedia Britannica* from Encyclopedia Britannica Premium

Service www.britannica.com/eb/article-9109421
[accessed 30 July 2005].

Chapter 8

1. William James, *The Varieties of Religious Experience*, Penguin Classics, 1985, pp.226–27.

2. George Whitefield, *Sermon on the 'Method of Grace'*, quoted in Dave Brown, *Whitefield and Wesley on Grace and Predestination* www.geocities.com/Athens/Forum/3505/Whitefiel dWesleyGrace.html

3. George Whitefield, quoted in J.F. Weishampel (ed.), *The Testimony of a Hundred Witnesses*, 1858, p. 121. www.mun.ca/rels/restmov/texts/believers/ weishampelthw/THW049.HTM

4. George Whitefield, quoted in J.F. Weishampel (ed.), *The Testimony of a Hundred Witnesses*, 1858, p. 121.

5. John Wesley, *Sermon 53*, 1872 edition I.11 http://gbgm-umc.org/umhistory/wesley/sermons/ serm-053.stm

6. George Whitefield, *Letter to a Friend*, quoted in J.C. Ryle, *George Whitefield and His Ministry*, p.4 www.iserv.net/~mrbill/ecl/ecl-gw01.html

7. John Wesley, *Sermon 53*, II.4.

8. William James, *The Varieties of Religious Experience*, pp. 238–39.

9. John Wesley, *Sermon 53*, I.14, 16.

10. J.C. Pollock, *Moody Without Sankey*, Hodder & Stoughton, 1963, p. 133.

11. Dwight Moody, quoted in J.C. Pollock, *Moody Without Sankey*, p. 87.

12. John Cairns, quoted in J.C. Pollock, *Moody Without Sankey*, p. 103.

13. Satirical poem, *Punch*, quoted in J.C. Pollock, *Moody Without Sankey*, p. 138.

14. Ira Sankey, quoted in J.C. Pollock, *Moody Without Sankey*, p. 122.

15. Arthur C. Benson, quoted in J.C. Pollock, *Moody Without Sankey*, pp. 205–6.

16. Athene Seyler, *Letter*, quoted in J.H. Oldham, *Florence Allshorn and the Story of St. Julians*, SCM Press, 1951, pp. 7–8.

17. Bishop Gresford Jones, quoted in J.H. Oldham, *Florence Allshorn and the Story of St. Julians*, p. 15.

18. Florence Allshorn, *Letter*, quoted in J.H. Oldham, *Florence Allshorn and the Story of St. Julians*, p. 24.

19. Florence Allshorn, *Letter*, quoted in J.H. Oldham, *Florence Allshorn and the Story of St. Julians*, p. 27.

20. Florence Allshorn, *Letter*, quoted in J.H. Oldham, *Florence Allshorn and the Story of St. Julians*, p. 28.

21. Florence Allshorn, *Letter*, quoted in J.H. Oldham, *Florence Allshorn and the Story of St. Julians*, p. 33–34.

22. Florence Allshorn, *Letter*, quoted in J.H. Oldham, *Florence Allshorn and the Story of St. Julians*, p. 29.

23. Florence Allshorn, *Letter*, quoted in J.H. Oldham, *Florence Allshorn and the Story of St. Julians*, p. 35.

24. Florence Allshorn, *Memorandum about training missionaries*, quoted in J.H. Oldham, *Florence Allshorn and the Story of St. Julians*, pp. 61–62.

25. Florence Allshorn, 'The Corporate Life of a Mission Station', *International Review*, 1934, , quoted in J.H. Oldham, *Florence Allshorn and the Story of St. Julians*, p. 59.

26. Florence Allshorn, *Letter*, quoted in J.H. Oldham, *Florence Allshorn and the Story of St. Julians*, pp. 71–72.

27. Florence Allshorn, *Letter*, quoted in J.H. Oldham, *Florence Allshorn and the Story of St. Julians*, p. 145.

28. J.H. Oldham, *Florence Allshorn and the Story of St. Julians*, p. 155.

29. Florence Allshorn, *The Notebooks of Florence Allshorn*, SCM Press, 1957, pp. 26–27.

Epilogue

1. Emily Brontë, *Wuthering Heights*, 1847, Penquin English Library, 1965, p. 150.

2. John Calvin, *Institutes of the Christian Religion*, 3.3.4.

3. Jerome, *Homily on Psalm 108*, quoted in David Lyle Jeffrey (ed.), *A Dictionary of Biblical Tradition in English Literature*, p. 418

4. John Dominic Crossan, *Who Killed Jesus?* HarperCollins, 1995, pp. 66–81.

5. *The Times*, 12 January 2006.

6. Jean Rhys, *Wide Sargasso Sea*, Penguin Modern Classics, 1997, p. 75.

7. Sir Thomas Browne, 'Religio Medici' in *Religio Medici and Other Writings*, Dent Everyman Library, 1969, p. 69.